SEARCHING

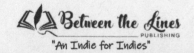
Between the Lines
PUBLISHING
"An Indie for Indies"

Between the Lines Publishing
1769 Lexington Ave N, Ste 286
Roseville, MN 55113
btwnthelines.com

First Published: October 2023

ISBN: (Paperback) 978-1-958901-33-5

ISBN: (Ebook) 978-1-958901-34-2

SEARCHING

Tim Stonecash

In memory of my mother, Elizabeth Buchanan Stonecash, and my father, Robert Othur Stonecash.

To my wife Kathy, children Matt, Jared, Ellie, and Aaron.

KILLERS

"Stop clock-watching and get some work done. We go by the bell, not the clock," shouted Mrs. Mc Daniels, my third-grade teacher. It was an unusually mild day for late November, and I was anxious to get home and play outside.

When the bell finally rang, I shoved my spelling book into my desk, grabbed my notebook, and bounded out of the classroom, down the stairs, and out the back door of the school. Like any other nine-year-old boy, I wanted to get away from school as fast as possible. I ran across the playground and headed to the alley that led to a shortcut toward home when the hood, Tommy Abraham, appeared, riding his bike directly toward me. He was a few years older than me; a hideous looking creature with a long chin and stringy hair bunched up on top of his head. The sight of him struck fear in everyone. Why was he coming toward me? Was he going to run me over? Was he coming to beat me up?

Tommy got about two feet from me then swerved his bike and said, "Fuck you, punk," as he spun his bike away from me. I wasn't sure what that meant, but I knew it was the worst of the worst words someone could speak, and I was glad Tommy was heading away from me. Then he yelled out, "Old man Kennedy just got his head shot off."

Hold up. *Was he talking about the president's father?*

My mind spun all the way home. When I walked in the back door, it felt different; something was wrong. There was a quiet stillness in the air, but I could hear the TV. I walked through our kitchen—the coffee pot beginning to steam—and into our small dining room and peeked around the corner. My nose fondly registered the familiar smell of dad—Old Spice and a hint of gasoline. Why was dad home at this time of the day?

Dad was standing in front of the TV watching the news.

"You bring that math book home?" he asked without much of a glance my way.

I didn't answer. I stood, mesmerized by the story unfolding. It wasn't the president's father who had been shot; it was the president himself. President John F. Kennedy had been shot. Kennedy was the most important person in the world. *How could this have happened?*

But there was more to it for Dad. They shared the same religious upbringing, they were both Navy men, and they were about the same age. Dad even resembled Kennedy to a degree. He had the same stature and slender build as Kennedy. Except Dad's hair was dark brown, almost black, instead of auburn. Both had a youthful, intelligent look about them.

Dad had shaken hands with the then Senator Kennedy when Kennedy's motorcade stopped briefly in downtown Miamisburg. Kennedy had been on the way to give a campaign speech in Dayton.

On that day, I was in school, but the Catholic school in town, Our Lady of Good Hope, had canceled classes. Many of those kids joined the more than four thousand people who crowded Miamisburg's Main Street to see only the second Catholic candidate for president. And after that day, the Kennedy name was revered in our house.

Sadness and hurt etched lines on Dad's face. And though he rarely watched television, today he didn't move from it.

I began to feel sad too. A sick feeling poured out of the TV into our house as though something terrible had happened to one of our own family members, and there was no way we could make it better. I had to get away from that overwhelming feeling, so I went next door to see what Doug was doing. Doug was my first friend. He came over to our house the day we

2

moved in and asked me to play. We had been best buddies since then. He was only a year older than me but a lot smarter.

As usual, Doug was ready to play. He stepped out into the mild afternoon and said, "Let's go down to the fort. We need to get some kind of roof on it before it snows. Did you hear about the president?"

I couldn't get away from it. "Yeah, Dad's got it on the TV now."

"Can you imagine if your dad was killed by a gun?" Doug asked. I thought about how terrible that would be as we walked to the far backyard where we had built a little fort in a grove of trees. My stomach ached and my anger rose.

"I would find that guy and kill him with a gun," I said.

Doug stopped, looked at me, and snickered. "Sure. I bet you would." He looked at me for a moment and then said, "Hey, I really don't want to work on the fort today. My dad's going to be home from work soon, and I want to see what he has to say about the president. Besides, we didn't bring any nails." Even the outdoors and my buddy Doug couldn't keep me from thinking about the killing of our president.

My grandma Susie, my mom's mother, usually came to stay with us on weekends. She looked just like mom, a little heavier and a little older but just as pretty. Her round face always carried a smile. She kept her grayish hair pinned in the back and always wore these weird looking cat-eyeglasses. I loved having her around; she made me feel safe and was always looking out for me.

Grandma didn't drive, so Mom would go get her on Fridays when she got off work. She lived alone since she and Grandpa had parted ways a couple years back. She seemed lonely and loved to be around family; she happily stayed with me if Mom and Dad went out on Friday or Saturday night. But this weekend, the only place anyone was going was to our living room to watch the never-ending news about the killing of President Kennedy.

The images from the TV fascinated me: Mrs. Kennedy arriving at the airport in Washington, DC from her flight from Dallas late that night—the front of her dress full of dark stains. The president's casket was lowered from the plane and placed in a black hearse.

Some of us hadn't seen the live video, but Grandma had, and when they replayed it, she narrated for us what was coming next. Our family was huddled around our small black and white TV—Dad in the recliner, chain smoking his Camels, and Mom, Grandma, and me perched on the couch trying to see deeper into the TV.

"Look, watch there. See Mrs. Kennedy? She tries to get in the hearse and can't because it's locked," Grandma recounted. "Watch, now she goes to the next door and gets in."

I felt so sad for Mrs. Kennedy. What a terrible day this must be for her. I wondered where her kids were. Later, the man on the TV explained who all the people were and what was happening and what was going to happen.

"President Kennedy will be the first democrat to lie in state at the US Capital," he said.

"Dad, what does 'lie in state' mean?" I asked.

"Well, that, ah, that means … you know how people come to a funeral home to pay their respects to a dead person? Well instead of that, President Kennedy's body will be placed in the Capitol building, which is the center of our government. He will lie in state, meaning in a government building. Does that make sense?"

"Sorta. Can we go there?"

"No, there would be too many people, and it's too far away."

I didn't argue with Dad. I knew that going there was probably unrealistic. In some odd way, I identified with the Kennedys. I had this yearning deep inside of me to be part of this somehow or at least to be there to see it all in person.

On Sunday mornings, Grandma went to work in our large country kitchen. She would rustle up a breakfast of eggs, bacon, fried potatoes, and her specialty—made-from-scratch biscuits and gravy. This Sunday morning was different.

"Mom, you go sit yourself down in the living room, and I will take care of the breakfast today. You're more interested in all that Kennedy stuff than me."

Dad gave Mom a quick stern look, then his attention was back to the TV. Mom was the sweetest, kindest person in the world, and I could tell she felt bad for the Kennedys, but it didn't affect her like it did Dad. Mom was Lutheran and brought up in a conservative home. She didn't romanticize the Kennedys like Dad did.

Our living room was small; a stone fireplace on one wall with windows on each side, a large picture window next to the front door. Only two lights were needed—a table lamp by the couch and a pole light next to the recliner where Dad always sat.

Grandma was having coffee three feet from the TV on the edge of a chair she had brought in from the dining room. Around noon, she jumped up and pointed at the screen and yelled, "Well, they just shot that man!"

"Who?" Dad yelled out as everyone rushed to the living room.

"They shot that man Oswald."

Later, I'd watch the replay where Oswald, a small smart aleck looking guy was being ushered out of a police station surrounded by men in suits and hats. One big guy with a white cowboy hat was holding onto Oswald by the arm, then suddenly a man in a black hat lunged forward from the crowd of reporters and shot Oswald in the stomach. Oswald let out a cry and slumped in pain; the man in the cowboy hat grimaced. We later learned from the TV man what the last words were between Oswald and the big guy in the white hat.

"Lee, if anybody shoots you," the man in the white cowboy hat had said, "I hope they're as good a shot as you were."

Oswald kinda laughed and said, "You're being melodramatic. Nobody is going to try to shoot me."

I was glad that Oswald was shot. He was a bad man and got what he deserved. Up until this time, the killing I'd known about had to do with cowboys and Indians on TV. It was all fiction. Mom had always made sure to tell me, "Timmy, you know that's all make-believe, right?"

But now I knew that not all the things on TV were make-believe and that scared me. I'd seen the first real murder shown on TV play out right in my living room! I had seen Marshall Dillon gun down many a bad guy in Dodge City, but I never saw anything like this before; this shit was real. We all stood staring at the TV in disbelief as replays of yet another killing continued to run.

It was a day of funerals. Besides the president, Lee Harvey Oswald was also buried that day, as was JD Tibbitt, a Dallas policeman that Oswald had killed with four bullets from his .38 pistol. I had never seen a funeral before—well, maybe a make-believe funeral on a TV show but not a real one. With real people. Real lives.

That Monday, the president's family and close friends led a funeral procession from the White House to St. Matthew's Cathedral. It was the first time I had seen an American flag draped over a coffin; in fact, it was the first time I had ever seen a coffin. Many people from lots of foreign countries walked behind them—a little Black man walking proudly with a chest full of medals, a tall dignified white man in a gray military suit beside him.

I wondered why they were all walking to the funeral instead of riding in their black cars; it seemed like a long way. My answer soon came from the TV man who spoke slowly and confidently, pausing as he said that Mrs. Kennedy insisted that she would walk in the funeral procession. The man said she copied what was done at the funerals of presidents Washington, Lincoln, and Grant because she wanted to follow that precedent. I wondered if Kennedy was as great as those presidents. I wondered if we would walk to my dad's funeral.

On the screen, a military man struggled to lead a big black horse with no rider; he called him, "Black Jack." There were big leather boots facing backward in the stirrups. *How odd*, I thought. Why didn't he just ride the horse? The question fascinated me as the TV man talked about the meaning: the boots facing backward in the stirrups signified the fallen leader would ride no more, but that he was taking one last look at the troops he

6

commanded. Black Jack tugged and pulled and even reared up on his hind legs.

"That soldier needs to keep a tight rein on that horse," the TV man said.

I'd heard Dad say that same thing to Mom about me more than once.

The horse just wanted to be let go, to be free. I imagined him getting loose and running away so fast nobody could catch him. He would be free to go where he wanted and do what he liked. I felt like that too sometimes, like I was being held back by a rein just like that horse. The horse looked like he just didn't want to be told what to do, and I felt bad for him. Did the horse have some sense of what was going on? Did he want no part of whatever was happening? I felt sorry for the soldier who was trying to control him. Did he wish he had a better horse or no horse at all? Did Mom and Dad ever feel that way about me?

Black boots. Black horse. Mrs. Kennedy wore a black veil covering her face. As she walked in the funeral procession, she looked so beautifully sad. At her side were the two remaining Kennedy brothers, Bobby, and Ted, both in sharp-looking black suits. I'd never seen so much black.

"Mom, why is everyone wearing black clothes? Is that because of death?"

"Yes, it just shows a sign of their sadness and that they are at a dark time in their lives."

The pageantry captivated me. I was sad and felt hurt even though I had no relation to the Kennedys. Their family wasn't my family, but I was strangely envious of their pain and their importance—their privilege. The Kennedys were the most famous family in the world; how could this happen to them?

I became fascinated with this spectacle that played out on TV for the next four days. All the channels were preempted for news coverage only. For four straight days, I watched intently. I cut out pictures from newspapers and magazines of the funeral, the Kennedys, and anything else that had to do with the president's death, and I pasted them into a scrapbook.

The scrapbook brought up more questions than answers, a few of which I peppered at my parents. I began with Mom, who was easier for me to ask questions of. She never expected that I should already know the answer like Dad did sometimes.

She proudly proclaimed she was a republican and said she had voted for Nixon, which didn't sit well with dad. Dad said she had just canceled his vote out.

"Mom," I asked. "Why did this man shoot the president? And why did this other guy shoot the guy who shot the president? And will there be school on Monday?"

Mom placed her hand on my arm. "That Oswald was just a bad man, Timmy, and I think that guy who shot Oswald felt sorry for Mrs. Kennedy. No, there will be no school on Monday."

Mom turned away and went back to chopping vegetables. I felt sorry for Mrs. Kennedy too, but becoming a killer by killing a killer? Well, that seemed wrong. I hesitantly turned my attention to Dad in the living room. "Will that torch really burn forever?"

"Well, that's what they say. Mrs. Kennedy got that idea from the French, who have an eternal flame at their Tomb of the Unknown Soldiers, and it's been burning for forty years."

"Dad, do we have a real gun?"

"Why do you ask that, Timmy?"

"I just want to know. We might need one."

Dad put his arm around me and said, "Don't be afraid son. We don't need a gun in our house."

"Why couldn't the Army or somebody protect the president?"

"I don't know, Timmy, I just don't know." Dad turned back and stared at the TV. That was odd. Dad always knew everything. The next day, November twenty-six, was my birthday. I got presents like always, and life began to move on.

Over the years, I read about lots of conspiracy theories. The mob was not happy about how Kennedy botched the overthrow of Fidel Castro, so they took their vengeance on Kennedy. Some said that our law enforcement was negligent in protecting the president, then covered it up. Others said that there were those who knew what Oswald was planning, and in some way, aided him or turned a blind eye.

Dad always said, "I wish I could have heard Oswald's side of the story." But the man in the black hat had made that impossible. "Son, the evidence points that Oswald, after learning the President of the United States was going to be passing in a motorcade right by the building he worked in, took the opportunity to express his anger toward our government and got off a couple of good shots." That seemed hard to believe, but dad was always right.

Until Kennedy, Oswald, and Tibbitt were killed, I never remembered anybody dying. I wondered where they went. Surely Kennedy and Tibbitt went to heaven, and Oswald went to hell.

I really didn't know much about President Kennedy, and I knew nothing about Oswald or Tibbitt. All I knew was that Kennedy was our president, Tibbitt was a policeman, Oswald was a bad guy, and they were all shot dead. The news man on TV said that Tibbitt had three kids, and one was the same age as me.

I thought, *How would it be if my dad were shot?* I wondered how growing up without a mom or dad would be. If you could kill the president of the United States, you could kill anyone, right?

And the killing had just begun.

I could tell on the first day of fifth grade that Mrs. Murphy liked me. I really liked her too though I thought of her as old and quite homely. My grandma had used that word about some man at work she knew, and I practiced it when I thought appropriate.

Mrs. Murphy's classroom was on the third floor of Kinder Elementary School. Kinder was the oldest school building in Miamisburg. There were long wide hallways with oak flooring, waxed and shined so well that you could almost see yourself in them. The classrooms were big with large windows that I spent a lot of time looking out of. On Fridays, my favorite day of the week, we had a special treat: *The Weekly Reader*. It had interesting stories about current events. Reading about what was going on in the world was one of the few things I liked to do in school. Mrs. Murphy would read some to us, then she would pick volunteers to read aloud an article they were interested in. I would be bouncing out of my seat, waving my hand to get her attention. She would glance around the room like she was looking right through me and pick someone who could barely read. I stopped raising my hand.

One Friday, there was an article in the *Weekly Reader* about our government's plans to send a man to the moon. I went to that story right away and began reading it to myself.

"Tim, wait up! You have something there you want to share with us?"

Was the teacher talking to me? Wasn't I the only Tim in the class? Maybe she said Jim. But I looked up and Mrs. Murphy was looking straight at me. "Tim!" she said. "Please stand up and read for us." That Friday was extra special. I got to read aloud about something that was really cool.

All Fridays were good days at school because I had the whole weekend to look forward to doing fun stuff, but that late February Friday was especially good. Reading about plans for space travel took my mind off the killings that poured from our TV, the streets of our country, and the jungles of Vietnam—at least for a little while.

But that night on the TV, news came that three killers had burst into the Audubon Ballroom in New York City and opened fire. Their target was a thirty-nine-year-old Black man who was mad about how Black people were treated in our country.

The man's name was Malcom X. As usual, I had questions. "Who was Malcom X and what kind of a name is that?" Dad's furrowed brow and stern face spoke just as much as his words.

"Well, he isn't Martin Luther King, Tim. He's not a peaceful man. He believed that if violence was necessary to change how Blacks were treated, then so be it."

The next day, with the newspaper in his hand, Dad had more to say.

"It says here, Timmy. Do you want to hear about this guy they killed?" He didn't wait for me to say no, not really. "Sit down. Let me read some of this to you," Dad ordered.

I could tell dad didn't think much of Malcom X. He spoke of him with disdain, anger, and fear. And it sounded like this Malcom had been killed by his own people. He claimed he was a religious man. But more of an "eye for an eye" kind of man where Martin Luther King was more of a "turn the other cheek" man.

The more Dad told me about this Malcom X, the more I was afraid. He was angry and wanted change and freedom from oppression that he believed was leveled on Blacks from a white-controlled society.

I too wanted freedom from the oppression I believed was being leveled on me by my parents and school. I had to do what my teacher told me all day long. Then when I got home, I had to do what Mom and Dad said to do. I went to bed that night with the image of Malcom X in my head, wondering why there were all these killings; was it dangerous to speak out about what you wanted? Was freedom only for white adults?

The next day Dad continued his lesson with the morning paper. "The paper says here that this Malcom X believed he would meet his end at the hands of his former associates who he had fallen out with. Just a week prior to his assassination, he said, 'I'm a marked man, and it doesn't frighten me for myself as long as I felt they would not hurt my family.'

"In a speech in New York City, he said, 'I believe in the brotherhood of man, all men, but I don't believe in brotherhood with anybody who doesn't want brotherhood with me. I believe in treating people right, but I'm not going to waste my time trying to treat somebody right who doesn't know how to return the treatment.'

"Timmy, do you hear this?" my dad commented. "The more I read here, the more this guy made sense; he's wasn't saying anything that I wouldn't say. But you know he's not a Catholic; hell, he's not even Christian."

I thought, *Do you have to be a Christian to be a good person?* I was sure I was a Christian, but what about Catholic? I know Mom wasn't Catholic; I wasn't sure if I was or not. I wondered if it was dangerous not to be a Christian.

"Well now they've really done it." Dad said as he came into the house from working out in the barn.

"Who's done what, Bob?" Mom asked.

"Just heard it on the radio—some kook just shot Martin Luther King. You can bet all hell is going to break lose now."

"Oh, Bob, that's terrible! Let's put the news on."

At the time, the killing of Martin Luther King didn't have as much of an impact on me as the death of President Kennedy. Probably because he was Black and held no political office, and I really didn't know much about him. I was becoming used to important people being shot and killed.

Dad kept Mom and me up to date on all the particulars of the assassination and the search for the killer. "I don't blame this King fella; he just wants things to be better for Black people, and the poor, too. Hell, things are better, aren't they? What's the big ruckus?" Dad said to nobody in particular. "If he was a man of peace, why is it everywhere he goes, when he leaves, a riot breaks out? Why are these people always in an uproar? They got their freedom; they can vote."

Mom in a rare occasion spoke up, "I don't think we heard King's message because we didn't think he was talking to us." Dad gave mom a questioning look and turned away.

All the people I knew were white, and while they all would have liked to have more money and a better car, they were pretty content. Nobody I knew was rioting in the streets. They didn't believe they were being held back by social injustice or by laws that prevented them from making a better life for themselves. Some, certainly not all, couldn't have cared less about civil rights for Blacks. I know the plight of the colored didn't come up at our house. The only thing that was holding me back was school and my parents. I was confused. I had never met a black person or even seen one up close.

I was always excited when my cousin, Pete Buckner, who lived in New York City, came to visit. Mom said he was he was a devout Catholic and a lifelong democrat. I didn't care much about that, but he was a big Yankees fan, loved to travel, and was always fun to cut up with, so we got along great.

I shared my bedroom with Pete when he came. It was a large room with two twin beds, a tall chest of drawers, and a small desk and chair in the corner. It was cool even on the warmest days of summer with two big box fans—one in a window blowing in and another in a window across the room sucking air out. On one visit, we were sleeping in late when Mom burst into the room.

"Bobby Kennedy has been shot!"

Pete jumped up. "What? Oh my God."

We hurried downstairs to the new color TV and began watching the unbelievable news that another Kennedy had been shot. Robert Kennedy had been celebrating his victory in the California primary at a campaign rally at the Ambassador Hotel in Los Angeles.

"Pete, do you think that's close to where Aunt Elizabeth lives?"

"No! Be quiet, I want to hear this," Pete said as he pointed to the TV.

I stared at the screen, trying to take in the series of events. Kennedy had given a short speech and began making his way through a small corridor that led to an exit through the kitchen. The area was crowded with campaign workers, reporters, hotel, and kitchen staff, and at least one assassin. When Kennedy reached out to shake the hand of Juan Romero, a seventeen-year-old immigrant Sirhan Bishara Sirhan shot him down.

At first, there seemed to be some hope that this Kennedy would survive his wounds, and we all prayed that he would pull through. Dad and Pete said a long prayer, holding beads and making a cross sign on their chests. But that sad feeling of dread which hung over us would not go away. And twenty-six hours and several surgeries later, another Kennedy was headed to Arlington Cemetery.

I couldn't understand why the Kennedys kept being killed. Was there something about them people hated, or were people afraid of them? Why were there such bad people in the world?

As I think about these killers now, did they believe they could change how things were or change the direction our country was headed? If so, I guess they were right. Arthur Schlesinger Jr., a noted historian and Kennedy aid, remarked, "We are a violent people with a violent history and the instinct for violence has seeped into our national life."

The following Sunday morning, Grandma was in the kitchen working her magic. We all were in the living room watching another Kennedy funeral mass, this time at St Patrick's Cathedral in New York City. I had been to St Patrick's and stared at the marvel: its looming structure, huge doors, and stained-glass windows. What would it be like to be there now? After the mass, a train took Kennedy and his family and passed thousands of people who lined the train track on the way to Washington DC. For the first time, there would be a nighttime funeral at Arlington Cemetery. Bobby was laid to rest near his brother under an oak tree, a simple white cross marking his grave.

Similar questions kept surfacing in my brain. Why were these famous people being shot? How could a life be taken away forever? Why did God allow that to happen? It was hard for me to understand these killings and how permanent death was. Should I be thinking about death?

I thought about my dad, how he was always sick with diabetes. What if he died?

I looked at the faces of the Kennedy kids; was that how you looked when your dad died? Is that how I would look if my dad died? At least the Kennedy kids had each other.

What would Mom and I do without dad?

Pete loved the Kennedys and seemed to know a lot about them. We spent some time together over the next day or so before he went home to New York. Maybe he'd help me understand a little better about these killings and the way the world worked.

"Do you think the same people had something to do with both killings? It's really weird and kind of scary that two Kennedys have been shot and killed."

"No, that's crazy. President Kennedy was killed a long time ago. Two different people were involved, but let me tell you something." He leaned in close like he had a secret. "As with his brother, there are people who believe there was a conspiracy to kill another Kennedy."

"Really? What do you mean?"

Pete lowered his voice. "Don't tell your parents any of this because they'll think I'm nuts. Some people say there were thirteen shots fired."

I did the math in my head as Pete counted out the shots. "Kennedy was shot three times, once in the back of the head just below the right ear and twice near the armpits; four other people were shot, and several audio experts say thirteen shots fired."

"So, what?" I asked

"Sirhan's gun only held eight bullets. And how could Sirhan have shot Kennedy if the fatal shot entered the back of Kennedy's head, and Sirhan was in front of Kennedy?"

I didn't have the answer to Pete's questions, and the concept of a conspiracy intrigued me. As time passed, even family members of the slain believed in the possibility of a conspiracy.

I watched the news of all these killings; I heard people talk about them. I cut out pictures and articles from magazines and newspapers and added them to my scrapbook. It all stood out to me—I paid attention to it. The details and circumstances of the murders. Who killed who and why? The elaborate funerals with parades and train processions, the eulogies that endlessly talked about how terrible this was—what these killings did to our country and what they took away. How things would be different now; how things would just stay the same. I was never afraid before.

I had Mom, Dad, and Grandma ... but what if I didn't?

That summer, the TV news turned to a wild and divisive democratic convention in Chicago. Hubert Humphrey was picked as the democrat nominee. His campaign came on strong toward the end but failed to recover from such a poor start. The man who said, "Well you won't have Nixon to kick around anymore," was elected as our thirty-ninth president.

Mom was pleased. Dad was not.

"That damn Wallace. Wished he stayed in Alabama. Talk about a racist; now there's a no count racist. They shouldn't allow third party candidates. He took away votes from Humphrey."

Wallace once said that "the only four letters that hippies don't know are w-o-r-k and s-o-a-p." That may have been the only thing he said that dad agreed with. I listened, and I watched. And while everyone else was talking about the country and the effects these killings had on us as a society, I wondered if I had changed, too. I was part of all this. I felt different. As though the world had become more real, that bad things, really bad things, could and did happen. I hoped that those things were still distant from me and that my family was safe.

Individual deaths were one thing, but my adolescence spanned the era of the Vietnam War which took millions of lives. Martin Luther King said, "One of the greatest casualties of the war in Vietnam was the great Society shot down on the battlefield."

By then, death had become commonplace. The fighting in Vietnam filled the nightly news with vivid war scenes—helicopters dropping off fresh soldiers in the jungle, then loading up with bloody soldiers on stretchers. They gave us the weekly tally of how many wounded and how many killed. It was on the front page of the daily papers. There was no escaping it.

Burt Linville III was a rough kid several years older than me that everybody referred to as a hard ass. Burt's mom would watch me at their house once in a while when both mom and dad were working. Burt was always nice to me, and one day, when a big kid in the neighborhood began picking on me, he'd even come to my defense. The big kid taunted me from the sidewalk, but when he took a few steps toward me, across the lawn, Burt tipped his head in my direction and called, "You better watch it! This kid is tough, and he'll take you down, man!"

16

I didn't move and tried to look tough. I was hoping this kid's respect and fear of Burt would be too much for him. To my relief, the kid backed down. Burt's confidence in me gave me courage to stand my ground.

I lost track of Burt, but I learned later he was killed in Quango Ngai Provence, Vietnam.

Despite the funerals, the killings, and the death of Burt, the war was distant to me at times, and my attention was on what was happening right in front of me. Going to school, playing sports, dealing with my parents, and eventually, looking for parties, trying to impress girls, driving hot cars, and avoiding school.

I thought everybody was for the war, except Muhammad Ali. I thought we were fighting against Communism, and everybody was against that. But I began to hear lots of voices saying this war was all wrong and we should not be in Vietnam. My favorite groups were singing songs against the war. Maybe it was becoming cooler to be against the war than for it. Why couldn't we just win the war? Then we would all feel good about it, like the other wars. Bobby Kennedy, who our family had admired had spoken out against the war.

Dad said, "He wasn't like his brother Jack—didn't have the backbone. He didn't really serve, you know; he was a damn reservist. He looked like a hippie with that hair. I don't think he understood what we were trying to do in Vietnam, but he was a Kennedy, so I guess I would have voted for him."

I watched the news with Mom and Dad; scenes of the war turned to people in the streets at college campuses, protesting against the war.

"Those kids think they're smart. What do they know about why we're fighting in Vietnam? We got to stop those commies before they take over the whole damn world," Dad told the TV and anybody else in the room.

Mom would look at me and say, "Don't you worry about all that, Timmy; it will all be over before you're ready for the draft." I wasn't sure if that was a good thing or a door that was going to shut for me. By the time I was about fourteen, more guys I knew of were going to and coming home from Vietnam. A couple guys who came home from the war were the ultra-cool ones you did not mess with. Eddie Back was one of those guys.

Eddie wore what he claimed was a "gooks ear" around his neck—one of many he claimed to have cut off a dead Viet Cong; it was nasty looking. Who knew if that were true? It could have been an old dried-up piece of pork rind for all I knew. Eddie was a skinny guy with a short, scrubby little beard and long black hair down to his shoulders. He had a southern drawl that made him sound like he was from Kentucky or Tennessee.

Eddie intrigued me because of all the experiences he'd had. Ones that for some reason I wanted to know more about. Some of my friends and I would hang out with Eddie in his parent's basement. Eddie had it all fixed up with a great sound system, cushy pillows spread out on the floor, and black lights hanging over rock posters on the walls. He even had a strobe light hooked up. It had the recognizable smell of pot which Eddie tried to cover by constantly burning incense.

One time, while a group of us were hanging with Eddie in his basement, I asked him to tell me about Vietnam. "How was it over there? Are we winning the war? I bet you had some good weed." Some things took precedent over others.

Eddie squinted and pushed his hat back. He was stretched out on a couch with some chick lying against him in a fog. "Here, try this." Eddie reached down and handed me a glass jar with a small pipe on one side and water in it. "It's my new bong; Candy here got it for me." He reached down and patted Candy on the head. I hesitated, not wanting to look like a square, so I took a toke. I sucked in and then exhaled and bubbles blew around in the jar.

"Don't blow out, dumb shit; hold it in."

"Thanks." I passed the bong to Candy. It was cool that I tried it, but I didn't see what the big deal was.

"I'll tell ya, Stonecash, we're winning that war, I guess. We never lost a firefight in my twelve months there. The dope was great, and nobody hassled you about it. We'd go out on patrol through villages and hook up with friendly girls for the night. Always had plenty of beer and good food. They even gave you a nice uniform to wear. It was fuckin great, man."

I became excited hearing this shit. I took another hit on the bong.

Visions of jungle villages teeming with cocky young soldiers filled my head. They strolled through, cigarettes dangling from their lips, a swagger in their steps. They served someone else, and yet they had more freedom than I could ever hope to realize. I wondered how it would feel to have that much freedom and power over life and death.

"Really? That sounds far-out. I bet you hated to leave."

Eddie took a long draw on his cigarette, nodded, and grinned. He looked first at Candy who smiled, then to me. I wondered how much of all that was bullshit?

"I hated to come back here to all this stress, man. My car needs a new stereo—weed here is worse than I remember. I have to buy my own food and cigarettes." Eddie's grin was gone. He looked me straight in the eye. "Seriously, you know what?" His foot grazed my chin when he moved to snuggle in deeper with Candy. "This isn't bad because when I go out tonight," he stood up suddenly and yelled, "I don't have to watch my ass cause nobody's trying to shoot it off!"

His words hit me hard, almost knocking the wind out of me. What I read and heard about seemed dichotomous. And just like everything else in a young boy's brain, I had romanticized the war. I wanted that freedom. I wanted to say "screw you" to the establishment. I wanted to find my place in this world.

Some of my friends and I jokingly talked about joining the army and going to Vietnam. That would be the ultimate statement, wouldn't it? Telling school and my parents where to get off. The big-time rebellion for sure. How could you top that?

We were too young though they wouldn't take us, and besides, there was a party this weekend someplace.

FAMILY AND FRIENDS

"It takes time to persuade men to do even what is for their own good."

Thomas Jefferson

I was seven years old in 1960. I didn't know it, of course, but while our country was entering a time of unprecedented social unrest, a transformative time for me had also begun. In that year, the first five American soldiers died in Vietnam. Mickey Mantle hit forty homeruns but lost the American League MVP award to Roger Maris by three votes. Our family was jubilant that the first Roman Catholic was elected president. Unknown to me at the time, a civil rights advocate was arrested at an Atlanta department store sit-in and an oddball named Charlie was arrested in Laredo, Texas, for a parole violation on a check-cashing charge and brought back to California to serve a ten-year prison sentence. And in August, a little-known band in Liverpool, England, changed their name from the Silver Beatles to The Beatles.

I had no uncommon talent; I had no great passion for anything, no exceptional hardship to overcome. I wasn't deprived in any way. My parents didn't keep me naked and chained up in the basement. I was just one of millions of ordinary kids growing up in the 1960s. At the time, my life didn't seem exceptional or different from any other time, but history has marked the decade of the 60s as an iconic, transitional time of civil unrest and social upheaval in our country. Looking back on that time now, it seems incredible that so many salient things could have happened all around me.

I wonder how it felt to step on the moon—how thrilling it would be to hit a home run in Yankee Stadium? Could I stand up if I was sprayed with a firehose? How scary would it be to have your father shot in the face? How cool would it have been to step on the stage in front of four hundred thousand people?

I wanted to be free to do what I wanted, when I wanted, and with whom I wanted—and I wasn't going to let Dad, Mom, school, or Tim Stonecash stand in my way.

I knew the difference between doing things that were good for me and doing things that were bad. My first priority: doing what was exciting and fun. Adolescence and teenage years are trying times for most boys—more so for those that demand large and regular doses of discipline to, as my uncle Goeble would say, "stay on the straight and narrow." For a likeable and endearing kid who was also described as unruly, rebellious, rowdy, and underachieving, with a propensity for high risk taking, staying the course was hard.

I'm sure today I would have been medicated. Conflicts with school, parents, and any authoritative figure happened on a near-daily basis. My friends and I smoked cigarettes, drank any kind of alcohol we could get our hands on, and ran wild in cars, chasing a good time—searching for who we were and that freedom we felt we didn't have.

After the depression and World War II, lots of men and women got married, and they had babies in record numbers. I was one of those babies.

By the time the baby boomers reached their teens in the mid 60s, they were taking up causes: the plight of the poor, the environment, and civil rights. They were dropping out, copping out, and diving into faraway places like Vietnam. They were questioning and rebelling against authority, and in particular, government, schools, police, and their parents.

The decade began by electing a Roman Catholic president and then killing him. It ended with a man on the moon, and for me, sadness, and confusion. John Kantor, the lead guitar player of one of my favorite bands Jefferson Airplane, said, "If you can remember the 60s then you weren't really there."

Well, I was there and this is what I remember.

On the fourth Thursday of November in 1953—a hundred and sixty-four years after George Washington's original Thanksgiving Proclamation—I arrived at Good Samaritan Hospital in Dayton, Ohio.

Thanksgiving—due to its falling on or around my birthday—was always an exciting time for me. I was either playing with toys that I'd just received from my birthday, or I was anticipating what toys I would get. And knowing there would be lots of family at our house made it special.

Thanksgiving Day began early with Grandma Susie scurrying about the kitchen. "Timmy, if you're going to hang around underfoot, you might as well be of some use," she said. "Can you peel some potatoes without cutting a finger off?"

"Sure, I can help, Grandma. What kind of pie are you going to make?"

"How about pecan? How would that suit you?"

"Oh, that would be swell, Grandma." I was all smiles.

"And of course, we'll have a pumpkin pie," she added.

"I'm also going to make some scalloped oysters."

I made a face.

Grandma smiled at me. "Oh, just for your dad."

By midafternoon, there was an elaborate display of food spread out over a large dining room table. Grandma would work all day on the feast. The pies from scratch, two kinds of dressing—cornbread, and the regular kind made with breadcrumbs—and always mounds of mashed potatoes.

Mom would lend a hand with the gravy, sweet potatoes, green beans, and cranberry sauce. Mom made her cranberry sauce with orange juice and pecans. It was an acquired taste, but I developed a liking for that tart, tangy treat.

22

We also had some kind of salad, but I never liked it much. Dad said it was called Waldorf Salad. It didn't seem like apples should be in a salad. And of course, the smell that filled the whole house, the centerpiece of the day: the celebrated bird.

Our table would be full of family this year. My cousin Pete had flown in from New York. He would later drive Aunt Wano back to Florida for the Winter. Uncle Goeble had made a surprise trip up from Florida to join us for the holiday and my birthday.

Aunt Wano—Wayland Hartney. Wayland was a difficult name for a kid to say, so we called her Wano. She was actually my great aunt. She was born in Campton, Kentucky in 1895. She married a man named Vince Hartney, who worked at Wright-Patterson Air Force base in Dayton, Ohio.

One cold January day, Vince was shoveling snow off his driveway and dropped dead; he was only forty-five. Shoveling snow was one chore I was never given—Mom ever the worrywart.

Aunt Wano was my grandfather's sister on my mom's side. She lived in Florida in the winter, and each spring, cousin Pete would fly down from New York and drive her to our house to spend the summer. She was a lot older than mom and dad, but she acted and talked like she was a lot younger. I loved having Aunt Wano at our house; she was so nice to me and just fun to be around.

Her brother, Uncle Goeble, was quite the character—a boisterous cigar-smoking die-hard Republican who claimed he was a Democrat. He captured my attention with his wild tales, always talking politics. I don't know how many times he told me, "You know, Timmy, the only thing the government should be doing is protecting the country and delivering the mail. I don't need them to do anything else."

On this day though, Aunt Wano couldn't resist. "What about that social security check you get every month? And what about that Medicare you're getting now?"

"Ah, oh well, you know that's all due me anyway—but they need to keep that going."

Everyone laughed. I didn't know what they were talking about.

Pete was about fifteen years older than me. It was like having a big brother around, even if it was for a short time. The more family at our house the better. With no brothers or sisters, it made me feel like I was part of something big.

Thanksgiving turned out to be one of my favorite holidays, and when in later years the first hint of turkey and pumpkin pie landed at the stores, my mind went back to those celebrations, those people; the warm feeling of contentment that settled over me during our dinners, taking away the loneliness at least for a moment.

DAD

Before Dad came Grandpa. Peter John Stankaquich. He died four years before I was born. So, I asked dad about him.

"Son, I wish you could have known him. He was a fun guy to be around, always had a smile and an encouraging word for you. You would have had to listen closely to him though, as he spoke broken English. He was hard to understand."

"Why was his English broke?" I asked.

Dad laughed and tried to explain. "It wasn't broke, exactly. English wasn't his native tongue. He was born in Calvary, Lithuania. He was a little older than you, I guess, when he took passage on a cattle boat to come to America and entered the country by way of Norfolk, Virginia—I think in about 1895. A naturalization judge asked him his name and occupation," Dad said.

"Peter John Stankaquich, tailor."

"Tailor," the judge said. "That's good, but a name like that won't serve you well here in America." So, he asked, "How about Stonecash?" Your grandfather could only understand a little English but enough to agree to the name. After five years, he met the citizenship requirements, which read, "'Having been in the United States more than five years, having conducted himself as a man of good moral character, and having renounced any

25

allegiance to the Czar of Russia.'" Dad went on, "Soon Dad had learned enough English to convince your grandma to marry him."

"What was her name?" I interrupted.

"Blanche Hall. She was only twenty; they were a good match. She was already an accomplished seamstress." Dad continued, "They moved to Brookville, a small village about ten miles northwest of Dayton. They set up housekeeping together in a duplex on first street, using the front room as a tailor shop."

My dad, Robert Othur Stonecash, was born there on June 11, 1923. The growing family soon moved to a larger house on Anderson Street in Franklin. Unlike Mom and me, Dad was surrounded by lots of brothers and sisters—ten in total. I had little or no contact with these aunts and uncles or their children with the exception of my Uncle Billy and my Aunt Katie and their children and spouses.

Their tailor shop on main street did good business, but there were many mouths to feed. Which meant that the kids lived with the minimum. Dad once told me, "If they had a decent football and a basketball that would hold air, they were happy kids." That thought always amazed me.

Despite being a good athlete, playing football and basketball in high school, and being a good student, Dad was unsettled. He wasn't interested in the tailor business and didn't want to go to college. Our country was at war, so he and his best friend Luke Blackaby joined the Navy Air Corp.

Perhaps they wanted to serve their country, maybe they just wanted to fly airplanes, or maybe they had just outgrown Franklin, Ohio, and were looking for an adventure.

Dad and Luke were admitted to Naval flight school and sent to Seattle for training. Dad was just nineteen years old. But he didn't last there. One summer, when I was about eight years old, Dad told me the story of what happened.

He was about eleven months into his enlistment, still in flight school when one day he woke up in the infirmary. The bright lights were blinding, and the place smelled like medicine.

26

"You feeling better there, Stonecash?" The words came from a man dressed in white standing over him. I could see the gold oak leaf on his collar, so I knew to show deference.

"Yes, sir," I said, looking around the room in confusion. "What am I doing here?"

"You remember what happened?" the man asked.

"Not really… I had just come in from a flight and…" I was working it out as I spoke. "And I was hanging up my gear, and I felt faint. I think I blacked out—woke up here."

"How many times has that happened, Ensign?"

"Not often. Usually, I get some orange juice, and I'm fine. Can I go now?"

The commander looked at some charts and motioned for me to sit down. "Just settle down there for a bit. I have some things to go over with you." He shuffled more papers before going on. "Ensign, your body is going too low on sugar, and that orange juice you drink brings your sugar level back up. I don't have good news for you. You have diabetes. You're going to need to start taking insulin, and you're going to have to watch your diet—beginning with no sugar."

I didn't like what I was hearing, but figured I could handle life with no sugar, no problem. "Ah okay. I can do that," he said.

"You're going to have to start taking insulin every day; your body cannot naturally regulate the sugar in your body. I'll have a nurse come in and show you how to do that, okay?"

"Okay, doc," he said nonchalantly. "But what's the cure for this diabetes?"

"Ensign, there is no cure, but we can treat it."

"Okay can I go now?"

"Listen, you have a serious condition. What if you would have blacked out today at ten thousand feet? Ensign, people who have diabetes don't fly airplanes in the United States Navy."

On December 17, 1943, Dad was given a medical discharge from the Navy. He headed back home, leaving his buddy Luke to fulfill their dreams of flying off aircraft carriers in the Pacific to fight the Japanese.

The story stuck with me. Things were not always good. Bad things like assassinations and war and disease just didn't happen to other people. Bad things could—and did—happen to my family. Just when Dad seemed to have found his way, he was told to go home; that disappointment still hung with him. But I could also see that he was proud to have been a pilot in the Navy even if for only a short time. I wondered if someday I could just quit school and join the Navy.

I didn't understand this disease. Dad couldn't eat candy except when he felt sick. I worried that I might get this same disease. Dad's poor health probably kept him from getting a really good job. He worked periodically at a filling station in Miamisburg, mostly doing the books.

Because of his medical discharge, he received a pension from the Navy and eventually because of his continued health issues was declared one hundred percent disabled. Mom always said we couldn't make it without Dad's Navy pension.

Dad helping me with my homework was most unpleasant.

On many school nights, as Mom was clearing the dishes from the dining room table, Dad, with sharp pencil in hand, would begin to write out math problems on a yellow pad. I dreaded this and was always anxious to get up from the table as soon as I had finished eating.

"Hold on their, son; let's you and I get a little work done here."

I was trapped. I impatiently waited, as Dad took his time. I hoped I would know how to do at least some of these calculations.

Finally, Dad slid the pad over to me. "Okay, here—see what you can do with these."

I stared at the pad, searching for something that looked familiar, but the numbers, letters, and symbols looked like gibberish.

Dad stared at me.

"I have to go to the bathroom," I tried to stall.

Dad shook his head no.

There were only six problems. I leaned in and completed two simple multiplication and division problems and I felt good about that. I grinned at Dad, hoping to make him happy in even the smallest way.

He grinned back and snickered, as if to say, "that's good but the easy shit's over."

Then came problems like: $5(z + 1) = 3(z + 2) + 11$ *What was Z?* I was lost; I just couldn't get the right answer.

"Damn it, Timmy, you know if you would work at this you would get it; it's not that hard." I was working at it. What did he think I was doing? Dad was a real math whiz and intolerant of anyone who didn't get it. Sadly, I didn't get it.

"Son, you don't know shit from shinola about this."

And he was right, but what I hid from him was that I didn't want to know shit from shinola about it. I survived Dad explaining the problems and how to get the answers. I breathed a sigh of relieve when Mom came to my rescue.

"Timmy, you better get your bath; it's getting late."

Dad often worked on small wood projects of all sorts. Sometimes, on cold winter evenings out in the barn, I'd hold a piece of wood or some metal thing, so he could hammer, glue, solder, or carve to perfection. I would be shivering, and Dad would act like he didn't notice.

"How long do you think this is going to take, Dad?" My arm would grow tired as I was thinking I could be in the house watching TV or playing with my army men. After what seemed like forever, he would look at me with a questioning eye. "Okay, you got your homework done?"

How did he always know the answer to that question would be no?

And while the thought of doing homework was about the worst thing I could imagine; it sure beat standing in a cold barn. Later, I wished I would have paid more attention to what dad was teaching me. My guess was it was more important than homework.

GRANDMA SUSIE

My mom's mom, Susie Lamb, was a sweet woman who always was there to meet my every need. She was born in Richmond, Kentucky, at the turn of the century. The story was her family came to Ohio in a covered wagon.

She took great joy in cooking for the family. She moved effortlessly about the kitchen with a pleasant look on her face, creating wonderful delights from pumpkin pie to biscuits and gravy from scratch. She made fried chicken and roast beef and her specialty pot pie. She always seemed to have an apron on and was either in the kitchen, coming from it, or going to it.

Grandma Susie had seven brothers and sisters. Jasper (Jap), Greene, and Monroe were among those she mentioned most often. I wondered about such funny names but never said anything. She married a Kentuckian named John Thomas Buckner (who went by John Tom) and settled in the small village of Springboro. They had one child, my mom Elizabeth, born on February 15, 1919.

Mom started school there, but her family soon moved to a nice little home along the Great Miami River in the heart of Franklin, about four miles west of Springboro. As Springboro flourished over the years, Franklin remained stagnant. "Remember," Mom would say as she quoted her own mother, "We moved to Franklin because Springboro was a one-horse town that would never amount to anything."

Grandma took a job just up the street with the Maxwell Paper Company where she worked for the next thirty-seven years. I often wondered if working at a paper company and living along the river defined something better than living in a "one-horse town."

Grandpa John Tom was a good-natured, fun-loving guy, but he had some bad habits, including drinking too much too often and lying out for days at a time. I overheard Mom tell Dad an old story about Grandpa and Uncle Goeble.

Grandpa John Tom was very close to his brother Goeble. But as Goeble would say, "He was a real pain." Goeble had a car parking lot in downtown Dayton. People would leave their car there, go to work or shopping, come back, and pay Goeble, and get their car. Gobble asked John Tom to watch the lot for a few hours one day. When Goeble returned, there was no John Tom. Soon a man who regularly parked his car there appeared and wanted his car. Well, it didn't take long to figure out that John Tom had taken the car for a joy ride. Goeble was fit to be tied. John Tom eventually returned, smelling of alcohol and wondering what the big deal was.

No matter how mad Goeble got at his brother, he would forgive—give him another chance. And sure enough, John Tom would disappoint again. When I heard that story, I thought about what I would do if my brother did that. Maybe having a brother would be a pain.

Grandpa never held down a job for very long. The one job I knew about was at the Logan & Long Paper Mill in Middletown. They specialized in making felt tar paper and shingles. Paper mills were known to have fires, and the Logan & Long had a big one. On that night, Grandpa held the end of the fire hose, waiting for the water to be turned on. When the water reached the end of the hose, it burst out with such force it threw him into the fire. He was engulfed in flames, melting asphalt, and shingles. He was in serious condition, and it was thought at first that he would not survive.

"Dad was never the same after the fire," Mom always said. "I think it affected his head. "He physically recovered for the most part, but his face

31

changed—wrinkled with a dark, rough complexion. And his drinking and carousing continued so that, finally, Grandma divorced him.

Over the years, Grandpa John Tom briefly and infrequently drifted in and out of our lives. I remember coming home with my parents and catching a glimpse of a shadow. "Someone is on the porch," I said, my heart skipping a beat.

Mom, embarrassed, whispered to Dad, but I could still hear, "Oh, its Dad, Bob. I don't want Timmy to see him like that; he's too young, and he won't understand. He was in town last week, just wandering around and managed to get arrested."

"For walking around?" Dad asked.

"Well, it was for public intoxication. I paid the fifteen-dollar fine and they let him go. I'll have to give him something."

Mom loved her father but resented how he had treated her mother. I could see in her tearful eyes that she loved him and felt bad for the way she was feeling. I could sense she wasn't sure how to deal with him or how to help him. Mom would shake her head and say, "He just let the bottle get the best of him."

After that, on occasion, we would come home to find Grandpa sitting in the shadowy corner of the porch so as not to be seen by any passersby. Did all people who drank end up like Grandpa? I hoped my dad didn't end up like that.

While I must have talked to Grandpa at some point, I really don't remember doing so. He would only stay long enough to get some money from Mom. He must have been impressed with where his daughter lived and thought surely she could help her dad out a little.

Poor fellow; what a sad life. I wondered why he was the way he was. How did a person get in that condition? It would have been nice to have had a real grandpa. Someone to build model trains with, to play ball with, to watch scary TV shows with. A man to teach me things I needed to know and a safe haven for when I didn't want to deal with my parents. But that's not how life was for Grandpa. I hoped he had a good life when he was young.

Grandma soon married again to a kind, thoughtful gentleman named Ralph Archdeacon, who was also a teetotaler. He was good to Grandma and Mom. They had a happy life together for more than twenty years before he died of a heart condition. At that point, Grandma devoted all her attention to me and Mom. And even as a child, I was grateful for having such a caring grandparent. I was very close to my Grandma Susie. When I would complain about being told I was too young to go somewhere or do something, she would say, "Oh, honey, don't fret; you're eating your sweet bread."

Grandma spent all morning frying chicken and making dumplings to bring to the annual Lamb family reunion.

Carloads of cousins—second, third, maybe even fourth cousins, as I had no aunts or uncles on Mom's side—gathered at Bob & Myrtle Lamb's farm under a large sycamore. It was a day of fun, food, and reminiscing. The adults sat around and talked about old times—who had died recently, who was sick and going to die soon, and why wasn't so-and-so at the reunion. My cousins and I played in the creek and chased cows around the pasture.

"Okay, let's get a move on, Timmy; let's get in the car. "Dad was ready to go and when Dad was ready—we went. I was glad to see my cousin Denny Lamb there and we immediately hit one of the coolers for a root beer and headed to the creek. I loved the creek, and we played in it every reunion. "Let's build a dam," I suggested. We piled up rocks we found along the water's edge and made a small wall all the way across the creek. Soon a small pond was formed.

Denny had been struggling to pick up a large rock when he screamed, "Ah! What's that?!"

"It's a snake; run!" I screamed back.

The fearsome looking creature had popped up out of the earth below the rock. It was big, black, and mad. Denny dropped the rock, jumped over the snake, and took off up the creek. I was ahead of him on the other side when I looked back and saw him fall. He grabbed his bare foot as he flopped into the shallow water and raised it up. Blood oozed from his heel. I needed to go back and help Denny, but the snake—my worst fear—stood in my way.

What to do? How could I help Denny? Would the snake get me? Fear like I'd never felt before gripped me, and then another thought emerged in my mind: Had the snake seen Denny fall, and was it now swimming up the creek to get him? *Oh no.*

"Denny!" I yelled. "Come on!" A cold sweat beaded on my forehead, and my heart almost burst through my chest.

"I can't!" he yelled, holding up his bleeding foot again.

So I made a decision. "I'm coming!" I yelled at the top of my lungs as I turned and ran back to Denny. I tried not to think about whether the snake and I would reach Denny at the same time. I scooped up my friend in my arms, looked around, and with no snake in sight, I took off. I carried him out of the creek and back to where everyone was gathered under the sycamore tree. His mom came running and took Denny from my arms. There was quite the fuss. I was a hero, and for a moment, I felt loved and significant, that I had done something good and that I was special in some way for saving my little cousin.

And later, I wished I had a little brother like Denny.

We lived in the largest of a small group of homes on old Route 25 that ran along the Great Miami River just south of Miamisburg. A farmer, who lived across the road, rented us a nice three-bedroom home with basement for ninety dollars a month. The backyard had an old brick fireplace and backed up to a large twenty-five-foot-high earth levy that held back the Great Miami River.

In January of 1959, the rains came, and the streams and small rivers rose over their banks. Mom and I were worried; there was talk of a flood, which just fed into my fears.

Dad assured us. "Don't worry, that big levy behind our house will protect us. It runs from the north of town all the way past our house to

Shephard Road. There's just a small stretch without it." It was that small stretch that kept me awake that night.

Uncle Billy had warned Dad, but by the time Dad met Mom and me at our house, the water was up to the windows. Uncle Billy and Aunt Sue Ellen owned the Ohio Paper Company which was on the north side of town. I am unclear how this came to be, but Uncle Billy was assigned to blow up a dam on the river to keep the flood waters in its banks. While blowing up the dam would protect a large number of homes and businesses, it would cause the river south of town to come out of its banks and flood the few homes along the river there.

Our house was heated by a fuel oil furnace that had a two-hundred-gallon storage drum in the basement. When the water rose, it floated the half-full drum and it broke loose, spilling gallons of fuel oil into the house. The water rose about two feet into the living room. All our furniture and anything that was on the floor of the house were either washed away or covered with dirty river water mixed with fuel oil.

"Dad, will our house float away?" I asked, trembling as I thought about the power of the water. The scene of our house surrounded by the river burned into my mind. I would carry a fear of dark rushing water for the rest of my life.

Dad looked down at me and pulled me close. "No, son. Don't worry about that. But those toy army men I stepped on this morning in your room? I wouldn't count on seeing them again."

Mom had told me to put away my toys the night before. I was worried about those little army men; they were my favorite things in life. Dad thought me playing with them was silly, but I would line one army up on one side of my room and the opposing army on the other side. Then I'd roll a marble into the enemy lines—the Americans against the Germans and the Japanese—and knock them down, alternating whose turn it was to die.

I played this for hours all by myself, and often, I wished I could be in the army. But as I stood there with the floodwaters rising, I thought about how I had always felt that doing what Mom told me to do was an option while doing what Dad told me to do was mandatory. I realized now that not doing what Mom said also had consequences. It would be a long time before I took that lesson to heart.

We moved in with Grandma Susie after the flood. And while most of my army men survived the flood, they were covered with mud and oil. We never returned to the house by the river.

We lived with Grandma Susie about a year. Then we moved to Miamisburg where some ten thousand people lived just north of our old house along that same Great Miami River. Most of the town lay on the east side of the river, running out a couple of miles. Only Siebert Plat and a few houses were along the west side of the river. Main street sat a couple of blocks east of the river, running parallel. The downtown thrived with several bars, Philhowers Drug Store, Suttman Men's Store, Phaffs Jewelry, a Western Shop, and the Plaza Movie Theater. Our favorite store was Star City Hardware; Dad and I visited it often.

Our new house—well, it really wasn't new—was made of stone and built around 1913. It sat about a mile east of downtown on Central Avenue. It had big archways made from large rocks cemented together, and there were two fireplaces inside and a huge one in the backyard. A large barn constructed with wooden pegs stood on the property; it had an odd smell— a mixture of old wood, oil, and animals—though we were told it had been a long time since cows were housed there.

Dad eventually put a little workshop in one end of the barn. At the other end, two storage bays housed a little camper and our garden tractor. The backyard seemed like it went on forever; two-and-a-half narrow, mostly wooded acres stretching back to Hillgrove Cemetery.

I was excited to find kids living next door. But under the excitement simmered the fear that they wouldn't like me. I didn't have any brothers or sisters, so I was unsure of myself around other kids. Would they like to do the things that I liked to do? Did they want a new kid around?

The Belville family lived next door in a nice two-story red-brick house. They had three kids. Doug was a year or so older than me, Spencer about four years older, and Margie was my age. Their dad George was a rotund man with dark hair and bushy eyebrows who wore black horn-rimmed glasses. George was an engineer who worked for General Motors. It took me a long while to understand that he didn't work on trains.

One Sunday, I went over to the Belville's house to see if anyone could come out and play. Mrs. Belville answered the door and said, "Come on in; the kids are all in the living room."

Doug smiled. "Hey, come on in; sit here. Dad is reading the funnies to us."

Mr. Belville was sitting in a big chair in the corner by the fireplace. Doug, Margie, and Spencer were cuddled around him as he read the Sunday comics to them. Mr. Belville motioned for me to join them. I was hesitant; I hadn't come over for a reading lesson. I thought this was a waste of time. We could be playing ball in the yard, or at the very least, a board game.

Mr. Belville read a short funny.

"And then just when Benny thought the Corporal was gone for the day, he put the mop down and reclined in Corporal's Chair."

"Benny!" The Corporal poked his head in the window.

"You know hard work never killed anybody."

"I know, but I don't want to take any chances."

We all looked at each other and snickered.

After a time, I became accustomed to Mr. Belville's bad breath and the slow cadence in which he read. His expressions and the way he enunciated his words made the caricatures come to life: Beatle Baily, Peanuts, Dennis the Menace, and my favorite, Snuffy Smith.

After that first Sunday morning, the warm feelings I got from the Belville kids and from Mr. Belville, helped quell any fears I still harbored about not being liked. If it was a rainy day, after the funnies, there were two games that we played: Monopoly and Stratego. I loved buying and selling houses and collecting the rent when somebody landed on one of my properties, trying to amass more property than anyone else. Monopoly was so fun; I usually won, and I liked that.

Stratego was a war game that pitted two armies—one red and one blue—against each other. I never understood why a Marshal outranked a General. Or why a Minor could take out a bomb. And since only two could play at a time, we would play a little tournament with each other. Buying houses and playing war games was something I was good at.

But in the summer, we played whiffle ball under the lights in Belville's backyard. Mr. Belville erected two thirty-foot poles on each side of his yard. He put two spotlights on top of each pole. Doug, Spencer, Marge, and sometimes a couple kids from across the street would play whiffle ball long into the night. I got a hit almost every time up, and many times I hit a home run out to the swing set. Spencer, the oldest by a couple years, was a poor hitter. He always swung too hard, but if he did hit the ball, he was so fast he just kept running. We could never catch up with him or with the ball. But overall, just like Monopoly and Stratego, I was the best. And being the best at something made me feel good inside.

My family sometimes felt small and I was lonely. And while the Belville kids weren't my brothers or sisters, they treated me like they were, and I cherished that. Just like with family though, life didn't always run smoothly.

One day as I was headed over to Doug's to play, I noticed a group of girls out in the backyard, which meant it had to be something to do with Margie.

They had set up a small plastic pool and were playing games, laughing, and carrying on. It looked like a birthday party. My heart fell. Why wasn't I invited? Didn't I mean anything to them? Had I been wrong in thinking they were my friends?

I went over and stood by the fence between our property line, trying to subtly get their attention in hopes they would invite me over to join them. Most of them ignored me but I saw Margie and a couple of girls look over at me. Margie whispered something in their ears, and then they all giggled.

Sometimes feeling bad inside makes you want to sit and cry. But other times, it makes you want to do something about it. And this time, I would do something. I took some jawbreakers I had and offered them through the fence to some of the kids, hoping they would actually invite me over, but no one did. So I just stood there with a sick feeling in my stomach, looking over at all of them. I felt dumb and embarrassed standing there with a hand full of jawbreakers, on the outside looking in. Why did I keep standing there? Shouldn't I just go back to my house? Something deep inside kept me rooted in the spot; I wanted to be included. Was Margie embarrassed that I was her neighbor, her friend?

It was okay that they had other friends besides me. But feeling left out hurt my insides. After what seemed like forever, when most of the girls had left, and just when I was about to go inside, Margie motioned for me to come over.

Anger rose in me. Why now? Did they want me over because most of the kids had already gone? But the two cutest girls were still there, so I was eager to join them. No sooner had I stepped close to Margie than those two cute girls came up to me holding hands and smiling. What? And then they stood right in front of me and kissed each other right on the mouth! What the heck? Why would they do that?

"Boy, I wish I could have been between you two," I blurted out. A kiss from the two of them on each cheek would have been swell. More than swell if I were being honest with myself. In an instant, my anger about not being invited over evaporated.

Go to the Coal Bin and Don't Eat the Snow

The 1960s was also a time of fear.

"The next war will be different; it will be unlike anything the world has ever seen. It will be nuclear with radiation killing millions of people," Dad warned.

Every snowfall, Mom would warn me, "Don't eat the snow; that radiation from the nuclear bomb testing comes down to earth in the snow. "Not only did we used to eat the snow, but Mom used to make us ice cream with it. Mom soon put a stop to that—she was the worry wart in the family. She would know because she worked at Mound Labs, where we thought they made atomic bombs.

In school, they talked about what we should do if we came under attack: Get under our desks and don't go near the windows. Dad said we would go down in the old coal bin and bring some canned food and a radio with us. I'd heard that radiation could come in through the cracks in the house, and I was worried we wouldn't have enough air to breath down in that coal bin.

We always watched The Twilight Zone on TV. One night, the show was about a family building a bomb shelter. That night I had a dream.

Dad had decided the best way to protect us was to build a bomb shelter. Uncle Billy brought his bulldozer over and dug a big hole in the backyard. All our neighbors were at our house—even some kids and a few parents that we didn't know from up the street. They'd come to see what Dad was doing.

"Hey, Stonecash, you digging a pool there or a little pond?" Mr. Belville yelled out sarcastically.

"No, George, I am building a bomb shelter to protect my family. Don't you know what's going on between us and the Russians? We could be attacked at any time!"

Everyone was standing around, real quiet, listening to Dad and Mr. Belville go back and forth. Then some snickers came from the kids, and they all started laughing. Dad was undeterred. "George, you're an educated man—an engineer, right?" Every time I heard Mr. Belville called an engineer, even in my dreams apparently, I thought, *Where's his train?* "You should know about what's going on in the world with all the Russians threatening to bomb us. You read the papers, all of you do—don't cha?"

Then somehow, the bomb shelter was all built. There were steps that led down to a big iron door that opened into an underground room that looked just like our coal bin.

There were beds, blankets, a big flashlight, lots of batteries, and stacks of canned food along the wall all the way up to the ceiling.

All of a sudden there was a loud boom and a blinding flash of light.

"Quick, get the radio and let's get down into the bomb shelter." Dad yelled. We hurried down the steps and just as we got to the door, we heard the Belvilles.

"Wait, Stonecash; let us in too," yelled Mr. Belville.

There was something wrong with the door. Dad couldn't get it open.

Then we heard kids yelling. "Please wait for us! Let us come in too!"

"There's no room for all of you," Dad yelled back at them. "This damn door is stuck; it won't open."

I looked at Mom and she was crying. There were now lots of people at the top of the steps and they were all yelling at us. I began screaming I couldn't breathe.

When I woke, my heart was pounding. I felt like I was going to throw up. I got out of bed and ran down the hall and jumped into bed with Mom and Dad.

That wasn't a dream; that was a nightmare," Mom said after hearing my tale. "Too much TV

IN THE NEIGHBORHOOD

Most of the kids I knew didn't have to do anything to be with other kids. They woke up every day, and they had brothers and sisters that they fought with, played with, loved, hated, and grew with. I didn't have that option though. So, when friends were scarce, I turned inward, to my imaginary friends, Rinke and Dinky. They were good guys, and I would pretend to do things with them. Hike through the jungle, play army in the backyard, guard the president of the United States, or pretend we were in a band. I would talk to them and tell my mom about them and how much fun we all had.

Then there was Pity Pat. He was bad. When I did something wrong or something had been misplaced and Mom and Dad would ask, "Who did that?" or "Have you seen this or that?" I would say, "Maybe Pity Pat did it" or "Maybe Pity Pat took it." It was usually me or Pity Pat, and I thought it better that Pity Pat take the blame than me.

Three doors down to the east of our house, lived the Zimmerman family: David, a year older than me; Jimmy, three years older; Teri, five years older; and Walley, a couple years younger. Their mom—a single mother, as their dad had moved away, and nobody ever talked about him—was very strict and a little scary. She was tall and skinny with a pointed nose on a face that never smiled. They were rarely allowed to leave their

43

yard, so I usually had to go over to their house to play. We played a lot of football and basketball in their backyard. Walley and I would take on Jimmy and David in football. We were so much faster we usually took it to them. One person would hike the ball and then go out for a pass. Then the other team would count—one Mississippi, two Mississippi, three Mississippi—before they could rush. It was so much fun.

Basketball was a different story. They had a dirt court, so it was hard to dribble past Jimmy, who was a gifted string bean of six feet, three inches. He would grow another four inches and later play college basketball. David would just lob the ball to him, and even if I jumped up with arms stretched out, he would just drop it in. Jimmy, needless to say, would dominate.

Jimmy Zimmerman was either playing basketball or passing papers; he had the largest paper route in town. He asked me to help him a couple times. It was the first money I ever earned. And I could spend it anyway I wanted. I liked the freedom that earning my own money gave me.

In between our houses were the Daileys. They had one boy Carl, who was about Teri's age and an older girl that had grown up and moved away. Carl was a short kid for his age, not much taller than me, but stocky and solid with broad shoulders. He carried around a big bullwhip that he would crack on his blacktop driveway; it sounded like a firecracker going off.

I had to sneak past their house on the way to the Zimmerman's to avoid Franky, Carl's little wiener dog that barked, snarled, and snapped at me. His short little legs moved him fast across the ground like a duck's feet in water, but I was always about two steps faster.

One day, not long after we moved in, all the neighborhood kids met up in the woods behind our house. The Belvilles, Carl, and even the four Zimmerman kids. I was happy to have all the kids at my house. Friends provided a distraction from anything I didn't feel like feeling—loneliness, discontent with my parents, problems with school. At the back of my mind, though, sat the notion that they were there because of the yard and the woods not because they wanted to be friends with me. So I wanted to hold their attention and keep them around to play.

"Hey, let's build a fort!" I said.

Everyone seemed excited about that. Carl Dailey went home and brought over a big machete and began hacking down small trees. The rest of us started stacking them on end in a big circle. Before long, we had a big clearing in the woods, but I began to worry that I had not asked Dad about doing this. What would he say? Getting in trouble with Dad wasn't something I wanted to occur.

"Hey, you know what? I'm not sure my dad wants all these trees cut down."

Everyone stopped working and looked at me. "Well, do you want a fort or not?" Carl said.

I wasn't sure what Dad would think. Did I want to risk Dad's wrath or disappoint all these new friends? I didn't want them to be mad at me and leave, but it was clear I should have asked Dad before we started. I felt torn, unsure of what to do. I looked at the faces staring back at me. "Ah sure," I said. Carl resumed hacking away and we all went back to work. The worry in my mind eased a little at least for a moment

I was surprised how fast things began to take shape with all of us working together. I began imagining what it might be like, all of us living in the woods together like the Indians did. String Bean Jimmy Zimmerman, a fun guy, mostly goofed off with Spencer. David Zimmerman, Doug, Carl, and I did most of the work. Only two girls were there: Margie, who was a little chubby and really didn't help much, and Teri, who was really cute and seemed a bit too cool to be doing this. After watching her for a moment, I realized that she was more interested in Carl than she was in building a fort. It all made sense. Carl took charge of the project. He would periodically look at me when he barked orders as if to say, "Hey, this okay with you, Timmy? We're doing it my way, but I want to check in with you." His voice commanded authority. It felt good to have somebody older than me asking for my permission, showing me some respect. What I said had some significance, I think.

All of a sudden, Dad stood before us. Everyone stopped work again and looked at me.

Dad glanced around. "All you kids live around here?"

Everyone started answering at the same time, a cacophony of voices reverberating off the woods.

Dad put his hands up in the air. "Hold on! That's great, don't let me get in your way." He glanced at me, then at Carl and his machete, and said, "Have fun but be careful." Dad walked away, and I stared after him, my heart thumping in my chest.

Carl looked at me, wide-eyed, eyebrows raised. I tipped my head. We continued our work. It was great having the whole neighborhood in my backyard. What if all these kids were my brothers and sisters? I figured that would be the end of it with Dad—after all, he didn't get involved in what I was playing—but I was wrong.

The next weekend, Dad got me up early. "Let's get the tractor out and get something done in that back yard," he yelled into my room. We used the tractor to pull out the smaller stumps and built fires to burn out the big ones. Our backyard soon began to look like a backyard with a few trees instead of a dense wood. Dad helped me and Doug move our fort and rebuild it with a second story at the far back corner of our property next to the cemetery. I never asked Dad about why he helped, but I was grateful.

We started a club; it was in my yard, so I was president and Doug was vice president. Having a club of friends that enjoyed working outdoors made life fun and exciting. My friends and I could get away from our parents and do what we wanted at our fort; nobody could see us. We scrounged wood from around the neighborhood and would work on our fort every chance we had.

On several occasions, a group of us kids would gather in our "back forty," as we called it, and choose sides and have BB gun fights. We would run around in the woods and go into the graveyard and hide behind tombstones. Once I thought my gun was out of BBs so I shot down at a small tombstone. I didn't see the BB leave the barrel of the gun, but I saw it bounce off the gravestone and come straight back toward my eye. It stung me right beside my nose. How dumb.

Summertime was great for campouts in the backyard. We would set up a tent or just sleep out on our covered patio. One night, Doug and I and the two brothers from across the street Andy and Bill camped out in the backyard.

"Let's get some cars," Bill urged. We had two crabapple trees in the yard that were full of little red, inedible apples. We would get a handful of them and chuck them at cars as they passed by the house and then run for cover. An odd way to pass the time? Maybe. But we were young boys.

"Okay, but let's wait until Mom and Dad are asleep." I pointed to the house. "The lights are still on."

"Well, if we wait too late, there won't be any cars," Bill replied.

Soon, it was completely dark, and there was only one small light in the house. We grabbed our supply of apples, and we hit a few cars. One even slowed down and some man yelled something at us. We started laughing so hard we almost wet our pants. But eventually, the game began to get old. Then we heard the fogger.

Once in a while late at night, a big truck with a round tank on the back would slowly make its way through the main streets of Miamisburg, puffing out some bug-killing chemical.

"Let's get our bikes and go after it," Bill said.

"No, you dumb shit! That stuff will eat your skin off," his older brother Andy said.

"I am not doing that," I added.

We saw some kids on their bicycles, already in pursuit of the fogger, riding right up behind the truck and into the mist. We settled on grabbing some hedge apples that were in the side yard and threw them, trying to hit the tank. These were pretty innocent pranks for the time, but looking back now, I would have been quite upset to learn what my kids were up to. Maybe

Mom and Dad would be too then if they had known.

GOLF

Dad loved to play golf and was always looking at ways to improve his game. He took an old driver, drilled holes in it, and poured lead in it. He thought if he practiced swinging a heavy club he would increase his club speed, thus increasing the distance he could drive a ball.

One day, Dad announced, "We're going to put a one-hole golf course in the backyard. We'll make the tee right here behind the patio and build a green on the other side of that big sycamore tree at the end of the property right in front of the cemetery."

Kids always thought their parents were at least a little crazy, but this time, I didn't know what to think. Over and over in my head, I kept imagining that a golf course might bring more kids over. Or at least keep the ones that did come over, coming. It might take a lot of work to build, but wouldn't it be worth it?

We built a mound about two feet high and about twenty feet square. We hauled dirt in from behind the barn and raked it smooth. We planted this special grass called "creeping bent" that dad said was designed for tees and greens at golf courses. I was excited about building the golf course, but I was wondering about how much effort we were putting into.

"Dad this is a lot of dirt and a lot of work; won't the Green need to be a lot bigger? How much more dirt is that going to take?"

48

"Don't worry; your uncle Billy is going to bring his bulldozer over to build the green," Dad said. A real bulldozer! I was excited. Riding on our tractor was fun, but how much fun would riding on a bulldozer be?

Uncle Billy brought the dozer over and began tearing down trees and moving brush like there was nothing to it. This machine was huge and made twice as much noise as our tractor. It puffed billows of black smoke out a small smokestack at the front of the engine. It jerked back and forth, ripping out trees and brush with ease.

After the trees were cleared, Uncle Billy stopped and motioned for me to join him.

I climbed up and sat in his lap. The rumble of the giant engine made my whole-body shake. I could feel the power of this huge machine. "Where's the steering wheel?" I yelled. Uncle Billy just smiled and answered by moving the lever on the left to turn and the lever on the right to raise and lower the blade. I looked down and his feet were on two pedals, moving back and forth.

By the end of the day, the ground was mounded up three or four feet—level on top with a gentle slope on the sides. Dad and I raked the dirt out smooth and planted the creeping bent grass. It felt good working with Dad on his one-hole golf course. I worked hard, and I could tell he appreciated it. He would tell everyone that, "Tim and I built this." That made me feel special. Dad was proud of me.

Many of Dad's friends would try using different clubs, mostly irons, to drive a hundred and fifty yards, then up and over the seventy-foot-tall sycamore tree and drop the ball on the green. Lots of bets were placed on that but nobody's ball ever cleared the tree.

CARNIVAL

Each spring a carnival would come to town. They would set up in a parking area that ran along First Street for about three blocks—referred to as the cinder path.

My buddies and I would get word as soon as the carnival hit town. We would hurry down on our bikes and see if they would hire us to help them set up.

Larry Russell was the quarterback on our school's football team, the point guard on our basketball team, a good student, and one of my best friends. We hit off right from the start in kindergarten when we both thought it fun to raise a little hell.

Larry and I were the first ones down to see the carnies this year and Little Pete—who billed himself as the smallest man in the world at only twenty-four inches tall and thirty-two pounds—hired us.

Little Pete rode around on a small skateboard, shouting orders as to how everything should be set up. During the carnival, Little Pete sat on a small box in a tent and talked to people, making funnies as people paid a dollar to come in and see "Pete the Littlest Man Alive."

While Little Pete was the main attraction, he also had The House of Mirrors. People loved to walk through the maze of different sized and

50

shaped mirrors and stare at their reflections, which were all strange-looking and out of proportion—some fat, some long, some skinny.

Setting up was hard work. Those mirrors were heavy and had to be placed in slots in the floor at just the right angle. Sandbags had to be laid over the rope poles so that the tent would be secure. With a high squeaky voice, Little Pete yelled out, "Hey boys, where can we get some sand?"

My friend Larry and I offered to head to the river bottom to get the needed sand. Little Pete said he would drive us there. So, Larry and I, along with Pete and a rather attractive young woman of normal size, piled into Pete's car. Special driving controls had been installed, which allowed Pete to operate the car with his hands. He sat on a little seat with his lady friend snuggled up close.

"Boys, this here is Freda, my wife. Isn't she sweet?" he said as he pulled her over to him and gave her a smooch on the cheek.

We drove out to the river bottom and Larry showed Pete where the sand was. We filled the sand bags while Pete sat in the car with his wife. Soon, Larry looked at me, hooked his thumb toward the car, and said, "Hey Tim! Check out what's happening in the front seat!"

I looked up from shoveling sand, and there was Little Pete, holding his wife's head in his tiny hands, making out like we weren't there. We had to stare; it was so strange watching this little guy necking with this hot chick. "Wow," I said. "I can't believe they're doing that right in front of us."

A short while later, she leaned over to him, her arms around his little head, and he squeezed her face with one hand and her tit with the other, the whole time kissing her passionately. My mind jumped with questions: What attracted her to him? How exactly would sex work?

As if Pete could hear my thoughts, he yelled, "Keep your mind on your work, boys! Don't be watching us. Just fill those bags." It was easy filling the sandbags but hard not to watch and keep from laughing. But since Little Pete paid us well, we did as we were told. And we all came back at the end of the week to tear it all down and pack it away so they could head onto the next town on their circuit.

I thought a lot about Pete and his wife after that. I thought about life, about being happy with what you have and doing something with it. If someone like Little Pete could be successful and happy, couldn't I too? If somebody like Pete could have a cute wife, couldn't I at least have a cute girlfriend?

There were rich kids, poor kids, smart kids, and dumb kids who lived in Miamisburg. My friends fell into all those categories. You generally knew what kind of kid he was by where he lived. If a kid lived on Sycamore Street, in the downtown area, or in Siebert Plat, across the river, they did without a lot of things they needed, and they got very little of what they wanted. We weren't rich, but there wasn't much I needed that I didn't get. But there were lots of things I wanted that I didn't get, in particular, a little brother. Understanding the birds and bees wasn't a problem, I got that. But I thought everyone should have a sibling. They made for instant friends, didn't they? You didn't have to go looking for someone to play with. You would share the same experiences with parents and school. You would have someone to tell secrets to and to plot with.

Alas, no sibling ever arrived. And instead of channeling my energies into something positive, I began to fill the void in easier ways. One of those was to think about not attending school, something I had no desire to be part of.

My growing interest in not attending school brought me in touch with a large group of kids with similar social and economic backgrounds who didn't always do the right thing. The kids, those who lived in poorer neighborhoods, got into trouble at school or with the police. And while some rich kids exhibited similar behavior, the poor kids were the badasses. Some of these kids were, at times, my closest friends. Why? Because for the most part, if you had something in common with a kid—you both liked playing baseball or had a dislike for school or enjoyed going to the pool— it didn't matter where you lived, how smart you were, how much trouble you got into; it was easy to become good friends.

But Mom and Dad became concerned about my choice of friends.

"The kind of kid you hang out with is the kind of kid you will be," Dad said. "So, make friends with good kids; kids with good reputations, who have character."

Good is a relative term though, right? What kids think are good kids and what parents think are good kids can differ. I didn't consciously and purposely try to speak and act like my friends or those who stood out to me, but I did.

I would imitate outrageous and wild behavior. I picked up their slang and accents.

Whatever someone did or said that was far-out rebellious and looked cool—I did or said that. If a kid smoked, then I smoked; if a kid had steel heel taps on his shoes, I put some on mine; and if a kid gave teachers a hard time, I did too. Later, when I saw kids driving fast and wild in cars I did too.

But I didn't just imitate bad behavior of friends and locals. I also imitated actions of accomplished men who were doing notable things, who spoke well and dressed sharply—like the Kennedys and my cousins in New York. While I was not able to do the things they were doing, in my mind I pretended that I was like them. I wasn't satisfied with who I was.

The people in my life—be it the company I kept, or those I was exposed to by the media—often determined the kind of person I was at the time. I began unconsciously code-switching, both in language and action. Still discontented, still grappling with who I was and who I would like to be, and still trying to fill the void—I morphed. I didn't know who I would become or what would come next. I began to think that there must be more out there than what was in Miamisburg.

Summer drew to an end—just like every other summer before it—and the dread and excitement of returning to school was on my mind.

GRANDMA'S STORY

My grandmother Blanche on my dad's side of the family was a lady with many talents. I once saw her playing the banjo and a harmonica at the same time. The only other person I saw do something like that was Bob Dylan. She was old even when I knew her. Born in 1885, she was in her late seventies as I remember her. She was tall and lanky with a dark, weathered complexion and grayish hair. We always thought she was part Indian or maybe even mostly Indian.

She lived on Main Street in the small town of Franklin, Ohio, above a five-and-dime store owned by Dad's sister Margaret and her husband Clair. To reach Grandma's home, you had to scale an old fire escape and then walk across a flat, black-tarred roof. It seemed that we always went there at night; there were no lights, and it was a little spooky. Her apartment, always poorly lit, was quite small—just one bedroom, a kitchen, and what Grandma called her sitting room.

She was so kind and thoughtful with a great sense of humor, always kidding with me and my dad. Dad would give it right back to her. I can still hear my dad telling her some wild tale and her laughing and saying, "Oh, Bob, that's not true."

Dad would respond with a grin. "Sure, sure it is, Mom."

Once in a while, when our parents would go out on the town, my cousins Lisa, Cindi, and I would stay all night with Grandma Stonecash. Lisa was five years older than me, smart, had long dark hair, was the prettiest girl I had ever seen, and she treated me like her little brother. Cindi, about three years younger than me, was a wiry, skinny little kid who idolized Lisa and was eager to do whatever Lisa wanted her to do.

Grandma's habit was to curl up in her rocking chair in a dark corner of her sitting room next to a small wood-burning stove; tonight was no exception. She was huddled up with her afghan blanket, only her head poking out. We begged her to tell us one of her scary stories.

She rocked back and forth in the chair. "No, you kids won't be able to sleep tonight."

"Oh, please!" we all pleaded. "We won't get scared."

But that's exactly what we wanted—to be scared.

"Okay; Lisa put another log on that fire, but be careful," she said as she reached up and pulled the string on the light by her chair. Now only the flicker of flames seeping out the cracks in the stove lit the room. We gathered closely on the floor around Grandma. And then, in the warmth and darkness of the room, she began her story.

"When I was young about your age, Timmy, a very strange thing happened to me one night. My dad had tucked me into bed and said my nighttime prayers with me. I hadn't been asleep very long when I was awakened by an unearthly presence. I had never seen my mother before, but I knew it was her; there was a feeling of familiarity—of warmth and trust. She looked just like she did in the photo that sat prominently on our kitchen hutch. Her voice was calm but urgent. I barely heard her over the terrible noises coming from the ceiling of my bedroom—the rumble of chains being dragged across the floor and a wailing cry. The noises were coming from the attic. I asked Mommy what the noise was."

Get dressed quickly, Blanche," she said. "We must get going."

"The wailing called out above."

"The boys. *The boys!*"

"Where are we going, Mommy?"

"The boys, Blanche! They're in danger, and we don't have much time."

Grandma turned to us then. "My mother smiled at me with kind eyes. I felt her love, but I was afraid. My mother had died when I was too young to remember her, and I knew this was a dream, but it seemed so real." Grandma glanced at me to make sure I was paying attention. She continued, "It was a chilly, foggy, pitch-black night, much like tonight."

"It's not foggy," Cindi said, popping up to look out the window.

"Shh," Lisa said, putting her finger to her mouth and pulling Cindi back to her seat.

"Blanche, come on! We must hurry! Put this coat on," Mom said. We hurried outside and started walking quickly up a gravel road.

"My feet...the gravel hurts them, Mom," I complained. We both looked down at my feet; they were bare.

"I am sorry we forgot your shoes, but we must get along."

We all looked puzzlingly at where Grandma's feet would have been below the afghan as she continued, "We came to a wide fork in the road. "Which way?" I asked.

"Mom looked at me and said, "Can't you tell which way; can't you see which is the better road for us? Haven't you learned anything since I've been gone? Can't you tell good from evil?"

"We took the fork that went off to the right. After we had walked a while, we began to hear voices in the distance. They became louder and clearer as we walked. Kids were yelling and laughing. We came to a sign that read "No Parking on the Grass." The road ended in a gravel parking lot. There were fences, lots of fences. Behind them was beautiful green grass that crept up to dark brown dirt.

"There was a man hitting fly balls to boys in the outfield, and another man hitting grounders to boys in the infield. Mom sighed, smiled, and said, "Oh, maybe the boys did make the right decision. Baseball will keep them safe! Please, Lord, let it be." Mom and I leaned on the fence and anxiously looked to see which boys were Danny and Marty. They all had the same blue shirts and hats on. They all looked the same, pretty much.

"Where are they? I don't see them," I asked.

"They have to be here." Mom looked worried again.

Cindi interrupted the story. "Grandma, why were they having baseball practice in the middle of the night?"

"Well," she said, returning to her story. "It wasn't night to them. We could not spot them."

"Mom ran around the fence and up to the man hitting the balls.

"Where are Danny and Billy?"

"You tell me, ma'am. If there not out there, they're not here."

"Oh, really? Are you sure?"

The man glanced back at Mom with a mean look in his eyes. "Do your boys know right from wrong? Can they recognize evil? Do they know good when they see it?" The man looked at me, turned away, and smacked another ball in the air.

"We must hurry, Blanche, back to the fork! We have to catch up with them."

"We ran back to the fork in the road. Why would they go this way? Couldn't they see that this way was not going to be good for them? That danger lies ahead? Come on, Blanche. They took the wrong road again. We still have time but we must hurry."

"Mom, stop. Please stop. I can't run anymore."

"Come on."

"We soon came to a river, which was riding high and swift on the bank. There were two little boys skipping stones across the river. The ground they were standing on was wet and sloped steeply to the river, and every time they threw a stone, they would slip and almost fall in. I told them to stay away from the river, and now there they were.

"Mom whispered, "Please, Lord, give me another chance with them." Then she called out, 'Boys, come to momma! Get away from the river.' They looked at us surprised and slipped to the edge of the river. They scrambled to their feet and ran off toward the road.

"Let's go, Blanche. We must get to them."

"Why, Mommy? Who are they? I'm afraid."

"Mom was running and pulling me along. To the relief of my sore feet, the gravel road turned to blacktop. "Let's stay to the left so we can see cars coming toward us," Mom said.

"Far down the road, through the fog, we saw the boys standing in the middle of the road. As we got closer, their smiling faces seemed to light up. Mom called out to them, but they were mesmerized, looking past us down the road."

"How many times have I told them to not go on the road?"

"A roar, as such I thought it was a train. A monster eighteen-wheeler came roaring past us with blinding lights, blasting its horn. It came within inches of us, and the wind nearly knocked us down!"

Grandma's voice rose, her eyes bulged, and her face blazed with fright. Her arms came out from under the afghan and into the air as she screamed their names. *"Danny! Marty!"*

Cindi scrunched down next to Lisa, and I leaned back and away from Grandma as she continued, "We ran down the road after the truck, but it disappeared into the fog. I was out of breath when I caught up with Mom, who was sobbing and beginning to walk. "What happened, Mommy? Who are those boys and where did they go?' There was no sign of them.

"Blanche, those boys are your brothers."

"What? How can that be, Mommy? I don't have any brothers anymore. Why are they running from us?"

"They're searching."

"For what?"

"Something they should not have. We must catch up with them before it's too late," Mom said.

"We spotted the boys high on a hill. There, Blanche! Up on that ridge, do you see them?"

"There was a hill that ran up from the road. The hill was covered with trees and brush, but halfway up the trees stopped as if someone had cut them near the edge of a cliff.

"Trying to sneak up on the boys, we climbed up the hill through the trees. The hill was very steep, and we fell to our knees and began crawling on all fours. I was huffing and puffing to keep up with Mom. It seemed to take forever, but we were making progress. I suddenly got dizzy, and the ground began to move around. I could not focus. I looked ahead and saw the boys only a few feet away from Mom who was reaching out to them."

"Then the sky traded places with the ground, and I felt sick. I could not be sure what was up or down. Mom reached out, but the boys leaned forward, and the two of them gently floated off the cliff, down, down, down. I reached the edge of the cliff just in time to grab Mom, who embraced me as we teetered on the edge. Looking down, we saw the boys standing at the bottom of the ravine on railroad tracks. The bright light of an oncoming train lit their smiling faces. The ravine was so narrow there was no place for the boys to go.

"The boys reached into their pockets for something. They knelt down and placed it on the tracks. The train's whistle blew loudly, and it wasn't slowing down. The boys looked up at us, not smiling this time, tears in their eyes.

"Mom yelled, 'The train! Move away!'"

"The boys did not move. Mom grabbed me and hid my view as we stood on the edge of the ravine, holding each other tightly, the long train rumbling along below. When the train passed, we looked down into the ravine. We could not see the boys.

"We climbed down the cliff to the tracks. There was no sign of the boys. We slowly walked in the direction the train had gone."

"'Mom, look.' I picked up two flattened pieces of metal. You could still see the face of St. Christopher smashed smooth from the train wheels. 'I gave those to Danny and Billy to keep them safe, I hope they did their job,' Mom said."

"Kids, let me tell you. I knew all this was a dream, but I couldn't figure out why it was going on so long. I wondered if this was how God talked to people? Lisa, stoke that fire a bit," Grandma said, breaking from the story.

"I'll do it, Grandma," I offered.

Grandma looked at me sternly, raising her hand. "No, Timmy. You stay away from the stove."

Grandma leaned in and looked over us all, narrowing her eyes as she went back to the story. "There was something eerie about Mom, the way she moved so effortlessly. She seemed to hover just above the ground when we walked."

"Grandma, it was a dream, right?" I broke in.

Grandma just looked at me, her eyes seeming to see through me to another place, her hands raised to quiet me. She didn't answer. I was scared now, more of Grandma than the story. I inched closer to Lisa as Grandma began rocking faster as she continued her story.

"We walked down the tracks and crossed over to the road we had been on before. Soon, we began to see houses, and they were getting closer together. We were coming into a little village; a sign said Brookville.

"I asked Mom, "Why are they running from us? What are they looking for?"

"They're looking for fun and adventure, but they're too young to see the dangers in life. They know if I catch them, I'll blister their tail, but what they don't understand is I will also keep them safe. I couldn't save them before, Blanche. I was always too late. Now we have another chance. We can save them now, but we must get to Dad's tailor shop."

"Why do we have to go there, Mommy?"

"Because that's where the fire will be."

"'How do you know?' I asked.

"Because that's where it always is."

"We both began running again, my bare feet smacking the pavement in step with the beat of my heart, Mom floating along just ahead of me."

"Grandma, wait. Wasn't your mother dead?" Lisa asked.

"Why yes, she was."

Lisa gave a puzzled look and said, "So, let me get this straight. You're running down the road with your dead mother, chasing your two dead little brothers, and trying to stop them from what? What were you trying to stop them from doing?"

"I was trying to keep them safe. And it should have been quite easy if they had just let me help them make the right decisions. It's getting late now, so let me get on with this." She adjusted her back against her seat, smoothed her hair, and took a sip of water.

"We soon came upon my dad's old tailor shop. It was a small frame home that Dad had converted. Dad was a fine tailor of men's and women's clothes, and Mom was an accomplished seamstress. They could make men's shirts, pants—even a complete suit—or blouses and dresses for women. They also dry-cleaned clothes. You see, dry cleaning clothes was not really dry at all. The clothes would be washed in a mixture of gas and kerosene. The mixture, if done right, was very good at making them bright and clean again, taking out stains and even grease, but it was extremely flammable. Mom closed the shop and boarded it after Dad passed away. It was mostly empty now. Those boys were warned to stay away from the old shop. Both Mom and I told them many times. There was even a big sign on the door. *No Trespassing.*

"We crept quietly up onto the porch of the tailor shop and peered into the window. We didn't want to alert the boys as they might run off again.

"There they are, Mommy. What are they doing?"

"Tempting fate, playing with fire," Mom said.

"There's no fire in there, Mommy."

"Just then, we saw one of the boys open the potbelly stove and throw some rags in while the other boy lit a match and tossed it in. As the flames leaped out the door, the boys jumped back, knocking over a can of liquid that spread across the floor, and fire quickly followed it.

"Stay here, Blanche."

"Mom raced for the door, but it was locked; she began pounding on the door and yelling for the boys to open it. The fire followed the rolling can as it emptied onto the floor. It finally came to rest against a pile of rags and a big red can marked, 'Danger."

Grandma stood and yelled, "BOOM." We all jumped with fright. She continued the story, saying, "A flash of fire exploded as Mom finally burst into the room. Mom slipped on the soaked floor as she reached through the flames for her boys. She struggled to get to her feet. She grabbed Marty, picked him up, and pitched him out into the darkness. She turned and went back for the wailing Danny, who was engulfed in flames; she swooped him into her arms, her hair and clothing on fire. She fell out the door onto the porch.

"I found a garden hose and sprayed them all with water. They both lay in a black smoldering clump, Mom moaning in agony and Danny not moving. Mom lived a few agonizing days in the hospital but soon we lost her."

"And Danny?" asked Cindi.

"He died that night; his charred little body had to be pried away from Mom's arms."

"Oh, how awful," said Cindi.

"And what of Marty?" Lisa asked.

"Oh, he lived through the fire; he had only minor burns. But with the cold and wetness of the night, he caught pneumonia and died a month later."

"What was Danny and Marty searching for?" I asked.

"Danny and Marty were searching for their freedom, but they weren't ready for that freedom; they hadn't earned it. They were too young to see the dangers in this world and how the decisions you make matter." Grandma looked around at us, then paused and stared me in the eye. "Did you like the story, Timmy? Were you scared?" She didn't wait for me to answer. "I hope you were." She rubbed her hands together. "Okay, kids, that's it. You all scat. Grandma is tired, and it's time for all of us to hit the hay."

I looked down at Grandma's feet as she walked back to her bedroom. "Lisa, that's not true, is it?" I asked.

"Which part?"

"Any of it—all of it," I said. "It was just one of Grandma's made-up stories, right?"

"Well maybe some of it was made up—maybe most of it." Lisa shrugged. "Grandma is getting old, and she gets her stories mixed up sometimes. But I do know Grandma had two brothers named Danny and Marty, and one died in a fire and one died of pneumonia."

I thought about Grandma's story and the way she looked at me.
Was Grandma trying to tell me something?

Before the Search Began

I have this sense that when I do a certain thing or say something in a particular way, I feel like it is one of my deceased relatives saying or doing it. It's usually a gesture or the way I pronounce something; it can also be a physical action. It's like somehow, I have subconsciously copied their behavior as my own. It's a surreal feeling that doesn't happen often, but when it does, it's clear and I can see the face of who I am copying. And it's always someone who was close to me growing up—my mother, father, cousin Pete, Uncle Goeble, or Aunt Wano.

I wonder how much of my family is in me in some way.

I know my penchant to kid around and my love of strong drink and longing for the road must have come from my dad. I know that my worrisome ways and kind heart came from my mom.

MORE OF DAD

I helped Dad remodel our kitchen. Well, I helped in the tear-out. The walls were covered with imposed tin, and I was ripping it off the wall with a crow bar when I got a small cut on my hand.

"Oh, Timmy, let me see," Mom cried.

"He's going to need a tetanus shot.," Dad said, taking the crow bar from me.

Just what I wanted to hear. Dad was very careful about health issues. If I got a cut or stepped on a nail, he would make sure it was immediately cleaned and sterilized with mercurochrome, which burned like hell. This was a cut from rusty metal and could get infected, so it was off to the doctor's office we went.

I can't believe now that we took out the marble that was on our countertops and windowsills and replaced it with Formica. Part of the countertop had to go around a corner, so Dad took a 100-watt light bulb and held it up to the Formica. He was able to bend the Formica to go around the corner.

Mom was proud of her new kitchen, and I felt proud that I had helped.

Dad was forever working on something in the barn. It always seemed like it was winter and cold when he needed my help.

65

"Son, hold this, will you? No, you need to hold it right here, and don't let it move while I screw it down. You have to hold it tight; do you see what I am trying to do here?"

I always answered with a "yeah" and a nod. But even with my winter coat, I was cold and wanted to go inside. I would start shivering and moving my feet back and forth, my teeth chattering.

Dad looked at me. "Are you really that cold?" he'd ask, and I would stop shivering.

"No, I'm fine."

Of course, he sported a light jacket and probably thought I was being a baby about it.

After what seemed like eternity, Dad said, "Okay, go on in the house and make sure you get your homework done. I want to see it when I get in there." While doing homework was the last thing I wanted to do, it was better than freezing in the barn

My buddy Doug and I loved to go sledding in the cemetery that bordered our property on the south end. A hill with only a couple of new graves on it ran down and crossed a narrowed gravel road and then went straight off a cliff that fell about ten feet onto our property. Off from school, a snow day, Doug and I headed to the cemetery. After a few fun trips down the hill, I was looking for something more.

"I'm going to go all the way and go off the cliff. Doug, you come with me and we'll take your little toboggan," I said. Doug had a small two-man toboggan. It had a smooth metal bottom and would really fly on snow.

"Okay, but I don't think we should go over the cliff," Doug said.

"Oh, come on, Doug! Let's do it!"

He finally agreed. We ran, pushing the sled to get it going before both of us jumped on. We flew down the hill, dodging a couple headstones.

At the bottom of the hill, the sled scooted across the road and off the cliff. We soared in the air and landed with a thud. Everything was quiet. I blinked at the gray sky until I got my bearings. I had landed hard on an old tree stump and my butt hurt. I started to moan and felt my behind. There was no blood and I managed to get up.

Doug, who had landed in the soft snow nearby, said, "You look okay."

I left my sled and slowly headed for home with tears in my eyes—something I didn't want Doug to see. I got about halfway back to our yard when I saw my dad. Despite the deep snow, he started to run toward me.

"Timmy, what happened?"

"I fell off my sled and landed on a stump on my tailbone."

Dad picked me up. "I thought you'd hit your head! With that red hat, I thought it was blood."

Dad carried me to the house and took me to the doctor right away. The doctor confirmed it was a bruised tailbone. Dad was always quick to take action in urgent times. That made me feel safe. The lesson that day was if you're going to be a show-off, don't be surprised if you get hurt.

DAD'S FAMILY

Of dad's ten brothers and sisters, I really only knew Billy, Katie, and Mary. I always wondered why I didn't have any brothers and sisters. Maybe it was because Mom had none.

Dad was close to his youngest sister Katie. She always had cookies or a special treat for me and asked me about school and how I was doing. She was full of compliments on how big I was getting and how handsome I was. She made me feel special.

Aunt Katie was very bright and enjoyed dueling with dad on the issues of the day.

She worked for a prominent attorney in Franklin. At tax time, she was always overworked, doing income tax preparation for the clients of the law firm. Dad would help her out and enjoyed the extra money. Aunt Katie married a great guy named Bill Chappie.

They had one child Lisa, who was five years older than me, but we were close growing up. She was always very kind to me; we were great friends. Dad and Uncle Billy were always fawning over their little sister's daughter. Dad and I would visit them often especially after Grandma Stonecash moved in with them. I always wished Lisa had been my sister instead of my cousin.

Dad was also close to his older brother Billy. He was a gregarious guy, always kidding with me and telling me wild stories like Grandma Stonecash did. He was a strong-looking man with a large frame, standing about six feet two. He was a great high school football player. Dad said he once threw a football seventy-five yards in the air for a touchdown.

He was bound for Notre Dame to play football until a freak accident. Uncle Billy was riding shotgun in a car and had his right arm out the window a little too far. His hand clipped a telephone pole, which nearly tore it off. They had to amputate most of his right thumb. Notre Dame had no use for a four-fingered quarterback. Dad always wondered how much better his life might have been if Uncle Billy had just kept his arm inside the car that day.

I had a habit of hanging my arm out the car window. Mom always yelled me, "Keep your arms in the car; remember what happened to your Uncle Billy."

Uncle Billy married an educated lady of sophistication named Sue Ellen Mays. Her father built a small fortune as a papermaker. He had a paper mill in Alabama and one in Miamisburg. When he retired, he gave the mill in Alabama to his son and the one in Miamisburg to his daughter and new son-in-law.

I wondered what it would be like if I owned my own business. I would be the boss, and nobody could tell me what to do. I would have the freedom to do as I pleased.

I heard Dad tell Mom more than once that Uncle Billy paid more attention to somebody named Jack Daniels and horsing around with plant employees than working hard and taking care of business. The mill soon began to run into financial difficulties. I remember Billy coming to our house one day. "Timmy, go play," he told me. "Uncle Billy and I need to talk."

I knew it must be serious as I always hung around Uncle Billy when he came over. loved how big and strong he was. He always acted like a tough guy and was in charge. But he always asked Dad questions and seemed protective of him. I was jealous. How great would it be to have an older brother? I overheard Dad telling Mom that Uncle Billy had asked him to work at the mill—just to straighten out the books and try to get the company on a sound financial footing. I had no idea what all that meant.

Dad was the smartest person in our family with Aunt Katie a close second. He only attended a few years of college but had a keen mind. He was class president of his freshman class at Ohio State University, and later he attended night school at University of Dayton. I don't know why he never finished.

He could figure out and build or fix most anything. And Uncle Billy knew Dad was also good with numbers. Dad loved his brother but was hesitant to jump onto a sinking ship. Mom told me Dad thought Uncle Billy had run the mill into the ground, and he advised him to file for bankruptcy.

One Sunday afternoon in the skies over the north end of Miamisburg, we saw large billows of black smoke. Dad thought the smoke had to be coming from the mill as a house fire would not cause that much black smoke. "That's tar paper burning," he said.

I was a bit surprised, but Mom and Dad brought me along to check it out. Sure enough, Uncle Billy's paper mill was on fire. Neighbors who lived close to the mill and many of the workers were gathered on a levee along a creek bed next to the mill.

"Bob, was there anybody working there today?" Mom asked.

"No, the mill reduced operations to only five days a week, so no one would be there today."

The mill was severely damaged and never operated again. There was always some suspicion of arson, maybe an insurance job, but nothing ever came of it. Uncle Billy filed for bankruptcy.

"I wish Billy would have just gotten a regular job," I heard my dad say. "But he always wanted to work for himself, be his own boss. But it takes a special kind of guy. You have to be smart and work hard if you want that freedom that comes with being your own boss. I'm not sure Billy had that combination."

Uncle Billy eventually opened a gas station on the west side of Dayton. It operated only a short time when it too went out of business.

Another one of Dad's sisters—Mary, the second oldest—never paid much attention to me nor I her. Some adults just talk to other adults and seem polite but distant around kids. Aunt Mary was one of those. Her husband Francis was a nice enough man, but I think he too preferred adult conversation. He worked at Uncle Billy's paper mill. When the mill went under, Francis was naturally upset and uncertain about the future, but Mary was uncontrollably distraught.

They had one child Donnie, who was a talented artist. Everyone would marvel at his drawings and paintings that were displayed around their house. There was something odd about Donnie, though. He seemed lonely, never said much, and acted bored at our family gatherings. He was several years older than my cousin Lisa, so I'm sure that had something to do with it. Being so much older maybe he just couldn't relate to us.

I had just come in the house from playing ball next door. Mom was standing near Dad, who was on the phone. Her arms were all folded up, and she had tears in her eyes.

"Mary is in the hospital; she apparently tried to kill herself," I heard Dad say. I wasn't sure who he was talking to. Mom and I stood by and listened in.

"Well, I'm not sure of all the details, but I guess Donnie found her this afternoon in the bathroom. She was unconscious, lying on the floor. Looks like she drank lye, mixing it with baking soda. Francis is taking it pretty well, but Donnie just sits and stares into space."

Mom and I watched and listened to Dad make several calls like this.

Aunt Mary was in the hospital for a couple of days before dying. I thought how awful that must have been to die like that. Dad said it must have been very painful, but that she'd fought the stomach pumps in the hospital. She wanted to die. Why would anyone want to die? And if you did, couldn't you have found a better way to do it? Could life ever become so bad that you didn't want to live?

Aunt Mary had lived on the same street in Franklin as Aunt Katie just up the hill a few doors. Lisa and I used to look up at her house, imagining the horror of poor Donnie finding his mother in such a state.

I never saw Donnie after Aunt Mary's suicide, but Uncle Frances did come to our house on Christmas a year or two after Mary's death. He had a present for me. I was excited. It was a book, not my favorite thing. In fact, it was the thickest book I had ever seen—as big as the Bible—and called *Don Quixote*. Mom and Dad both "oohed" and "aahhed" about it. I thanked Uncle Francis, looked at the book, and thought, *Wow, if I could read that, I would really be smart.*

I opened the book and brought the pages to my face It had a musty, woody smell that told me there was something in there I should know.

I took it to my room, and it rested on my bed for a while until it made it to the night stan, and finally over to a little bookcase where it remained for a long time, until it finally disappeared.

Mom

One day my friend Jeff Harty's mother came over to my house. She didn't even get out of the car when she began to lay into me. She rolled down the window.

"What did you think you were doing with those balloons today. Did they belong to you?"

"I didn't do anything," I answered. "What are you talking about?"

"Timmy Stonecash, you look at me. You know darn well that's not true." Her face began to swell as her voice rose. I always thought her a rather pretty woman, for a mom anyway. She had a slender figure, a youthful face, and her short blonde hair looked natural. But she wasn't pretty today, she was scary. "Those balloons belong to those Girl Scouts. You and I know Jeff was in on it too. Took the balloons out of those girl's school bags, filled them up with water, then hid in the alley. You guys pelted them on their way in to their Girl Scout meeting. Did you think that was funny?"

"No, no it wasn't me. I was there but I didn't throw anything," I lied. I had thrown one balloon and hit Connie Blackwood right in the head.

Her nose was beet red, and her nostrils flared out. I thought smoke was going to come out of her ears. I think she knew I was lying, but she wasn't there, so she couldn't prove it unless one of my buddies ratted me out. "Well, let me tell you, I got a phone call from two of those girl's moms, and they were none too happy. One of you two knocked off Connie's glasses and they broke. Do your parents know about this?"

I wanted this to be over with. What could I say to get her to leave? I grabbed my stomach and winced. "I...I'm sorry but I have diarrhea and I have to, ah, go, you know."

She looked at me hard then looked down at my pants. "I bet you do. You haven't heard the end of this, young man." She quickly backed out of our drive, almost hitting our trash cans.

I was shaking and ready to cry. Dad was in the shower. It was just as well; I didn't need him getting in on this. Mom got home a couple hours later, and she could tell I was still shaken up about something. "What's the matter with you?" Mom asked.

"Nothing," I lied.

"That's baloney. Out with it. What's up?"

I broke down in tears as I related the story. "That old bag Mrs. Harty came over here and yelled and screamed at me over something that happened after school today. She really bawled me out."

I didn't have to tell Mom anymore. She had Mrs. Harty on the phone asking her to come back over to our house. "Bob, where were you when all this was going on?"

"I was in the shower," Dad said innocently.

Mom glared at him. "Convenient for you."

Mrs. Harty had just got her window down when Mom leaned into her space and read her the riot act. "How dare you come over here and yell at my son when I am not at home?" Mom let her have it for about five minutes without taking a breath.

I went back in the house. Dad and I watched from the kitchen window.

"Wow, I wouldn't want to be on the wrong side of her tonight. Never seen her like that before," Dad said, looking at me.

It felt good that Mom was sticking up for me. When Mom came back in the house, she had a last word on what had happened. "Timmy, whatever you did that prompted all that fuss today didn't give Mrs. Harty the right to do what she did. But it didn't excuse whatever it was you did; just remember that. And remember to show some respect; she's an adult—not to be referred to as an old bag."

Mom or Dad never asked what I did. That night we had dinner on the patio. Dad had gone out to the barn to work on something, and Mom and I were cleaning up. "Oh, what a beautiful sky tonight," she said. "Look at all those stars."

I stood close to her, holding onto her arm, thinking about what had happened today. I gazed up at the brilliantly lit sky. "Look at the moon, Mom. It's so bright," I said. It was a special moment of closeness and bonding between us, sharing such a wondrous sight. She hugged me and I felt loved.

"Timmy, let's always remember this moment, you and me together, looking up at the stars."

"I will remember," I said.

"Always?"

Yes, Mom, always."

We stood there gazing up at the stars, holding each other—thinking about what the future held for us. And that we would always be together.

If I got in trouble at school, I would always try to hide it from Mom and Dad. Mom, because she would yell and scream at me and threaten to tell Dad, and Dad, because he would kill me. While I received numerous whippings from Dad, I never really felt in fear of my life, or that I didn't deserve it. Mom was always my go-to person for whatever I needed. If I begged her long and hard enough, I usually got what I wanted. Dad usually got what he wanted too.

We had a really cool house with a big stone fireplace in the middle of the living room and a huge yard with a big barn with lots of hiding places. The best thing was a wooded box built into the wall of my room; that's where I kept my secret things. Even so, Dad wasn't satisfied. He always talked about another house that he would like to build. He drew plans for a ranch-style home with a large patio. I don't know why Dad was looking to move someplace else when we had such a great place. But if Dad got excited about something, Mom and I did too.

Dad looked into buying a lot on Linden Avenue in Miamisburg. The lot was owned by Ben Suttman, who owned a clothing store in downtown Miamisburg. We didn't have the money right then, so Mr. Suttman said he would wait and not sell it to anybody else until we did. I asked Dad if Mr. Suttman was telling the truth. I wasn't sure he would really wait to sell that lot until we had the money. "We'll see. I think Mr. Suttman might be a man of his word."

"What does that mean, Dad?"

"It means if you tell someone you're going to do something, you make damn sure you do it. If you're a real man, that's what you do." That was about 1965. The lot is still vacant as of this writing.

When I was five years old, I got interested in dancing—or maybe Mom got interested in it for me. She enrolled me in dancing lessons at Vicki Jane's Dance Studio. It was located in a room above the entrance to the Miamisburg Swimming Pool.

I was the youngest and the only boy in my class. There were all sorts of other dance groups and they had this big revue at the end of the year at the Memorial Building in Miamisburg. Each group had a routine they performed on a big stage in front of an audience of admiring moms, dads, grandmas, aunts, and uncles.

At some point during our short dance routine, I began looking for Mom and Dad out in the audience. I couldn't see them because of the bright lights. So I took my hand up to my head to shield the lights and began scanning the audience for them, forgetting our routine and walking back and forth, side-to-side until I spotted them. The audience began laughing. The dance team—in particular, their parents—were not amused and later complained that I had ruined their dance number.

Vicki Jane told mom, "I think Timmy is a little young for this. Why don't you bring him back in a couple of years?" That suited Mom and me fine.

A number of years later, Mom enrolled me in jazz and acrobatics. The jazz was kind of weird, but I liked the acrobatics. Again, I was surrounded by girls. I thought maybe boys weren't supposed to do this sort of thing. They even had me working with a young girl on an adagio, which never went anywhere. It wasn't long until I moved on to something else.

They announced that there would be a special meeting after school for anyone who wanted to learn to play a musical instrument. Mom and I went to the meeting, where a man and his wife gave a little talk and demonstration of different instruments: the trumpet, saxophone, flute, a French horn, and drums. "Mom, I wanna play the drums."

"Oh, Timmy. What about something more musical? You know, Dad plays the clarinet and he could teach you."

Oh boy, I thought. *A dumb clarinet and Dad teaching me? No thanks.* "That's nice, Mom, but drums would be so cool."

She smiled. I ended up with a Signet clarinet—not the top of the line but a nice instrument. Mr. Coffman, the junior high band instructor, also gave lessons. Dad had taught me how to play a few notes, so I was ahead of everybody else in the class; that didn't last long.

A boy named Robert Glanderous brought a rubber snake to practice and began teasing everybody with it. When he saw how afraid I was, he went after me with it. I was petrified and threw a piece of my clarinet and hit him right in the nose. There was a big uproar, and we both got into big trouble with Mr. Coffman. I went on to be a mediocre clarinet player for the junior high band. I quit in the eighth grade to play football. I wish now I would have stayed in the band.

CHRISTMAS

Christmas was my favorite time at our house. Every Christmas, Dad would wrap a small box with colorful paper and decorate it with a hand tied bow, put my name on it, and place it under the Christmas tree. It would be the first package I'd open, and every year, it was always a new baseball. He began disguising the package so it wouldn't look like another ball in a box. One year he put a spring on top of the box and wrapped it all up. While I thought it was the usual baseball, I wasn't sure.

Our family Christmas traditions were dear to me. I relished and looked forward to the atmosphere that all the decorations, special foods, and the excitement of a visit from Santa created. Our house looked and smelled Christmassy with candles around the rooms, evergreen garland on the mantel and—on many nights—a roaring fire in our fireplace.

Dad could draw anything—plans for a new house or a futuristic spaceship. Another trait, along with an aptitude for math, that I did not inherit. He would paint a Santa Claus on the oval window we had in our front door and make special decorations throughout our house.

One day near Christmas, Dad said to me, "We are going to make some candles for Christmas, and you can help; go get some of your old crayons." Dad put a large pot on the stove.

"What's that stuff, Dad?"

"It's paraffin. We'll melt this, then you'll peel off the paper on your crayons and throw them in. This will add the color to the candles." Dad poured the melted mixture into old milk cartons. After they dried, he painted Santa Clauses or Christmas trees on them.

Dad took great care in the decoration of our Christmas tree, making sure each ornament was placed just right. Once he scolded Grandma for just haphazardly throwing the icicles on the tree instead of carefully placing each one separately and evenly on the branches. We would fill the massive evergreen bushes in the front of our house with Christmas lights. A large plastic Santa Claus was placed on our chimney.

Dad loved to wrap presents and would take great care and time making sure each gift package was carefully decorated with ribbons and fancy bows that he would tie. Each gift looked like it came straight from the North Pole.

I wish I would have inherited some of his artistic talent; I was lucky to draw a stick man.

At precisely five o'clock on Christmas Eve, we would load up Christmas packages, stop and pick-up Grandma Susie, and head to Virgil and Angie Lamb's house for dinner. Virgil was my mom's first cousin, but he grew up with her and was like her brother. Virgil's mom and dad had died when he was a baby, and my Grandma Susie (Mom's mom) took him in. Virgil was one of my favorite people. He was gentle and soft spoken. He had a dry sense of humor and was always ready to laugh.

Virgil and Angie had two boys: Ron, a few months younger than me, and Steve, about two years younger. We loved playing cowboys and Indians and pretending we were in the army. It was always fun to get together with them especially on Christmas eve.

"Virgil, tell us about the army and the war," I would urge.

"Yeah, Dad, tell us what you did; did you shoot anybody?" Ron asked.

"Well, as I've told you boys before, I spent my time in the Solomon Islands, where I did reconnaissance. My job was to go out ahead of the main army group, spy on the enemy positions, and report back to headquarters.

79

It was always hot, and I was always wet—it seemed to rain every day." That's about all Virgil would say about his time in the army.

That sounded exciting to me—a great adventure. I thought about that. Why did he join the army in a time of war? Why didn't he finish high school? But it all must have worked out for him. don't remember much about Christmas Eve dinner as we were so anxious to open presents. Mom and Dad would get Ron and Steve the same thing every year: a set of six shooters, cowboy hats, or an Indian headdress. I would get the same from Virgil and Angie.

Around about eight p.m., we would pack up and go across town to Aunt Katie's and Uncle Fred's. I always hated to go because by now Ron, Steve, and I were having a great time playing cowboys and Indians. The only consolation for leaving was I knew I would get more presents at Aunt Katie's and Uncle Fred's house and my cousin Lisa would be there to update me on all the cool, hip things she was doing—things that I would like to do.

I never saw Virgil or Angie take a drink of alcohol. But the booze was always flowing at Aunt Katie and Uncle Fred's. Mostly beer and an occasional highball.

Uncle Fred was always nice to me but was quiet and reserved. I guess because Aunt Katie had so much to say. Aunt Katie was so kind and always making a fuss over me.

"Get over here, young man, and give your Aunt Katie a little sugar— right here on the cheek. You're looking so spiffy tonight. That bow tie makes you look all grown up." Aunt Katie led me into her kitchen. "I want you to be the first to sample these Christmas cookies I just took out of the oven."

"Oh great! Can I have two?"

"Of course you can, and look what else I made just for you: dried beef rolls."

I loved her dried beef rolls—cream cheese, diced scallions, and horseradish all rolled up. Yummy. Aunt Katie's home was a Christmas wonderland, smelling of fresh evergreens and lit with Christmas candles and sparkling lights from a huge Christmas tree. A crackling fire warmed the house from a brick fireplace. There were decorated wreaths and garland along the bookcases. A wooden carved crèche with straw scattered about, adorned with a ceramic angel at the top.

There were brownies, hard tack candy, fudge, and buckeyes (peanut butter dipped in chocolate) on small plates throughout her home. I made sure I sampled all the goodies.

My Grandma Stonecash was always there, and in fact, lived with Aunt Katie and Uncle Fred for the last five years of her life. She was a great story teller. We could never tell if what she told us was true or not, but it was most always scary.

Uncle Billy, Aunt Sue Ellen, and their daughter Cindi would sometimes be there. I had a great time and never wanted to leave. Being with family was so fun for me, and Christmas made time together the best.

On the way home one Christmas Eve, Dad complained to Mom, "Did you see what Katie gave Billy for Christmas?"

"The booze, you mean?" Mom asked. From the backseat my head swiveled between my mom and dad.

"I can't believe she did that knowing that's the last thing he needs," was Dad's answer. I wasn't sure what he meant. Maybe whiskey was bad for a person or maybe it was just bad for Uncle Billy.

"Did you say something to her?"

"I did later when I got her aside. Not much good then, though; Billy had already dived into it." Dad paused for just a moment before suggesting, "It's not too late; let's stop at Luke and Betsy's for a nightcap."

"Okay, Santa, but only one. I mean it," Mom cautioned.

Luke was Dad's best friend and best drinking Buddy, so Mom knew to set the ground rules upfront. Luke and Betsy lived just two streets over from Aunt Katie's.

"Bob, these roads are getting slick; this snow is really starting to come down. I'm serious; we can't stay long"

Once inside the warm house, Luke served Dad a beer in a globe-shaped glass. Dad would carefully sprinkle a little salt in it. Mom had a coke with me because she said she was driving.

Luke and Betsy had no children, so at Christmas they would splurge on me. Dad and Mom would say, "Oh my goodness, you guys shouldn't have."

I was thinking, *Sure, they should have.*

Luke would say, "Well, Santa was here and left this for Timmy."

I always had my eye on the shotgun that hung over the fireplace mantle. One Christmas Eve, Luke got the gun down and let me hold it; I must have been about twelve.

"When you get sixteen, it's yours," Luke said.

My eyes lit up. Wow, a real gun. Dad looked at me with glassy eyes and nodded, Mom just stared ahead. Sixteen seemed like an eternity away, but I finally made it. Luke, however, was long gone by then. I never got the shotgun.

By this time in the evening, I was tired, Dad was having a great time, and Mom was ready to go home. Dad's plea for one more round fell on deaf ears. Mom knew I would be up at the crack of dawn Christmas morning, begging to start opening packages. It was after midnight when Dad and Luke finished their third Hudepohl.

Most Christmas Eves, I put some cookies and milk out for Santa, but one year, Dad suggested that we put out a cold beer and some chips. Mom thought that was a bit much, as Santa certainly didn't need another beer.

I was the first one up in the morning, or that's what I thought, until I came downstairs and saw Grandma already in the kitchen working her magic.

There would be one toy that was not wrapped, so as soon as I came down the stairs, I went for it. I had to wait until everyone was downstairs, had their coffee and a roll, and then I was allowed to tear into the packages. Most of my presents were from Santa Claus. There were always a couple that were labeled from Mom and Dad.

Mom and Dad would exchange a couple of gifts. They would get Grandma something nice. I was always the center of attention and had lots of presents to open. Some clothes, but mostly toys. One year I got a huge train set my dad had mounted to a piece of plywood. It was really cool. You could put oil into the smoke stack and smoke would come out as the engine heated up.

I always hoped a little brother or sister would be in one of those packages, but that wasn't to be. Regardless, Mom and Dad did go to great effort to make it a special time in our house that gave me many sweet memories.

THE GARDEN

Dad looked at Mom and me and said, "I've laid the garden out, tilled the ground, and bought the plants; now we all have to get them in the ground."

By mid-April, the lettuces, radishes, and onions were already in the ground. The first week of May or so it was time to get the hot weather plants in as well. Tomatoes, peppers, and green beans.

Dad had done most of the work; now it was time for Mom and me to do ours. Keep the weeds out, water the plants regularly, and stake the tomatoes when it was time. It was a rule at our house that every weed had to be out of the garden before we could leave for vacation.

We grew rows and rows of half runner green beans, planting them at two-week intervals for about six weeks. Dad would take them to Bob Heck's Hi Spot and trade them for steaks. I don't remember what the exchange rate was, but it seemed like a great deal to trade green beans for steaks.

We grew big Spanish onions that Dad sold to another bar and restaurant in downtown Miamisburg named Mobley's. It was right across the railroad tracks from the Pure Oil filling station where Dad worked. On occasion, Mom and I would meet Dad there for lunch. A short white-haired lady named Pearl waitressed there. She was a sweet lady who would joke around with Dad. I would sit and stare at the huge airplane propeller that hung from the ceiling in the dining area. There were four lights that hung down from each of the blades.

"Pearl," I was brave enough to ask one time. "If that propeller started spinning, would it fly off the celling and cut our heads off."

"I 'spose it would if it got spinning too fast, so if you see it starting to spin, you duck under the table." She chuckled a little and walked away.

Surely she wasn't serious.

Pearl would put a big slice of one of our Spanish onions on a roast beef sandwich with some mayonnaise, and it was to die for. Dad was enterprising, always looking for ways to make a little extra money. Growing lots of vegetables in our garden, filling our table, and selling and trading them to local eateries.

That inspired me. I ordered vegetable and flower seeds from a seed wholesaler and then peddled them around the neighborhood. Our next-door neighbors, Charlie and Dorothy Schroder would always buy lots of seeds, mostly vegetable seeds. Charlie was very discriminating, looking at each packet carefully.

"Oh, Charlie, get them both! Help Timmy out," Dorothy said.

He remained methodical in his selection, making sure he knew what he was getting, turning them over in his hand, and reading all the plant descriptions on the back. Charlie had a gruff voice and would clear his throat just before he spoke. "Okay, how much we got here?" he said as he placed two more packets in his stack.

I really liked the Schroders. They were kind, earthy people. They had a small but incredibly productive garden behind their garage. I would often peer over the fence and marvel at how lush and vigorous their garden was. In the summer, Charlie and Dorothy were always out there. It was amazing how much they got from such a small space. All the vegetable plants were in nice, neat, weedless rows: lettuce, radishes, tomatoes, swiss chard, green beans, and onions. There were bright Marigolds all around the edge. Mom said he had a green thumb. I knew she was kidding, but I always looked. I only saw leathery calloused hands; his thumb was dirty, but I never saw any green.

Charlie was a measured man in his manner and tone. When I thought Charlie was going to say something, he would hesitate and just clear his throat. I could tell he was thinking. Then he would speak with some wisdom and usually end with a funny story.

"Timmy, when I was a kid about your size, I had a neighbor friend who every time I came outside with anything to eat, he always wanted some whether it was a piece of candy or a bite of my sandwich. So one day I came outside with a sandwich, and sure enough, the boy next door wanted a bite. I usually had a ham or peanut butter sandwich. But that day I had spread lard between two slices of bread." Charlie let out a big laugh. "He never asked for a bite of my sandwich again."

Charlie's garden bordered our property on the east side and the ground lay a little higher. He was able to keep an eye on the comings and goings at our house and he did. One day I was playing out in the back yard when I spotted Charlie puttering around in his garden. I wandered over to see what he was doing. That day Charlie gave me a little lesson. Much later, I realized the lesson was more than just about gardening.

"If you want a strong tomato plant that produces lots of nice fruit, you have to make sure they get off to a good start; they need to be planted in rich soil. You mix your compost of leaves, grass clippings, and kitchen scraps in with some good top soil. You have to work the dirt," he said. "Turn it over and mix in your compost and if you can get some cow manure—that's the best. Then you must keep all the bad things away from your vegetable plants; they try to get right up next to them. The first thing you know you won't be able to tell the bad plants from the good ones." He paused and looked sharply at me. "Now remember, get the plants off to a good start and then keep the bad things away from them." He was trying to tell me something.

"What bad things?" I asked.

"Weeds!"

One day, Dad asked me what I knew about the broken windows on the back of the barn. I told him that the Belville kids had done it. So he brought me over to their house and asked them if they had broken those windows. I started to cry when they told him they had nothing to do with the incident, that they had seen me throwing the rocks and breaking the windows from their yard. I cried even more when Dad cut down some switches from a willow tree. "I want you to know it's not about the windows—I was going to take those out anyway. It's about you lying to me." I always told the truth to him after that.

I always liked going places with Dad. He was always going to strange places and meeting strange people. One evening just before dark, Dad asked me if I wanted to take a ride with him. Without hesitation, I ran to the car. We were driving down Central Avenue when a car pulled out right in front of us.

"Damn!" Dad yelled as he hit the brakes and threw his right arm across me to keep me from hitting the dashboard. Dad and Mom's right arm acted as my seat belt on numerous occasions. Dad gave the guy a stern look as we pulled into a long gravel lane that led to an old run-down house.

Come on, I want you to help me pick out some things," Dad said.

I got out of the car and a big German Shepherd came running at me from out of nowhere, barking and growling. I barely made it back into the car. He jumped up and put his paws on the passenger door. I thought his snarling teeth were going to bite right through the window. My heart was pounding.

Dad kept walking and then looked back at me. "Just stay in the car." That's exactly what I was going to do. That dog finally calmed down, and wagging his tail, ran up to Dad. Maybe he wasn't a kid dog or maybe he knew I was too young to be here.

It wasn't long until Dad was back at our car with a big sack. "Scazooley had some good stuff."

"Scazooley?"

"Yeah, that's the man's name in there."

87

"What kind of name is that?" I asked.

"I think it's just something he made up. He doesn't want people to know his real name."

I pulled on the sack to look in.

"No looking! Wait until we get home." When Dad finally emptied the sack on the kitchen table, I cried, "Oh, wow! Fireworks!"

"Bob, you know those are illegal. Where did you get those?" Mom asked, crossing her arms over her chest.

"Scazooley, Mom. Dad got them from Scazooley," I blurted out.

"That's just a little law," Dad said. "Nobody cares about that."

The next day was the fourth of July. We shot them off our fireplace in the back yard up and over the levy and into the river.

The first time I saw Jim Creager I didn't know whether to laugh or cry. His head twitched side to side, and he would sort of spit his words out. If you were patient and listened closely, you could eventually understand what he was saying.

"Jim this is my son, Tim," dad introduced, "and you know my wife, Betty."

Jim's head bobbed up and down, he stuttered, and his arms jerked. "Nice t..t..to meet you Tim. Yep—know the Mrs."

Jim would come around every once in a while and have a couple of beers with Dad.

Mom pulled me aside. "Timmy, don't stare at Jim."

It was hard not to. I wondered what affliction he had and how he got that way. He walked with near convulsive movements that made me think he was going to fall down at any moment.

"You know God made us all different; none of us are exactly alike," Mom explained. "Some of us are more different than others. But you should know that no matter what, one person is no better than another person."

"But what about bad people? Like robbers and killers? Aren't we better than them?"

88

Mom gave me a patient smile. "Yes, there are bad people, but they didn't start out being bad. People make themselves that way; they choose to be bad. Jim didn't choose to be the way he is; he didn't do anything to make himself that way. He's different but he's not bad."

I could hear Jim and Dad laughing, hooting, and hollering in the living room. I could tell Jim's affliction made no difference to Dad; he never mentioned it, so I never asked about it.

I thought about that; how strong a person Jim must be to carry on with life. Mom said Dad had stood up for him at his wedding. What could a woman see in Jim? I had lots of friends, but it was easy to be their friends. I wondered what could you do with Jim? You couldn't ride bikes; you couldn't play baseball—could Jim swim? I doubt he could even pass a football. It wouldn't be easy to be Jim's friend. But Jim needed a friend just like everybody else, and my dad was Jim's friend, and I felt good about that.

Aunt Katie's basement was our family's favorite wintertime party venue.

Dad, Uncle Billy, and Uncle Fred were all accomplished drinkers. Mom, Aunt Katie, and Aunt Sue Ellen were not far behind. They always had a high old time together, many times ending the evening singing the Lord's Prayer, which I always thought was kind of odd. My Aunt Mary and Uncle Francis would occasionally be there. Lisa, Cindi, and I would dance the twist with our aunts and uncles. Uncle Billy said, "Feels just like I'm putting out a cigarette with both feet."

In the summer, our family parties moved to our patio in our backyard. It had a big double-sided fireplace with a roof and a cement floor. Dad strung fancy Chinese lanterns down the center rafter and filled an old refrigerator that sat in the corner with RC Cola, popsicles, a bottle of wine or two, and plenty of beer. After someone stole a bottle of wine, Dad put a chain and lock around the refrigerator. I later found out the wine thief was one of my friends.

At one of those parties, we challenged each other to a race. Uncle Billy was there with his two boys, who were from Sue Ellen's first marriage; they were quite a bit older than the rest of us. Anyway, we were all lined up to race: Lisa, Cindi, Jeff, Chris, and me.

Just before Dad said go, Uncle Billy jumped on the line. Dad restarted, "Ready, Set, Go!"

Uncle Billy took off and looked back to see us all trailing in his dust. He hadn't lost much from his football days even with a few highballs in him. We knew he was the strongest in the family; now we knew he was also the fastest.

Lisa, Cindi, and I would play around the fire and roast marshmallows, laughing and cutting up, having fun with each other while our parents were having a good time with Strohs, Carling's Black Label, and highballs.

Aunt Katie noticed it first. "What's that light back there? Is that up in the graveyard?"

We all looked for ourselves.

"Wow what is that?" Cindi asked.

"Let's go check it out," I suggested.

"I'll go if you all will," Lisa said.

"Cindi, you'll go, won't you?" I coaxed.

"Only if a big person goes."

"Come on, Mom, go with us," Lisa begged.

"No, I am not going way back there! It's dark," Aunt Katie said.

"Of course, it's dark! That's the whole idea. That's what makes it scary; it's dark." I pleaded, "Come with us, and let's see what that light is." I was excited -- an adventure was about to begin.

Aunt Katie turned away from us, then quickly turned back and looked at us really hard. "You know, that's up in the graveyard, and all of you will chicken out before we get there. You'll take off and run back here, leaving me alone in the dark." Aunt Katie really wanted to go as much as we did, but she wanted to see if we would really go.

"Please, pretty please! Go with us," we all begged.

Finally, Aunt Katie relented. "Okay, let's take a couple of flash lights, and let's all stay together," she said as she began to lead us into the dark a couple hundred yards through some trees. We climbed over a short, barbed-wire fence and then up a steep hill that led to the edge of the graveyard.

"You can barely see the fire on the patio," Lisa said, looking over her shoulder.

"Maybe we should go back," Cindi whined. With no moon and an overcast sky, it was pitch black.

Crack! We all jumped and yelled. "What was that?"

"I just stepped on a stick—or was that someone's back I stepped on?" Aunt Katie joked.

Our laughter rang out into the darkness.

"Oh, look at all the headstones, all the different sizes and shapes. Each with a dead soul under it, *ooooh.*" Aunt Katie was trying to scare us.

"Why do they call them headstones?" I asked.

"When they bury you, they place your head where the stone marker is. If they put your head at the other end, they would have to call it a footstone," Aunt Katie explained.

That was the last time we all laughed.

"Okay, where is the light?" Lisa said.

"It's coming from that big mausoleum. Let's go over there," I said.

"No, I'm not going," Cindi cried as her grip on Aunt Katie's hand grew tighter.

"Yeah, let's go. I want to see what's up there," Lisa pleaded.

We began walking carefully between the headstones toward the mausoleum. "Are there dead people in there?" Cindi asked.

"No, they're not dead. They're just sleeping, and you have to go up and knock on the door and wake them up," Lisa said.

"No way! I want to go back." Cindi was really scared now.

"Okay, honey, don't be scared. We will go back," Aunt Katie assured her.

"No, I want to go knock on the door," I said. "Come on, Lisa." I grabbed her hand and we began running as fast as we could toward the mausoleum.

When we got within a few feet, we stopped. "Well," Lisa said.

"It was your idea. You go knock on it."

"Chicken," she said.

That was all it took. I reached out and pounded my fist on the door. A monster-like growl came from inside the mausoleum. We looked at each other, struggling in vain to move and speak.

We both just stared at each other, frozen in place. I tried to scream, and nothing came out. We couldn't move—it was as though our feet were in concrete. We reached for each other's hand. I had this feeling that said, *Run away and don't ever come here again*, but I couldn't move.

Then, all at once, we were free and our screams came out. We turned away and ran as fast as we could. We caught up with Aunt Katie and Cindi, who had heard our screams and were already running toward the patio. They were now climbing over the barbed-wire fence. Lisa and I leaped the fence, and I yelled, "Come on, hurry!"

We were all out of breath when we reached the campfire. We looked back toward the graveyard. The light was gone. We had lots more family parties in our backyard, but that was our last night trip to the graveyard.

On Decoration Day, Grandma Susie would haul me off with her to bring flowers to our family who had moved to the Springboro and Franklin graveyards. On this day the graveyards would spring to life with a plethora of beautiful flowers of all shapes and kinds.

Grandma would explain, "My people are resting here, and I remember and honor them on this day by decorating their graves with flowers. We especially honor the men who served and died for our freedom."

"Why did they have to die for our freedom?"

"Shucks boy, because there's always been bad people in this world trying to take our freedom from us. If we want to keep our freedom, sometimes we have to fight and sometimes we have to die."

"Why are they trying to take our freedom? Don't they have any?"

"Now, Timmy, you're being silly. But you know you may have a point there. Now go fill this bucket. There's a pump down at the end of that lane." Grandma pointed in the direction of a well pump. The bucket she gave me held several gallons, so when it was full, it was really heavy. I struggled when bringing it back and water splashed over the rim. "Go get another one. I want to soak them. No guess as to when it's gonna rain, and I won't be back here for, well, no telling. I want these flowers to last as long as possible."

I liked going to the Franklin graveyard on Decoration Day. Grandma's Mom and Dad and a few aunts and uncles were spread over a steep hillside. At noon, old soldiers fired their rifles in the air. They ejected the spent shells, and we kids scrambled around the ground to pick them up.

Off in the distance, a trumpet played, and everyone stilled.

I enjoyed the time with Grandma at the graveyards, but we always stayed too long. I never liked to stay in the same place too long, especially a graveyard. I had places I needed to get to and things I needed to do.

She would point out all our "kin folk" as she called those who had passed.

Other kinfolk and friends would also be watering flowers and Grandma would have never-ending conversations with them. I always thought our family small, so I was surprised to be introduced to so many of us even if most were dead.

Grandma had her own gravestone with her name and date of birth on it. It seemed odd and a little scary to be standing there with her, looking at her grave. Grandma showed a lot of sorrow and respect for the dead. It was all foreign to me; I hadn't been. touched by death.

BASEBALL

I loved being around my family, but it seemed like they were mostly adults. So, if there was a chance to be with other kids, I jumped on it.

And baseball gave me that chance.

Playing whiffle ball in the Belvilles' backyard was the first thing I remember doing when we moved to our house on Central Avenue. We spent many afternoons smacking that plastic ball around their yard, long games beginning as soon as the weather broke in the spring. We pretended one team was the New York Yankees and the other team was the Cincinnati Reds. I liked the Reds because they were only fifty miles down the road from where we lived and the Yankees because they had the best player in baseball: Mickey Mantle, who also had the coolest name. At that time, baseball was America's national pastime, the most popular sport in America. The 1961 season was special for both the Yankees and the Reds.

That summer, while the Belville kids and I blasted balls until dusk in the backyard, Roger Maris began his second year as a Yankee, and he and the great Mickey Mantle chased Babe Ruth's record of sixty home runs in a season, a record that had stood for thirty-four years.

Doug spoke up, "I bet you Mickey gets to sixty first. That Roger Maris acts cocky, and I heard he spit in the umpire's face."

"Yeah, I heard that too," I added.

94

My friends and I really couldn't fathom it happening—after all, the only one who had come close to hitting sixty home runs was the Babe himself in 1921 when he had hit fifty-nine—but boy, did we want to see it happen. We all agreed if the Babe's record had to go down, we wanted Mickey to do it.

In September, Mickey became ill and missed some games. So, it was Maris who passed the Babe on the last day of the regular season, which saw the Yankees at the top of the American League and my Reds, led by Frankie Robinson, the National League Champions.

All the World Series games were played during the day, so after school I would race home to catch the last few innings. I kept waiting for Mickey to hit a home run or do something great. The announcer said he was hurt, so he didn't play that much in the series, coming to bat only six times with one hit. But the Yankees didn't seem to need him.

"I feel bad for the Reds," I told Doug. "Heck, the Yankees go to the World Series all the time, but the Reds rarely make it. So getting there for them was a big deal, and they only won one game."

"I know," Doug agreed. "It would be like getting to the championship game in your little league then only scoring one run and losing. What a letdown that would be; thinking you found a taste of victory only to have it taken away."

The next year Mickey Mantle won the American League MVP award again, and the Yankees beat Willie Mays's San Francisco Giants in the World Series. The Reds, meanwhile, came in third place. That same year, still crazy about major league baseball, I began my own organized baseball career. I was nine years old.

Being young, I was anxious and a little scared to go to my first practice. I envisioned hitting home runs like the great Mickey Mantle and pitching like Whitey Ford or Jim Maloney. I just didn't want to play right field. They always put the worst player in right field because most kids were right-handed and would naturally hit mostly to left and center field; rarely would a ball be hit to right field. So, if you played right field, everybody knew you were the worst player on the team, just one step above the kids on the bench.

It was raining on that early spring day of my first practice. Mom thought practice would be canceled, but I begged her to go just in case. She drove us to Bell Civic Park in our new Rambler station wagon. The diamond had been built on land that was donated by Bell Vault Moment; they sold headstones. The park backed up to a twenty-foot earth levy, holding back that same Great Miami River that had flooded us out of our home just a couple of years before.

The hard rain had let up, but it was still drizzling when we got to the park. We drove around by the concession stand and then over to the other side of the park; there was no sign of anyone. I rolled down the window, feeling the spit of moisture on my arm. The air was clean and cool and had that earthy, musky smell that was familiar after a hard rain.

Suddenly, a man on a bicycle came from the alley across the parking lot. Mom rolled down the window as I slumped in the back seat.

"Well, Mrs. Stonecash, how are we doing this fine rainy day?" His brown hair was soaking wet and glued to his skull.

"Dicky Hanna, what are you doing out here?" Mom asked with friendly enthusiasm.

"Oh, just riding my bike in the rain," he said breezily, leaning on one leg with the bike resting against his thigh. "I live just down the road there in the yellow house. What are you doing since you left National Cash Register—or "The Cash" as we called it?"

"Dickey, I was so worried after they let us all go. I worked at Grants for a while, but we needed something more. I finally got on at Mound Lab."

"Wow, that's nice. How's that working out? What do you do up there?"

What was with all the questions? I wished this guy would just hit the road already. "Oh, it's great," my mom answered with a grin, "and it only takes me five minutes to get to work; but I can't tell you what I do... it's all secret up there. You know, government work."

I stared out the window at the soggy field. All I wanted to do was play baseball, but since practice wasn't going to happen, I wanted to go home. I gently pushed my knee against the back of Mom's seat, hoping she'd get the hint. I could be a rude little shit. But she kept on talking.

"It's not much of a day for bike riding," Mom said.

Dicky peered into the back seat. "I thought I would ride down here to the park and see if anybody showed up for my practice."

I straightened up. Did he say *his* practice?

"This your boy, Tim?" Dicky asked.

"Yes, he's my one and only." Mom beamed.

How did he know my name? Who was this guy other than someone Mom knew from her old job? His tone livened up at that and he said, "I'm the coach for Gastinos! Tim's on my roster!"

I wondered what or who a Gastino was, but Mom's voice wouldn't let me linger there long. "Oh, really? Did you hear that, Timmy? Dicky—Mr. Hanna here—is your coach."

Coach Hanna glared at me with a forced smile then looked back at Mom and said, "I thought he was nine?" I sat up straight and tried to push my belly out. I might not be a big leaguer yet, but I could play.

Mom looked at me and said, "He *is* nine. See, Timmy. I told you to eat your vegetables."

My mind raced with the thought of me sneaking green beans off my plate and stuffing them into pockets so I could leave the table. I hated green beans, especially after they'd gotten cold sitting on my plate while I hoped they would somehow just disappear. Did they really make a difference as to how big I was? Maybe I'd need to rethink my vegetable eating.

"That's okay; we'll find a spot for him," Coach Hanna said, grinning at me, showing a missing tooth in the corner of his mouth.

He and Mom continued talking for what seemed like an eternity. I caught the part about there being no practice that day and that regular practices would be on Tuesday and Thursday nights with games on Saturdays. All good information, but nothing really interested me. I just wanted to play.

The team was made up of kids nine to eleven years old. There were six of us first-year players, four second-year, and three third-year players. So that meant four guys sat on the bench. I didn't want to be one of those four guys.

The first day of practice, all the first-year players were put in the outfield to catch fly balls hit by the assistant coach, a big guy named Bill Williams, who called me out.

"Tim, get over here and shag for me."

I had to catch the balls coming back in from the fielders and give him the ball so he could hit it again. I liked that; it made me feel special. Every so often he would hit a ball almost straight up and yell at me to get it. I would jump toward the ball, catch it, and toss it back to him.

There was one big kid on the team, Bill Williams Jr., the coach's son, and one very big kid on the team, Alberto Biggalo. He asked everybody to call him "Big Al" and we did.

He was about six foot tall and just about that wide—not fat, just big, thick-necked, with muscular arms. Both were third-year players—both pitchers and good hitters.

Big Al could throw smoke and hit the ball harder and farther than anybody else on the team. He had several long home runs that year. After one long ball, I yelled at him, "Hey, next time put it over the lights!"

He responded, "I did! It did go over the lights!"

I laughed. It had been a towering blast, but there was no way the ball went over the lights. Big Al was a great hitter but not quite as good as he thought, but I sure wasn't going to argue with him.

Our catcher was Buddy Green. He would jump up after a fastball from Big Al, throw his glove off, and rub his hand, all the time complaining under his breath about Big Al, "throwing so fuckin' hard." Buddy was a good catcher: he had a strong arm and would dare kids to steal on him. If Buddy caught the ball cleanly, he would throw most kids out going to second. Anyone trying to steal third was dead meat.

But Buddy had a bad habit of flinching and turning his head if the ball was thrown in the dirt or even real low. Buddy would likely miss it, the ball would run all the way to the backstop, and if there was runner on base, he would advance easily.

Bill Williams Jr. was also a good hitter and a better overall pitcher than Big Al. He and I got along really well. One day, just before our game started, Bill said, "Hey, Tim, do you see those two girls over there in the stands?"

"Where?" I asked

"Right up there, sitting at the top. See the old man with the hat. That's my Grandpa; there is a girl sitting on each side of him. The one to the right is Debbie."

I followed Bill's finger and my eyes landed on a cutie with long blonde hair and tanned face. She smiled at us, but she got a little shy and looked away when she noticed Bill was pointing her out.

"Yeah, so."

"Well, they think you're cute," Bill said with an air that suggested he was in the know.

"The bigger one does anyway."

"Yeah?" I said, considering. "How do you know that?"

"Cause they're my little sisters," Bill said as he playfully jabbed me in the side.

I had a buddy Mitch Sparks. He wasn't a real big kid, but he had a fiery temperament and wouldn't take shit off anybody. But what I liked most about him was he was always up for anything. I soon found out he was sweet on Bill's sister Debbie and lived in the same housing plat. He and Debbie's family were friends and had been on vacation together. So, needleless to say, he had the inside track with her.

One day, Mitch came over to my house. We went to the far end of my backyard and climbed a big sycamore tree. The first branch was way over our heads, so we took turns jumping up, grabbing it, and pulling ourselves up. Mitch was on one side, and I was on the other as we slowly made our way up this mammoth tree.

"This about far enough, don't ya think?" I asked Mitch.

Mitch looked down, "Oh shit yeah; this is high enough."

Taking out our pocket knives, we carved *TS+DW* and *MS+DW* into the bark. The limb must have been about twenty feet off the ground; no one was ever going to see it but us, surely never Debbie. But it amused us. And we didn't stop there. He and I even pretended we got in a fight over Debbie at Bell Civic Park one night. We went over the river levy and hid and ate some Reece's Cups, telling some other kids to go tell Debbie we were fighting over her. We had a big laugh over that.

I never had much of a relationship with Debbie. In fact, the only time I can remember talking to her in person was at her birthday party. I was surprise to be invited and even more surprised that Mitch wasn't.

We had the usual cake and ice cream, and everyone gave Debbie a present. Mom had wrapped a couple books for me. Debbie thanked me, but I could tell she wasn't impressed.

We played pin the tail on the donkey for a while and some other dumb game.

"Hey, Mom, we're going to go down in the basement and listen to music," Debbie announced.

Debbie whispered to me, "Come on, were going to play spin the bottle."

That sounded good to me, especially if Debbie was playing. There were three groups of kids, only three boys, one in each group of three girls, sitting in a circle on the floor with an empty coke bottle in the middle. Somehow Debbie wasn't in my group. *How could that happen*, I wondered. There were two girls I didn't know and Debbie's little sister in my group.

Then, just as I started to spin the bottle, Debbie ran over said, "Sara, you switch with me and go over to that group." It was Debbie's party, so there was no objection. I smiled at Debbie and spun the bottle. It stopped and pointed squarely at one of the girls I didn't know.

"Ah, that was a practice spin," I said as I gave the bottle another whirl. Unbelievably it stopped again pointing at the same girl.

"Oh, give it one last try," Debbie said as she pushed the bottle toward me.

This time it stopped right in front of Nancy, Debbie's sister.

"Okay, that's it, come on, no more cheating," Nancy said as she grabbed my hand and pulled me up.

You had to go behind a curtain for the kiss, and once hidden away, as Nancy closed her eyes, I gave her a quick but soft kiss on her check. When we immerged from behind the curtain, Debbie pulled me aside and said, "Well, we tried. Sometimes things just don't work out, but here's a friendship ring to make up for it."

"Oh, wow that's great! What does this mean?" I asked.

"It means we're friends—what do you think it means?"

It wasn't long after the party that Debbie and I had an argument on the phone. She thought I paid more attention to some of the other girls at her party than I did her. Debbie didn't think I should be talking to other girls in front of her; she said that that made her look bad. I thought she was crazy and that she was just being jealous.

I told Mitch all about it as we were standing on the curb in the street near his house. He leaned over the sewer and said, "Go ahead, toss that ring in the gutter; that'll show her."

"Why would I want to do that?"

He didn't let up. He kept encouraging me to throw her ring in the gutter. To make him shut up, I finally tossed it. Immediately, I had second thoughts and dove toward it, yelling, "Wait! Don't go in!" The silver ring stopped rolling, landing right on the edge of the gutter grate. I nearly felt relief until Mitch bent down and flicked it off the lip and into the drain.

Those rings were a big deal in those days; they usually meant you were "going together," something that I didn't think Debbie and I ever were.

Mitch wasted no time in telling Debbie I had thrown her ring into the gutter. And that was the end of my brief and superfluous relationship with her. But somehow, my friendship with Mitch was not diminished in the slightest and continued to grow over the years.

Back on the field, Coach kept telling Buddy that turning away when the pitch was in the dirt was dangerous as he had no padding on his side

101

or at the back of the head. "Sometime, you're going to get hit!" Coach would say. But being the only catcher meant lots of playing time, so Buddy always said he wanted to catch even though he didn't like it. I was relegated to the outfield, usually left field. I felt alone out there, just me and my glove. I'd cover my face with my glove—the strong scent of leather pleasing—and peer through the tiny holes to watch Big Al winding up and throwing smoke as usual. I was safe—nobody was going to pull the ball to left field on Big Al.

I was in the outfield with my legs crossed, bored, chewing on a piece of grass when I heard the scream. Buddy threw off his mask and gloves and rolled around on the ground crying. It seemed that Mike had thrown a wild one that bounced just to the right of the plate. When Buddy turned his back, it had caught him right in the kidney.

"Hey, Stonecash!" Coach Hanna yelled. "Get in here and get the equipment on!"

Was this my time to shine? I ran in fast but not too fast; I wanted to enjoy everyone watching me come in to catch.

"You ever caught before?" Coach asked.

"Nope."

"Well, how tough are you?"

"Pretty tough."

"Get in there and see if you can handle this, Stonecash," Big Al yelled from the mound.

No further encouragement was needed. I tried to hurry but had trouble with the knee pads. Coach Williams bent down and loosened the strap for me, offering a few pointers. "Keep your right hand in a fist behind the glove like this," he said, demonstrating with his own glove. "You don't want to get a broken finger. And keep your eye on the ball. You got a chest protector—if you miss the ball, it's not going to hurt. Keep your hand in a fist until the ball hits the mitt, then squeeze it. You have knee pads, see—" He knocked his knuckles against them. "Hard plastic—good protection for those kneecaps." Then he took the ball and pushed it up to my face mask.

"See? The ball can't get through these metal bars. Now remember this above all else: never turn your head or body away from the pitch. You see what happened to Buddy? Got it?"

I nodded because I couldn't do anything else. My heart galloped in my chest. Is this how a major league catcher felt?

"You have no protection back here," Coach said as he slapped my side and back of my head with his glove. "Okay, you're ready. Kneel down and take some pitches; you can do it."

Despite the nerves, I did it, and not a ball got past me. I got a lot of playing time that year, especially for a first-year player, largely because nobody else wanted to catch. I actually got pretty good at it too. I was no Yogi Berra or even a Johnny Edwards, but I was better than Buddy, throwing out a few guys trying to steal third and nailing a couple of the guys going to second.

Once in a while, I would let one get through, but not many. The pitchers appreciated that, and most importantly, so did the coaches. That first year was a lot of fun because the two best players, Bill, and Mike, took a liking to me. I was respected and looked up to by the other players because I was playing catcher, a key position on any team.

My organized baseball career lasted a mere six years. I spent three years in what was referred to as the minors for nine- to eleven-year-olds and two years in the majors (thirteen- and fourteen-year-olds). Then it was E-League for fourteen- to sixteen-year-olds.

Fun wasn't the only benefit to being on the team. It provided structure in my life. It required me to be organized and cooperative—everything my teachers wanted me to be in school. Coaches demand you to be where you're supposed to be, when you're supposed to be there, doing what you're supposed to be doing. And I did it because I loved being around kids on a baseball field. I couldn't wait to get to practice or a game. The exhilaration of playing buoyed me—my confidence, my spirits—though I was also afraid. A fear that I would strike out or let a ball get past me—that I would be sent to right field, or worse, to the bench.

But my enthusiasm and hard work led to limited but meaningful success and a feeling of achievement, which fueled my interest in the game even more.

There were only two things to do in the summer: play baseball and go swimming. Miamisburg had an Olympic-sized pool built by the TWA in the 1930s. The pool had low, medium, and high diving boards in the deep end, which was twelve feet deep. The other end had a huge slide that emptied into about three feet of water. The pool was a big no-no on game days. The coach said that swimming out in the hot sun wore you out, and you would be no good for the game that night. If you came to the game that night and Coach found out that you went to the pool that day, you didn't play. The chlorine in the pool and the sun had a way of making your eyes bloodshot and bleaching your skin, and that was a dead giveaway that you'd been at the pool, so there was no sense in lying. Plus, some kids would snitch on one of the starters in hopes they would get more playing time that day. There were rules, of course, *on* the field in baseball but also *off* the field—none of which I minded; it was nothing like school.

I continue to follow the Yankees who won the American League pennant again in 1963 for the twenty-eighth time. They fell, however, to the "Left Hand of God" and the Los Angeles Dodgers in four games, the first time the Yankees had ever been swept in a World Series. Sandy Koufax had an incredible year, going 25-5 with a league-leading 1.88 ERA and becoming only the second player to win both the Cy Young Award and the Most Valuable Player Award.

That fall after our organized baseball season had ended, our games began again in the Belvilles' backyard. I pretended to be Koufax. He was a southpaw, so I couldn't imitate that, but I did copy his high kick and long stretch. Even though he put it to the Yankees, I rooted for him but pulled in vain for the Yankees to win the series. Koufax struck out fifteen in the opening game and pitched two complete games.

The next year, my Reds came in second place. That was a good season, but in those days, there were no playoffs; if you didn't finish in first place, your season was over. My team understood that same anguish of not winning too, but something in the game still called to me.

Even when we lost—and some years my team lost a lot—playing the game was fun and that's what it was all about. I wondered if major league players had fun even when they lost.

The Yankees fell way behind in the pennant race that year; they came on late in the season to win the pennant for the fifth straight year. The St. Louis Cardinals also rallied late in the year, and to the surprise of everyone, including the team's management, won the National League pennant. My Yankees lost to the Cardinals in the World Series. Mantle had a good series wining the third game with a walk-off home run. In the sixth game, Mantle and Roger Maris hit home runs on back-to-back pitches.

Mickey Mantle's record of ten games in which he hit a home run from both sides of the plate sealed his position as the greatest switch hitter the game had ever seen. He was my baseball hero, but I learned much later that Mickey had some bad habits—drinking too much and staying out too late. At the time though, he was my baseball idol, and his feats on the field overshadowed his transgressions off the field. Playing baseball and keeping up with my teams kept me occupied in the summer.

In December of 1965, the unbelievable happened: The Reds traded our best player Frankie Robinson to the Baltimore Orioles for some guy named Milt Pappas and a couple other chumps who would only be with the Reds a couple years and never amounted to a hill of beans.

Dad said, "The team thought Robinson was over the hill."

"Over the hill?" I exclaimed. "Who do they think they are; why would they trade our best player?" Under my breath I added, "That sucks."

The next year Robinson won the triple crown and the Orioles the World Series.

One season, our entire little league team took several buses to see the Reds play at Crosley field. The only thing that stood out about that trip was this badass kid named Woody, who for some reason, buddied up with me. We sat together on the bus, but most kids kept their distance from him. He was the same age as the rest of us, but he had a look about him that said "tough and experienced." You could see, even at his young age, that he had seen some hard times. He and I got along great, laughing and joking around the whole way down I-75 to Crosely Field.

When we got to the park, the first thing I did was buy a miniature baseball bat.

"Hey, let me see that," Woody said, reaching for it. He was messing around, and somehow, he managed to get it wedged between the seats, smashing a big green dent into the plastic from whatever coating was on the green seats.

I'm sure he could tell I was mad, but I just said, "Oh, it's okay, it's not broke." I wasn't about to cause a fuss with him.

All of a sudden, he jumped up and said, "Well, I'll just take this!" as he snatched the bat from my hand and got up. "Come on!"

I followed him off the bus and up to the concession area where I had bought the bat. Woody bought another one and gave it to me, keeping the damaged one, and said, "Now we both have billy clubs." He gave a menacing grin and smacked the bat hard against his hand.

I don't remember who won the game that day or even who the Reds were playing. I just remember having a fun time and getting a billy club. I felt sorry for Woody; I could tell that he had a tough home life and got his respect from people through his fists. He just needed a friend that day and I was handy.

Long after the baseball season, I got into a fight with some kid in the front of the junior high building. We were sort of dancing around each other trying to box, neither one of us landing anything. A big crowd of kids formed around us. All of a sudden, my badass teammate, Woody, came out of nowhere and hit the kid—*boom-boom-boom*—knocking him to the ground. I just stood there in shock, glad he wasn't after me. I felt bad for the other kid, who didn't know what hit him. Badass gave me a pat on the back and walked off as the crowd parted to let this gunslinger through. I never saw Woody again.

As the decade progressed, The Reds, Yankees, and Mickey were on the downward slope, and the American League in 1967 belonged to the Boston Red Sox, who took the pennant, and their star Carl Yastrzemski—Yaz—became one of my favorite players. I thought he was from Lithuania where my grandfather was from, but he was actually Polish. He also played left field, and that was my position at the time. He held the bat straight up and high in the air, a stance I began to imitate. Did the stance help me hit home runs in the Belville's backyard? Who knows? But I felt mighty and free as I swung that bat around like Yaz. And I hoped that with this new stance I'd be able to hit home runs at my games too.

I almost did hit a home run in little league one time. That night, my Great Uncle Steve Buckner took me to the game. My second time up to bat, I hit a dinger that cleared the left field fence by thirty feet! The problem was, it landed two feet to the left of the foul pole. My foul ball home run!

When I got home, I told Dad and Mom how close I had come to hitting a home run. Dad loved sports and wanted me to be successful. "Go get that old bat you have, Tim, and bring it out to the barn."

Dad drilled a couple holes in the top of the bat. He heated some lead with a torch and poured it into the holes.

"Why are you doing that?" I asked.

"This will increase the weight of the bat a little. You swing this bat one hundred times every day, and it will strengthen your arms and wrists. Then when you swing a regular bat, it'll seem light. Your bat speed will increase, which in turn will enable you to hit the ball farther. Remember, I did this with my golf driver—same theory."

I just stared at Dad, not sure how he knew that. But he seemed to know a lot about everything.

"It's not how hard you swing the bat," he continued. "It's how fast you swing the bat."

"Really? How do you know?"

"Ted Williams told me." Dad smiled, and we went back in the house, letting the bat cool down.

I wasn't completely sure whether to believe Dad or not, but later I found out that Dad was right. When I picked up a regular bat after swinging the leaded bat, it was as light as a feather, and I felt like I could really whip the bat around. Whether it made me hit the ball farther, who knows?

I was lying on the couch one day, playing with that leaded bat. One of the pieces of lead was loose and as I fiddled with it, I thought if I used some model glue, maybe I could seal it up and keep it from falling out.

I scrounged around in my desk until I found a tube, then squeezed the tube onto the loose piece, thinking that it would just seal the lead in. The glue didn't settle in the way that I thought it would and—forgetting gravity—I positioned the bat upside down over my head to get a really good look at the situation. Before I could blink, a drop of glue fell into my eye. A painful burning sensation exploded onto my eyeball. I screamed bloody murder, threw down the bat, and began howling and running around the living room.

"What's the matter?" Mom yelled, concerned, as she and Grandma rushed into the living room.

"My eye is burning!" I rubbed my eye frantically, but the burning persisted. "I have glue in my eye."

Mom held me down while Grandma took a wet rag and cleaned my eye out. It stung like hell, but she finally got the glue out. I thought I would be blind, but the sting and blurry vision didn't last long.

"Child, what caused you to do such a foolish thing?" Grandma asked.

I didn't answer.

That summer of 1969 was my last year of playing organized baseball. I played E-League at Beachler Field. I didn't catch much anymore, which was fine with me since I loved catching long fly balls. I would crouch down, my hands on my knees, chewing on some Double Bubble. The bill of my hat was pulled down far enough to shield my eyes from the sun but up a little so I had a clear and wide view of the field before me. I focused on our pitcher as he wound up; I followed the ball as he released it from his hand, spinning quickly to the plate. My eyes zeroed in on the white ball as it met the bat. *Crack*—the sound echoed across the park as the ball rose in the air, coming my way. My eyes trailed the ball, guiding my legs and hands. My first instinct was to take a few steps in; cautiously I judged the flight of the ball, the worst thing that could happen would be to come in too far and then realize the ball was going farther and faster than I judged. A decision loomed: back pedal and catch up to the ball, or turn completely around and sprint to catch up to the ball. I back pedaled. Quickly the ball became much larger, and smacked solidly into my glove. My fingers closed the glove and the empire signaled. "Out!"

What a great feeling.

The Reds played in their last full season at Crosley Field and finished in third place. Pete Rose was coming into his prime, and with Tony Perez and Johnny Bench, the Big Red Machine was coming together. Great things were on the horizon for the Reds. I hoped good things were on the horizon for me too.

Whether at Bell Civic Park or in the Belvilles' backyard, baseball had played a big role in my life during those years. Wining gave me a great feeling of accomplishment and pride whether it was my team or the Yankees or the Reds. I learned though that the real fun was just watching and playing the game.

I missed baseball, and I was anxious and restless.

There were lots of places and opportunities to get into trouble in Miamisburg. I tried to find as many of those places as I could; there was only so much time. But on the baseball field, it was hard to get into trouble, and even harder not to have fun.

There was only one thing more fun than playing baseball, and that was going someplace. Visiting family in distant states or going on family fishing trips. It gave me an opportunity to be somebody else, and like Aunt Wano, I was always ready to go most anywhere anytime.

SITTING ON MY SUITCASE

I liked going places with Aunt Wano. Unlike most of my family, she was not a smoker but loved her Jack Daniels—Black Label. She was always old and always up for most anything. A trip to the grocery store or a trip to the Holy Land. I still have a now almost-empty bottle of water from the Jordan River she gave me.

She was a product of the Great Depression and fervent admirer of Franklin Roosevelt. A dyed-in-the-wool Democrat who spoke her mind. I asked her one time why she always voted for Democrats.

"They are always the best candidate," she said.

"What if Fidel Castro ran on the Democratic ticket?" I thought I was being clever. "Would you vote for him?"

"Well, if he were on the Democratic ticket, he must be the best man for the job."

Aunt Wano was set in her ways but she was fun to be with. She asked me to come along with her to the grocery store one day. She always insisted on going to Liberals Market even though Kroger was much closer and had more variety. I think her affinity for the market had something to do with her political bent.

Part of my interest in going with her had to do with being able to push the cart and speed up and down the aisles, something that never would have been allowed with my mom. That day, Aunt Wano and I got separated in the market, so I started speeding through the aisles with the grocery cart, going around corners on two wheels and looking for her. There were very few people in the store, so I continued to go really fast down one aisle, turning quickly and heading up another aisle. Suddenly, Aunt Wano stood before me, and I swerved, crashing the cart right into a huge display of bottled beer. Shards of glass and foamy beer went everywhere.

"Come on, let's get out of here!" Aunt Wano said. We hightailed it out of the store before anyone could see the wreckage.

When we got to the car, Wano was out of breath. "I should have told them," she said as she wiped a hand across her forehead. "Timmy, we will never speak of this to anyone, okay?" I went to lots of places with Aunt Wano again but never to Liberals.

This little episode became our little secret, and years later, we always winked at each other when somebody did something similarly dumb.

"Remember the beer," she'd say.

"Remember the beer," I'd say back to her.

Aunt Wano would periodically take me shopping downtown in the heart of Dayton. She insisted I dress up smartly with a little sport coat and sometimes a tie. She would do some shopping for herself and then buy me something nice, usually a shirt or pants. Rikes, the premier department store in Dayton, had a nice restaurant on the sixth floor, and sometimes she would take me there for lunch. "Order anything on the menu you want, Timmy," Aunt Wano would say.

The freedom to order what I wanted sometimes seemed overwhelming, but it added to the feeling of being a grown up. There was a thrill and a sense of importance, being well-dressed in a bustling city, complete with several large department stores, movie theaters, and restaurants.

There was one very memorable shopping trip to Dayton that included Aunt Wano, Mom, and Grandma. That day, at Elder's Department Store, we were riding the escalator—one of my favorite things to do when shopping. I had my hand on the rail when I started daydreaming, and when we came to the end, I kept my hand there, trailing it all the way down to the end of the track where it got caught in the brushes. I thought the escalator was going to suck me in! I knew I did a dumb thing and felt suddenly panicked.

"Oh my God, Timmy, let go of that!" Mom screamed.

"It's got his arm! Pull him back!" cried Aunt Wano.

Fortunately, a store clerk standing nearby saw the whole thing and immediately shut the escalator down. Aunt Wano, eyes popping, was aghast and seemed embarrassed at the whole thing.

My hand didn't hurt much until they pulled it out from the brushes. When I looked at my bloody fingers, I joined in the wailing. The clerk took me to the security office, and I had my hand all bandaged up. After, Grandma asked, "Timmy, why didn't you let go of the hand rail?"

"I don't know," I said. And I didn't.

In today's times, we'd probably call our lawyer, but then we were worried that I'd be in trouble for messing up the escalator. Nothing came of it. In the end, my hand was fine, and it made for an exciting trip! It gave us all a story that we retold many times over the years.

The happiest times in my life were when I knew I was going somewhere. The anticipation of how fun it was going to be, the things I would see and do, people that I would meet. Thinking and planning for the trip was as much fun as the trip itself.

It didn't matter if we were going to a vacation cottage on a lake in Michigan, to Uncle Goeble's house in Florida, to NYC to see my cousins, a trip to Martha's Vineyard, or to Star City Hardware Store.

Going somewhere excited me and gave me a sense of freedom. I loved being on the move, and when I was away from home, I was allowed to experience different things. I saw people who were not like me or anybody I knew. They lived in places and ways that seemed strange to me. I slowly began to understand that the things that were important to me were not always the same things that were important to other people. I was lucky my parents seemed to love to go places as much as I did. Mom and Dad made traveling and going on vacation a priority. It was something we made time for and found money for.

NEW YORK CITY

In the summer of 1964, Aunt Wano took me to New York City to visit her nephews—my cousins Richard and Pete Buckner and Richard's wife Emma. I could hardly sleep the night before we left, thinking about all the neat things I would see and do in New York. I was up early, dressed, grabbed some cereal, and was on the porch sitting on my suitcase before anyone else was awake.

We boarded a train in Dayton, Ohio, and about a day later, we pulled into Pennsylvania Station. Richard and Pete met us there and drove us to Richard's apartment on east Seventy-sixth Street. This was my first visit to the Big Apple, and I was excited to say the least.

I was enthralled with New York City. The smell of freshly steamed hot dogs, the salty stale tasting pretzels coming from vendors on every street corner, newspapers everywhere, horns honking, cigarette smoke filling the air, sirens in the distance, the sound of a jackhammer making room for more cement, the click and clack of millions of shoes hitting the pavement – the streets were alive with people moving fast and with a purpose.

The city excited me and gave me a sense that anything was possible. I could be, I *was*, one of these important people. There was a buzz in the air; this is where it was happening.

I couldn't believe how all these people lived so close together. Where did they come from? Why did they all come here? Black people, white people, Italians, Asians, poor people, rich people. People walking, jogging, riding bikes.

People lying on newspapers on the ground and on park benches. Others hailing cabs, some hopping on buses. Some riding in long stretch limousines, many riding on graffiti-covered subway cars. Lots of people smoking, some even drinking right on the streets. People eating or reading on benches. Some strolling aimlessly about but most moving fast to someplace. They had someplace to be, to work or to play, and they wanted to get there soon.

There were so many people doing so many things. I was excited to be here.

Richard was a fun guy, quick witted and well read. He married a lovely girl Emma while serving a stint with the US Army in Germany in the early fifties.

He worked at The Metropolitan Museum of Art and rose to the position of Chief Registrar. He would travel the world arranging for the transportation of loaned art going to and from the MET. I would marvel at the places he visited and wondered of the adventure and freedom. When he retired, he took up writing books about the American Revolution.

Like me and Mom, Emma was an only child, born in Goeppingen, Germany, and grew up in Tuttlingen on the upper Danube. I was intrigued by her thick accent; I had never heard anyone speak like that before. She was petite but strong and had a keen mind. Emma paid a lot of attention to me, sharing fascinating stories about her life in Germany during World War II, which astounded me, and unlike most things, held my attention.

Emma lived with her mother during the war years as her father had been conscripted into the Wehrmacht and sent to the Russian front; she didn't see him for five years.

"Timmy, let me tell you, one day, as I was hanging wash in our backyard, I heard the roar of an engine and looked up to see a plane heading straight for our house. The plane's engine whined so loudly I was scared it was going to crash into our house. I jumped behind a large tree just as the plane strafed our yard with machine gun fire. The plane was so close that I could see the blue star on the plane. Americans did bad things too during that war."

Emma was an antiquarian book dealer. She bought books at private sales in the city and sold them at book fairs and to small used book stores throughout New England. I don't think she ever made a lot of money from it, but it was fun for her, and she became well known on the antiquarian book fair circuit. Emma encouraged my interest in books and suggested I start collecting books about a particular subject. So I started collecting biographies of US Presidents. And over the years, Emma would send me presidential biographies to add to my collection. I don't remember ever reading any of those books, but I liked collecting them. And I knew that what was written inside was important. These people led significant lives; they had made a difference.

Richard walked to work every day from their modest but well-appointed upper east side apartment. On that first visit, Richard wanted us to see where he worked. So we spent a day getting a behind-the-scenes tour of the marvelous exhibits at The Metropolitan Museum of Art. Richard gave us exhaustive narratives of the history behind so many things that I didn't know which way was up. My feet hurt, I was tired, I was thinking about baseball. All I remember was being overjoyed when I looked up and saw we were headed toward a red sign that said Exit.

This was the first of what was to be many visits to museums around the world. It took a while, but I learned to appreciate art. The historical context of when the painting or sculpture was done. The artist, who they were, and what motivated them to paint or sculpt this person or that scene. This art took me to faraway places in different times. I saw myself as a Roman soldier having a glass of wine with a beautiful girl by a stream, a knight ready for battle, or a Pope giving a blessing. Looking at art took me to another world where I could be a different person, still searching though, for who I was and who I wanted to be.

116

On that first trip to New York, in the summer of 1964, my biggest thrill was going to see the Yankees play. We attended a night game where the Yankees beat the Washington Senators 7-1. We had great seats right along the third base line, only about ten rows up.

I couldn't believe I was in Yankee Stadium; and there was the great Mickey standing by the batting cage with that big smile and those broad shoulders. He was hurt, so he didn't get to play, but I was thrilled just to see him. I took several pictures with my new Kodak Instamatic.

We saw all the famous places: the Empire State Building, which at the time was the tallest building in the world; the United Nations, with all the flags; and St. Patrick's Cathedral.

Richard, ever the historian, gave us a little background. "This is the seat of the Archdiocese of New York and the largest Roman Catholic Cathedral in the United States," he said. "It seats over two thousand and first opened in 1879." Perhaps to get my attention, Richard added, "And its where Babe Ruth's funeral was held and a memorial service for the Yankee Clipper, Joe DiMaggio." And for Wano's benefit, he also mentioned that Judy Garland's funeral mass was held there.

"Who is Judy Garland?" I asked.

"She played Dorothy in the Wizard of Oz," Wano exclaimed. Oh, I knew who *she* was—that was my favorite movie. She was afraid for her little dog, so she ran away, and what an adventure she had. I thought for a moment what cool things I could do if I ran away.

We visited the New York Stock Exchange. I had no idea what was going on there but was amused by all the men running around with paper flying all over the place; I wondered at the time why there were only men. But I didn't ask.

We spent a full day at the World's Fair that was being held in Queens. Over fifty million people attended the fair during the two-year run. It wasn't a fair like I had ever been to before. No rides or cotton candy that I remember. Mostly large buildings called pavilions. The General Motors pavilion was really neat; it showed you what living in the future would be like through intricate models and elaborate dioramas. I peered off the tram and through the glass at flying cars and machines that cleaned your house for you. AT&T displayed a "picture phone." I would have loved to have had one of those.

Richard explained that, "Pope John II gave special permission for Michelangelo's only signed work of art, La Pieta, to be brought from St. Peter's Basilica in Rome to be displayed at the fair. It was the first and only time La Pieta had left St. Peter's since its installation in 1500 A.D. At the fair, it was displayed behind a bulletproof glass."

I wondered why anyone would want to shoot a statue?

Richard, like his father, was a prize fight fan, and he even boxed a little in college. He was keen on the card for the July 31st fight at Madison Square Garden featuring Dick Tiger. You had to be at least fourteen years old to get into the fight, and I was only ten. But Richard and Pete both agreed I was big for my age. And it was worth a try.

We got to the Garden and waited through a long line. When we finally approached the ticket counter, I stretched as high as I could up on my tip toes, but when that cigar-smoking ticket man looked down his nose at me, he had three words for us: "No way. Next!"

"Let's hurry home; we can catch it on the CBS station," Richard said. We rushed home and watched the fight on the black and white television. Tiger had a TKO in the sixth round against Jose Monon Gonzalez, and all was right in Richard's world.

Early the next morning, Emma asked, "Timmy, you want to go with me to take Lady for a walk?" Emma asked.

"Sure, where do we go with her?"

"Oh, just down to the river and back."

We walked east on Seventy-sixth Street to a sign that said Gracie Mansion. "What's Gracie Mansion?" I asked.

"That's the home of the Mayor of New York."

"Wow, nice place," I said.

We turned and walked down along the East River for a few blocks.

"Wow, where are all those barges going?" I asked.

118

"Those barges are full of garbage going down the river, headed out to sea," Emma answered. "That's all the trash collected in the city each day. They take it way out in the ocean and dump it."

I looked at her in disbelief.

"There are millions of people who live in the city," she said, "and they have lots of garbage. It all has to go somewhere," Emma explained. That seemed wrong. Wouldn't that pollute the ocean—the ocean I loved to swim in? *There should be a better place to put all of that,* I thought.

Being in the city filled me with excitement; it made me feel important, that I had a purpose and could be significant. I wanted to explore all that was going on. I knew that I would return to New York City soon and often.

MICHIGAN

Our family spent many summer vacations on various lakes in Michigan. One summer, Mom and Dad, Grandma Susie, our cousin Virgil, and his wife Angie, and their two boys, Stevie, and Ron, rented a big cottage on White Lake. Uncle Billy and Aunt Sue Ellen, their daughter Cindi, and some friends of theirs named Nick and Mary Lou rented a cottage on the other side of the lake.

White Lake was a seven-hour drive from Ohio—twenty-five hundred acres that emptied into Lake Michigan. Dad had convinced everyone it was full of hungry, walleye, and smallmouth bass just waiting for us to load them into our boat.

One morning, all the dads went fishing. Dad and Virgil took the rowboat that came with the cottage and mounted his fifteen HP Evinrude on it. Uncle Billy and his friend Nick had a small runabout.

I was disappointed that I was not going along, but I got up early and went out to the dock to see them off. It was cloudy, and the air was still, warm, and smelled of fish. Someone had done a poor job of rinsing off the fish cleaning station at the end of the dock.

I thought Uncle Billy was a big man, but this Nick guy was huge. His stomach was so big he could barely turn the steering wheel. I thought to myself, *Why is he driving? If the boat overturned, he would be stuck and never get out.*

"Hey, let's get our poles and fish from the dock," Ron suggested once the dads were out of sight. We caught a couple of nice sized bluegills and a big catfish that we never got unhooked.

"Ron, cut the line; he's jumping around," I said. "I'm not getting stuck by one of those barbs and he'll be a bear to clean; he's not worth it."

Ron took his needle-nose pliers and snipped the line just outside the catfish's mouth. While neither of us had had any first-hand experience in cleaning fish, we gave it a noble try to impress our dads. We salvaged a little meat from the bluegills and mom let us put them in the fridge.

By late afternoon the wind had picked up and a light rain began to fall. In the distance, dark clouds were rolling in; a storm was brewing.

"They should have been back by now," Mom said with a worried look. The rain was heavy now, coming down in sideways sheets, pushed by the strong wind. The waves were lapping over the dock, white caps everywhere.

"Okay, boys, everyone inside," Mom ordered.

We all stood in the screened-in porch, all eyes searching the lake for two small boats.

"I hope they don't get blown out to Lake Michigan! They'll be goners," Grandma said.

Mom gave Grandma a stare and said, "We're at the other end of the lake. They would know to stay away from the channel that leads out to Lake Michigan."

Grandma's concern continued. "Those waves on Lake Michigan are like the ocean and would easily swamp the small boats they're in."

"Mom, please! That's not going to happen. They're experienced boatman. They can handle a little storm. They'll be fine." Mom looked over toward the door; the life jackets still hung on their hooks. "Damn. Why didn't they take those?"

The rain was pounding so hard you could barely see the end of the dock. The owner of the cottages Mrs. Crock came running over. "Don't you have a boat still out?" she asked.

"Yes, Bob and Virgil have been out most of the day. They should be back by now."

"I've not seen a storm like this in quite some time," Mrs. Crock marveled. "You know, we lost a boat out there just this last spring. Too much water and too little boat. The wind is blowing from the northeast. That never happens … she's blowing right out into the big lake."

Those words were just what Mom did not want to hear. She shared distressed glances with the other adults then moved to the screen door, looking out into storm, straining to see some likeness of a boat.

We waited, Mom and Angie walking back and forth between the two windows.

The porch lit up with a big flash of light accented by two sharp booms that grew in intensity. The cottage shook, and we all jumped and screamed. Stevie started crying, and Ron and I huddled around Grandma.

"It will be okay. We're safe; the storm will soon pass," Grandma assured us.

Mrs. Crock sensed our fear. "I'm sure your men must have put in somewhere. They wouldn't want to be out in this. I have the light on at the end of the dock. You can spot it halfway across the lake."

There were lots of times I was afraid of things. But I had never been afraid for my dad. I always thought he was big enough and strong enough that nothing could hurt him. That night things changed for me. I learned to fear for someone else.

It was almost dark when we saw the outline of a boat bobbing in the water and a faint light could be seen through the blowing rain. Someone sat at the front of the boat holding a flashlight. The small rowboat moved slowly and was being tossed back and forth by the large waves.

Mom and Angie ran out to the dock, and Ron and I tried to follow, but Grandma barred our way. Virgil was in front, holding the flashlight while

Dad sat in the back of the boat, one hand on the steering arm of the motor and the other hand holding onto a rope.

"Bob, what happened out there?" Mom asked Dad.

"We've had a hell of a time! Billy's boat conked out, so we had to tow them, but the damn bracket on the stern broke off."

"Oh, honey, look at your poor hand," Mom said, reaching for my dad.

"It was hard to hold onto the rope. It cut into my hand, so I wrapped a rag around it. My hand is cut all to hell. I didn't think I could hang onto the rope, then finally my hand just went numb. We got all turned around in this storm until finally we saw that light at the end of the dock. We were lucky."

Virgil hopped out and helped Mom secure the boat to a dock post. Together they pulled Uncle Billy's boat up to the dock. Uncle Billy helped Big Nick, who was struggling to free himself from behind the steering wheel. A bolt of lightning lit up the dock like daylight, and a crack of thunder brought them all to their knees. They all huddled together, keeping low.

"Come on we can't stay here," Dad yelled. They all rose up, secured the boats, scrambled off the dock, and ran for the cottage. I missed the fun and adventure of being out on the lake, but I was glad Dad didn't allow me to go with him that day.

It's usually not good fishing after heavy rains, but we only had a couple more days at the lake, so Dad, Uncle Billy, and Nick headed out again the next day in Dad's boat. I wanted to go, but I was told they were going way out in the lake to look for some big fish and that it was no place for kids.

Virgil, who didn't go with them, said, "Hey, boys, get your cane poles, and we'll go get something for dinner right out there." He pointed to just beyond the dock. He took Ron and me out in the extra rowboat about a hundred yards from shore. Virgil sat in the middle seat rowing and baiting our hooks with nightcrawlers.

Fishing requires a pole, bait, and a body of water. Catching fish requires lots of luck. Your chances of catching fish, however, go up appreciably if you know where to fish, what bait to use, and the best time to fish. Catching fish also requires patience, quiet, and calm—none of which I had much of.

We weren't catching anything. I was ready to move to another spot and Ron agreed.

"Let's go out deeper; that's where the big fish are," I suggested.

"Patience boys—patience," Virgil whispered.

"My Mom says patience is a virtue I don't have," I admitted.

"Well, if you're ever going to be a good fisherman, you better get some. Just remember, patience is sacrificing the present for the future, but you can't overdo it. You must recognize when enough is enough when you've been patient long enough. Just like knowing when it's time to move to another spot to fish."

"How do you know when you been patient enough?" I asked.

"That's not easy to know—that's why it's a virtue—but you will get better at it; it comes with experience."

"Hey, I got a bite," Ron yelled. "Yeah! I got one!"

Then I got one. We spent most of the day filling up three large stringers with bluegills.

When that bobber goes under, the line tightens, the pole bends, and your heart jumps with excitement. How big is he? What kind? Once he's on board, a feeling of satisfaction, of accomplishment, overwhelms you; all in the world is well even if just for a few moments.

Dad and Uncle Billy returned with a couple of good-sized largemouth. They were surprised to see how well we had done so close to shore.

"How'd you catch so many fish, Virgil?" Dad asked.

Virgil smiled, looked at us, and said, "Oh just used a few of those night crawlers, and—"

I interrupted, "Patience, Dad; patience. Lots of patience."

Virgil had lots of patience and a good deal of knowledge about fishing. He was soft-spoken, calm, and had a gentle way about him. The fish must have trusted him. He may never have caught the biggest fish, but he always caught the most.

Coldwater Lake was about a three-and-a-half-hour drive from home, just over the state line into Michigan. It's a two thousand acre lake connected to four smaller lakes: Middle, Long, Mud, and Marble.

We always tried to get this one particular cottage on the channel that led to the other lakes. One year there were a couple boys just a little older than me who checked into a cottage right next to ours. I made friends with them right away.

We began taking a rowboat out every day and hunting for little turtles that sunned themselves on the banks of the channel. It was great fun. One evening, my friend's dad asked if I could join them on a night fishing trip. I was excited to go, but Mom said I had to wear a life jacket.

"Oh, please. I don't need that!" I said. "The other boys don't have to wear one. I'll take it along and keep it right beside me in the boat."

"They're older than you, and you have to wear it or you can't go."

Dad didn't say anything; he was digging around in his tackle box. He glanced up at me as if to say, *I'm with your mom on this, so do what she tells you*. Then he went on about his business. I wasn't a little kid, or at least I didn't want to look like one. I wanted to be like the others.

"It's up to you; do you want to go?" Mom asked, holding the orange life jacket in her hand.

I would have just run out the door and hopped into their boat, but Dad kept looking up to see what I was going to do. Should I put it on and look like a little kid or be stubborn and miss the fun? "Okay, I'm not going."

My friends kept coaxing me into putting on the life jacket. I thought about the fun I had on boats, the sense of freedom that washed over me, the idea of an adventure. As much as I hated wearing a life jacket, I swallowed some pride, wiped the tears away, put the dumb life jacket on, and climbed into their boat. Being out from under Mom and Dad gave me a sense of independence, of freedom I was on my own; even if it was just for a little while, it felt great. I even caught a couple of bluegill.

Mom and Dad would cut corners and try to economize wherever they could. One way dad did this was by not having a separate battery for the boat. Dad would trailer the boat down to the boat ramp and then unhook the trailer and drive the car the two blocks back to the cottage, take the battery out of the car, and bring it back and use it to start the boat. Then, when we brought the boat in, he would take the battery out of the boat and put it back in the car.

Our boat was light so Mom and Dad would just pick it up by the trailer tongue and push the trailer and boat into the water. Then, Dad would start the boat, pull it over to the dock, and come back and pull the trailer off to the side. We'd all hop in the boat and off we'd go. On this day, a strong wind was blowing in, and waves splashed up high against the stern.

As Mom and Dad pushed the boat deeper into the lake, water began coming over the stern. The boat became heavy, and even with my help, we could not push the boat out farther or pull the boat back out of the lake.

"Bob, we're going to lose the boat!" Mom screamed.

"Keep pulling!" Dad yelled. Mom had that worried look about her. I sensed her frustration as she strained, pulling as hard as she could. Dad was calm and looked determined.

I spotted a man in a pick-up truck parked on the road, hopeful to see he had a trailer hitch. I ran up to him. "Mister, can you please help us? Our boat is about to sink, and we can't pull it out."

He looked at our predicament and immediately whipped his truck around and backed it down the ramp to our boat. He and Dad hooked his truck up to our trailer, and he easily pulled our water-laden boat out. Dad reached in and pulled the drain plug to unload the gallons of water. Dad thanked the man profusely. He shook Dad's hand, tipped his hat to Mom, and gave me a little smile.

"Timmy, that was quick thinking to go get help for us!" Mom said.

I just smiled and looked at Dad, who looked at me admiringly but said nothing. He knew I had done a good thing. It was the right thing to do; he expected it of me.

Dad insisted I try to water ski. I was a little afraid but was eager to give it a try. It looked like great fun. I put on a ski belt and jumped off the boat. Dad floated the skis out to me.

"Keep the rope between your legs, lean back, keep your arms straight, and let the boat pull you up," Dad said.

I gave Dad a thumbs up that I was ready, and he hit the throttle. The motor responded with a roar. The boat moved slowly at first, then quickly picked up speed and pulled me forward. I felt the power of the engine and heard its loud whine as I rose out of the water. I got up on my third try.

I could see Dad smiling through my water-soaked eyes. The wind blew my face dry, and the water churned white just behind the motor. Thirty feet back, my skis were riding on smooth water created by our boat pushing the water aside. What a feeling.

Soon, the wake from another boat hit me. I wobbled and panicked and pulled in with my arms. It felt like the motor had quit and then just as quickly, our boat jerked, and I was dumped. Dad spun the boat around quickly to pick me up.

"You ready to go again?"

I nodded.

That night at the cottage, I felt pretty good about myself. I knew I had done good that day.

"Now, that's what I like to see you do," Dad said with a big smile. Dad was excited and broke his silence. He had to voice his approval; he was proud of me. All kids want their parent's approval. They want them to be proud of what they do. I was no exception. It was nice to be recognized even for small compliments that didn't come often; it was nice to hear them once in a while.

Dad and I loved to race other boats. We used to pull up across from boats that had fifty or sometimes seventy-five horsepower and challenge them. They could see we only had thirty-five horsepower, so they thought we would be easy pickings. They didn't know that it wasn't an ordinary thirty-five horsepower motor. Dad had souped it up, and our thin fiberglass boat was light. Most times, we'd be beat straight out of the hole, but we quickly edged ahead of them when the boat planed, and we would cut across in front of them at a good distance. Then we would slow down so Dad could light a cigarette. We would smile at each other with some pride in our little boat. Speeding around the lake, I had a sense of freedom and power, and to share that with Dad was special.

HOLLYWOOD

The year we bought a new Rambler station wagon, we took a cross-country trip to California to visit my aunt and uncle.

My great aunt Elizabeth (Buckner) Hammond, Mom's namesake and the oldest of the Buckner siblings, lived in Hollywood, California. Her husband Victor, a pretentious and eccentric man from Naples, Italy, fancied himself a wine and food connoisseur and a man about town. Victor had written several non-descript movies in the forties. Jean Parker starred in his only recognizable movie, *The Adventures of Kitty O'Day*.

The first day out, we started at four in the morning and drove six hundred and thirty-five miles to the Mickey Mantle Holiday Inn in Joplin, Missouri. Grandma and I took the back seat with me sleeping across her lap much of the time. Dad gave me several maps and a road atlas. I took on the job of plotting our route and how many miles we'd travel each day.

I had two questions for everyone: "Is there a chance Mickey Mantle will be there?" and "Does the motel have a pool?"

"Yes, there is a pool, son, but I think Mickey might be a little busy with the Minnesota Twins today," Dad said.

"I thought they were playing the Angels," I answered.

We stopped in late afternoon, so I had plenty of time to swim. Dad was right—Mickey wasn't there, but one of his bats was. It was in a glass case in the lobby with a couple of his home run balls.

The next day, we hit the road early. "We're sleeping in the desert tonight," Dad said. We picked up Route 66 in Joplin and followed it west. We spent the second night just east of Albuquerque, New Mexico.

We crossed the desert on the third day. I was wearing Grandma out by lying on her—sleeping and futzing about. Mom was always saying, "Sit up, Timmy! You're missing this or that." So I would jump up, see a big cactus or distant mountain, check out our maps, and lie back down.

Route 40 took us by the Painted Desert and Petrified Forest. The Painted Desert was a weird place; it looked like it had been painted purple, pink, and orange. The Petrified Forest was full of big pieces of stone strung along the ground that were once trees millions of years ago.

Grandma was quiet on the trip. She just seemed glad to be going along. She never said too much to Dad as he always thought she was kind of dull and wouldn't give her much time. She did speak once though, directing her question to nobody in particular. "When are we ever going to get to Litter Barrel? I keep seeing signs that say 'Litter Barrel, half mile.'"

Dad just looked at Mom with a slight smile and said nothing. Grandma looked first at Mom, then at me; nobody said anything.

We stopped briefly at the Grand Canyon. Grand is a good word for that incredible place. It was so much bigger than anything I had ever seen. I wondered how something like this came to be. I stood close to the edge. A bird soared in the air. My eyes followed it back and forth, up then swooping down. It was free to go where it wanted and to instantly change its mind and go the other way. I jumped back from the rail, my heart pounding.

The third night, we stayed at the Stardust Hotel in Las Vegas. I had a great time in the big pool. But at five o' clock a guy came out, blew a whistle, and told everybody to get out.

"Why do we have to get out of the pool" I asked.

"The pools closed son; it's time for everybody to hit the tables. But that's not for you, young fellow, you have to be twenty-one."

I rolled my eyes. "What's a kid supposed to do in this town anyway?"

The man laughed. "Kid, this town isn't for kids."

In 1963, there was always something, somebody, or some rule keeping me from having fun. *Okay*, I thought, *I'll be back.*

We finally made it to Aunt Elizabeth's and Uncle Victor's house. They lived in an old Spanish-style brick and stone apartment complex, not far from the renowned Grauman's Chinese Theater where famous people imprinted their hands in cement.

We walked through a beautiful courtyard with lush flowers, palm trees, and a large cement fountain. I stopped, focused on the naked woman with water spraying out of her breasts, and set my suitcase down.

"Come on, Timmy! Her door is down here." Mom motioned for me to keep going.

Dad glanced at me, the statue, smiled, and walked on.

They had a fancy home. The living room and dining room were on two levels. The furniture looked old but plush with two big couches with large flowered covered pillows. There were lots of cabinets filled with glasses and plates, and a large chandelier hung over a glass dining room table; visions of swinging from it danced in my mind.

We all looked around and stared as if we were in a museum.

"Don't touch anything," Mom whispered to me.

"Oh, Aunt Elizabeth, your place is so beautiful," Mom said.

"Oh, thank you darling. We've tried to make it comfortable, and please all of you, make yourselves at home." I wondered how I was supposed to make myself at home and not touch anything.

The first night, Victor announced in his Italian accent that he wanted to make a special Sicilian dinner for us. "Yes, I make my favorite dinner for you, Pasta Alla Norma, but I will need your help."

We all gathered in the kitchen. Grandma stepped toward Victor and was about to speak, but he stopped her. "Ah yes, Grandma, you sit right here and relax." Victor pulled out a stool and motioned for grandma to sit down. "Liz, please, glasses for everyone. Roberto,"—He called dad Roberto, how funny! —"take the wine here and pour for everyone! We going to be working hard."

Victor's voice sounded funny at times, but I knew better than to laugh at him. Instead, I tried really hard to understand the words between the ahs and uhs and asked for some wine. "Me too?" I asked, looking at Dad.

"Yes, Timmy, you also have but only a tiny bit," Victor said. "Okay, salute!"

Everybody raised their glasses and took a sip. Except for Grandma, who stood up and raised her glass, but no wine touched her lips. I could tell she wanted to be polite but strong drinks were "against her religion," as she would say.

The wine tasted bitter—root beer was much better—but I felt cool, like an adult. I could do anything at least for a moment.

Victor placed a big pot of water on the stove and turned up the fire. "Ah, Momma, you watch the pot for when it boils and cut up this eggplant," Victor said, looking at Mom. He said watch like "watcha" and then placed a large frying pan on the stove.

"We start with some oil, now a little garlic. Liz, please cut up the onions and red peppers, and—wait—let me a put on some Tebaldi." I didn't know what Tebaldi was, but I soon found out; it was terrible and loud.

"Roberto, please, more wine for everyone." Victor held out his glass to Dad.

Victor looked at Grandma and reached out and pinched her cheek. "Make sure Grandma has a full a glass!"

Grandma leaned back and smiled, but I knew she didn't like that.

"Sure, Victor, but it's Robert."

"Ah, yes, Roberto."

"You could just call me Bob."

Victor smiled, raised his glass to Dad, and said "Mucho grazie," or something like that. It was funny watching Dad and Victor talking back and forth. I don't know if Victor couldn't understand or just couldn't hear him. Victor just continued. "Okay, add pasta to the pot, now four minutes only. You time, Momma," Victor instructed, looking at Mom.

Grandma stood up and said, "Here, let me cut up that eggplant. It should be in chunks, not slices."

"Oh, Grandma is a right, in a chunk like this." The words sounded more like "like dis," and I was getting used to the way Victor spoke. It was different, but he seemed nice, and I wondered what growing up with more family around would have been like. Victor grabbed the knife from Mom and demonstrated how to cut. "See? But Grandma, you sit and watch, have some more wine, you not like?"

Grandma looked at Victor with a snarky smile, raised her glass, shook her head back and forth, and in a loud voice, called out, "It's a fine, Victor," she said, mimicking his accent. "But I a cook, not a wino like you!"

The smile left Victor's face; he put down his glass and moved close to Grandma, and I thought he was going to cry. The music had stopped, and everyone looked at Victor and Grandma. What would he say?

He nodded and put his hand on her shoulder, then patted the stool and invited her to sit. "I know, Grandma, you a fine cook. You have worked much a hard in your life. You have a wonderful family you brought to see me and Aunt Liz. We honor you with this meal, for without you, no family come to California to visit. You all here is a so special for us. Please—this is a time for you to enjoy, no work in kitchen for such a lovely lady today."

Grandma blushed a little, smiled, then stood up and gave Victor a big hug. Glancing over her shoulder at the rest of us, her eyes rolled. I had never seen Grandma hug anybody except Mom and me. How else could she respond to such a romantic lush?

Suddenly the music was loud again and blunted out any further conversation. Steam rolled from the boiling pasta, the smell of garlic filling the air. Victor resumed dancing around the kitchen with a big spoon in one hand and a glass of wine in the other. Everyone seem to be having a great time, even Grandma. I never knew cooking could be so much fun.

"Now we add the tomatoes, an eggplant, salt, pepper, and pinch of basil as well.

Your Caesar salad looks wonderful, Liz; add a few more anchovies. Now we sprinkle a little fresh ricotta. And we have dinner!"

The food was really good. Except the anchovies; I picked them off and shoved them to the side of my plate.

"Ah, Roberto, here's another bottle. Please pour more wine."

Dad smiled. "Sure thing, Vic."

The next night, Uncle Victor offered to take us all out to dinner at a famous steakhouse.

"Only the best for my dear kin folk from back home," Aunt Elizabeth said.

We were all dressed up. Mom had packed a sport coat and tie for me for "just in case," she said. Aunt Elizabeth was all decked out in what she called "her finery."

She and Uncle Victor then got into a big argument about when we were leaving and exactly where the restaurant was. Mom and Dad stayed out of the argument, and the four of us all went into the living room.

Finally, Aunt Elizabeth announced that Victor had said he was not going to be joining us, that he didn't feel well and would be going to bed. We had a great dinner at what Aunt Elizabeth said was the oldest restaurant in Hollywood—The Musso & Frank Grill.

When we returned, Victor had a tuxedo on and was perched on a stool in the kitchen; he looked like a big bird who was waiting to be fed.

"Well, where have you all been? I am ready to go!"

"You've got to be kidding, Victor," Aunt Elizabeth tore into him, and we all quietly and quickly slipped off to bed, letting the two of them go at it.

I enjoyed our time with Aunt Elizabeth. She was a first-class lady who insisted on things being just right—up to par, as she would say. Uncle Victor, well he was nice to me and kinda funny but sort of an odd fellow. I was glad he wasn't a blood relative.

There were two baseball teams in Los Angeles—the Dodgers and the Angels. The Angels were having a new stadium built, so that summer they were playing in Chavez Ravine, the Dodgers Stadium.

The Angels were having a poor season, so Dad easily got tickets to a game. I was hoping they would be playing the Yankees.

Reading the sports section of the paper, Dad announced, "Sorry, Tim, the Angels are playing Boston; the Yankees are at Cleveland."

"But hey, we're going to get to see Carl (Yaz) Yastrzemski; they say he's the next Ted Williams."

"I never heard of him, but he has a cool name."

We got there in time to see batting practice. There weren't many people there yet, so I was able to get five foul balls that were hit into the stands, adding them to my collection of baseballs that I got from Dad every Christmas. My mind went to my baseball team and the games I was missing, but traveling to California was a great adventure for me. I don't remember anything about the game other than the Angels lost and someone telling me they were owned by Gene Autry, the singing cowboy on TV Westerns.

California was beautiful. There were trees covered with striking violet flowers, orange poppies growing along the roadside, and of course, lots of palm trees; never saw anything like that in Ohio. The cloudless blue sky, sun always shining brightly. I would have loved to be on my own out here, just free to do what I wanted. I thought about how much fun my friends and I could have.

The trip home was four long, uneventful, hot days in the car. I laid my head on Grandma's lap with the window open and hot air blowing on me. Going home from a vacation was always a drag. I would have liked to have just kept going, someplace.

KENTUCKY

It seemed like every year we would take a short weekend trip to Kentucky. We toured the beautiful horse farms that covered the Bluegrass State. We once saw the great Citation at Calumet Farms. There was a plaque on the stable that read: *Citation won sixteen straight major races, including the Kentucky Derby, Preakness, and the Belmont Stakes, making him only the ninth Triple Crown winner. His jockey, the famed Tony Arcaro, said of him, "Citation was the best ever. He was so fast he scared me."*

I thought about Black Jack. How fast was he? I wondered if he ever got to race. Maybe he wasn't that kind of horse. I wondered if all he got to do was go to funerals and how sad that would be.

Mom's dad's side of the family, the Buckner's, hailed from Campton about an hour's drive south of Lexington in Wolf County, which at one time held the distinction of being the poorest county in the country.

Roy and Cora Buckner lived just outside of Campton. Roy was Aunt Wano's first cousin. As cousin Richard told it, Roy and Cora had been sweethearts when they were young, but Roy never could find his niche and never stayed at a job long. Roy abruptly picked up and moved to Middletown, Ohio, to live with his brother and his wife. Cora stayed in Campton and eventually got married to a fellow named Crocket.

136

Years passed, and when Roy's brother died, his wife had had enough of Roy's trifles and threw him out. Roy had heard that Cora's husband, who had worked for the railroad, had died and left Cora with a pension. Roy hightailed back to Campton and rekindled his relationship with Cora, and soon they were married.

One warm day in September, Mom, Dad, Grandma, Aunt Wano, and I headed to "God's Country," as Aunt Wano described anything south of the Ohio River. It was cool in the morning as we started out, but by the time we got to Campton four hours later, it was hotter than a firecracker.

Roy, Cora, her daughter Jane with a small baby—no father in sight— were sitting on the front porch of a small cabin, tucked back into a hollow just off a gravel road. Cora seemed elderly, not as old as Aunt Wano, but she had rough, weathered face and graying hair tied in a bun at the back. Roy was short, balding, a little chunky, with an ornery look on his face. They were most gracious and very pleased to see us.

"Ah, lordy, lordy, Wayland ain't seen you in a month of Sundays," Cora said as they embraced. "And are these some of my Yankee kin?"

Wano introduced us all around. Cora and Roy's home was small but adequate, kind of primitive, but clean and tidy. The inside had a woody, musty smell, and the floorboards creaked when you walked across them.

Cora went to a pump in her kitchen sink and gave out glasses of water to everyone. It tasted awful. Roy, seated in a wooden rocker, whittled on a piece of wood. He finally stood up and looked us over, not saying a word. Dad reached out his hand, and Roy looked him in the eye. He took Dad's hand, and a little smile crept over Roy's face.

"Glad to make your acquaintance. Bob, is it? I'm Roy Buckner." Aunt Wano, of course, knew them but had not seen them for many years.

"Roy, take that whittling outside!" Cora demanded. "You're making a mess that I know ya won't be cleaning up. You're getting more chips on the floor than you are in that box. Go fetch a chicken, and we'll make these fine people dinner." Roy sat back down, glanced up and grinned at Cora and then at Dad and kept whittling.

Cora shook her head, smiled, grabbed a cleaver off the wall, and headed out to the backyard. Aunt Wano frowned at Roy and followed Cora to the backyard. We all looked at Roy. Roy kept whittling.

Mom, Grandma, and I looked out as a group of chickens scattered. Cora grabbed a big one, held it by the legs over an old tree stump, and let the cleaver do its work. She held the chicken by its feet as it bled out. What a sight! That poor chicken, so free, running around the yard, then in an instant, her life snuffed out with one swing. Now we were going to eat that.

Cora was back in the house in no time with that chicken plucked and cleaned. "Roy, think you can get some greens, break off your work there for a bit?" She threw a small wicker basket to him, which surprisingly he caught. Roy just sat there and looked tired. "Come on, Roy. Show me your garden," Dad said.

"That boy! He is the laziest thing, but I just love him to death," Cora said with a big smile spreading over her face. So even if you don't do much, you could still be loved. Mom and Dad loved me no matter what I did, I think.

Roy and Dad brought some green beans, tomatoes, and a couple cucumbers in. Grandma peeled potatoes. Cora put flour on the bird and threw a hunk of lard into the skillet, turning the fire to a simmer. Cora set a nice table and was proud of her meal. It was fine, but the chicken didn't sit well with me. I kept seeing all that blood draining out its neck.

After dinner it was sweltering, so we all moved out to the front porch. Jane took the rocking chair and "worked it hard," as Aunt Wano would say. Jane had not said a word to anyone since we got there, and it didn't look like she was going to. She just held that baby and looked in wonderment at all of us. I heard Mom tell Dad later that the baby was a doll, and Jane looked a little addled. I had never heard that word before, but I knew right off what it meant.

"What you got in the big barn there, Roy?" Dad asked.

Roy's eyes lit up, and for the first time, it seemed like he was alive. "Come on, I'll show you," Roy said with a proud smile.

I was curious too, so I followed along. As Dad went by the back of the car, he said, "Hold on. Roy, how about a cold one?" Dad popped the trunk and opened a red cooler. Dad, of course, didn't know this until later, but Roy had been on the wagon for nearly a month by then. Dad took out two Stroh's beers and handed one to a beaming Roy.

He hesitated a moment and peeked around the car toward the house. "Oh, much obliged, Bob." He took the beer, Dad handed him a church key, and we headed up to the barn.

The barn was full of drying tobacco. Roy reached up and pulled a piece of tobacco off. "It's still a little green, Bob, but it'll smoke." Roy crushed a small leaf in his hand and gave some to Dad. Dad rolled one up and looked to hand it to Roy, but he was ahead of him and had already lit his cigarette and was handing a match to Dad. They breathed in the tobacco smoke and took long draws on their beers as Roy proudly explained to Dad all the work that went into growing tobacco.

They seemed to really enjoy the smoke and beer. I wondered how that beer tasted and how that smoke felt. I would have joined them if they offered. I was ready to try new things even if I knew they probably were not good for me.

We didn't visit Roy and Cora too often; I think only a couple of times. Their life was so different than mine. I couldn't imagine living the way they did, and I felt sorry for them, in a cabin wedged back between two small mountains—no neighbors around and the nearest town miles away. I loved the wilderness aspect of it, but I would be afraid of the loneliness. I asked Aunt Wano, "Why do they live way back in the woods like that?"

"Well, that's where they're from; it's their home. And they're poor and poor people don't have the freedom to just up go and live in a different place. Besides, don't you think there're happy? And isn't that what's important?"

"I don't know. Can you be happy if you're poor?"

"Sure you can," Aunt Wano assured me. "You just have to decide on what makes you happy."

I thought about that for a moment then asked, "Why are they poor?"

"I don't know, honey; they just are."

I thought of how different their lives were from my cousins Richard and Pete in New York City. Or Aunt Elizabeth and Uncle Victor in California. I thought how differently I lived in Miamisburg.

FLORIDA

I stood waist-deep in the waters of the Gulf of Mexico, the wind blowing gently on my face. The water was a beautiful marine blue and as smooth as glass.

In the sixties, the beach at Destin was a magnificent, sparsely developed playground of pure white sand on the panhandle of Florida, stretching from Ft. Walton beach to the government-owned land–perhaps ten miles. It is still one of my favorite beaches even though it's now cluttered with hotels, condos, and those damn hotel beach umbrellas.

I first came to Northwest Florida with my mom and dad in 1962. We visited my great uncle, Goeble Buck Buckner—quite a name for quite a character. He was my grandfather John's brother on my mother's side of the family.

Goeble was born in Campton, Kentucky, in 1900. As a young boy, Goeble fell off the front porch of his house. After a time in bed, his parents finally took him to the doctor. The doctor said he would probably walk again but would always need a crutch. Goeble was a very determined little fellow. He walked again, albeit with a distinct limp, and became a good athlete, playing catcher on his high school baseball team. He served his country in the U.S. Coast Guard. Later he became an accomplished bowler, competing in tournaments throughout Florida.

By the time I got to know this man who would become like a grandfather to me, he was in his sixties. He was loud, dominating, kind, and full of life. I was captivated by his gregarious character, his staunch conservatism, and his love for God and his country.

He claimed to be a Democrat, and in fact, ran for the state legislature; he was narrowly defeated. For a Democrat, he had a lot of conservative beliefs.

Goeble often repeated his favorite mantra: "The government has two purposes, to defend the country and run the post office." He loved the Kennedys—except Teddy. He thought Jimmy Carter was a wimp, and he voted for Nixon against McGovern. Goebles' family struggled through the Great Depression. He credited Franklin Roosevelt for pulling our country out of the Depression and leading the Allies in defeating Axis powers. In his opinion, FDR was to forever be revered as a great man and wonderful president. It was hard for me to understand his political views. How could you like both John Kennedy *and* Richard Nixon?

The story went that Goeble and his wife moved to Dayton after Goeble was discharged from the Coast Guard shortly after the end of World War II. Goeble was soon offered a job as a civilian back in Florida at Eglin Air Force Base near the small village of Valparasio. They packed a few things and headed south. They were in such a rush they didn't even take their dishes or pot and pans. They even left the dog tied up in the backyard.

Uncle Goeble would visit us periodically, and sometimes Marie would come with him, but most times not. His car would be packed full of blankets, toilet paper, metal chairs, towels, and ammo cases. "Goeble, where does all of this stuff come from?" Mom would ask.

Uncle Goeble laughed and said, "Hell, it comes from Uncle Sam."

I had never heard of Uncle Sam.

"This is all surplus; if we don't get rid of it, they throw it in the ocean. Or else our budget will get cut for next year."

Mom looked puzzled. "I don't think I want to know any more about that."

None of that made any sense to me. One time, Goeble brought a long, thick rope that Dad tied up to a high limb on our big Chinese Elm tree.

Dad showed me how to climb the rope. "Watch this, Tim. Wrap the rope around your right leg and let the rope rest on your right foot like this … now pull yourself up, then clamp your left foot down over the rope which is across my right foot. Keep repeating this maneuver, and you'll go right up the rope." I couldn't believe how easy it was. Dad was proud of how quickly I learned to climb the rope.

Aunt Wano had told us that her brother Goeble was a very generous man. If he could find a way to help you, he would. It didn't have to be family or a friend; he was there for anybody who asked him for help. Goeble had been working at the base a few years when one day a couple of the city fathers paid Goeble a visit and explained that Valparaiso needed new sewer lines, but they didn't think the citizens could afford a new tax to pay for it. The next week a military truck began unloading black sewer pipes along all the roads in the village of Valparaiso.

The mayor and council of Valparaiso were pleased, but the colonel in charge of base supply was not. He paid Goeble a visit.

"Well, Buck," the colonel said. "What the hell gave you the idea that the government didn't want that sewer piping?"

Goeble spoke up calmly, "Colonel, since it's been lying out in the field behind the base hospital for the last ten years, I figured if we were going to use it, we would have done so by now."

The colonel's face went red and Goeble knew he could be charged with misappropriation of government property—a serious offense. But thankfully, the colonel knew it was good for the Air Force to be on good terms with the locals. The City of Valparaiso and the base depended on each other. Of course, Goeble had known this as well; he figured he was covered, and he wasn't afraid of breaking the rules if it meant helping someone out.

If Goeble was your friend, you were a fortunate man. One day while we were visiting, a scruffy looking man wearing a t-shirt and a baseball cap showed up on Goeble's front porch.

"Hi, I'm Rex Tilton, a good friend of Goeble's. Is he around?"

I listened from the hall while I heard Mom answer, "He's in the bathroom. Come in and have a seat; he'll be out in a few minutes. I'm Betty, Goeble's niece. We're visiting from Ohio."

"No, that's fine, ma'am. I'll just wait out here in the yard. I've heard so much about you. I've known your Uncle Buck, as we call him, since he first came here to the pine woods."

Mom would say she never remembered Goeble speaking of this fellow.

"Oh, I remember going with Buck when he bought that Buick out there," Rex added. We didn't really know Rex or how good a friend he was of Uncle Goeble's, but one thing was for sure—we knew he was a liar. That Buick was Aunt Wano's car, and she gave it to Goeble. What we didn't know was that he was also a murderer.

Goeble and Rex had a long talk out in the back yard. Mom and I watched and tried to hear what they were saying from the open kitchen window. We couldn't make out much, but every so often we'd hear Goeble raise his voice, and he would jester up in the air with his hands. After Rex left, Goeble filled us in on his friend Rex's situation.

"Well, I'll just tell you like it is," Goeble said. "Rex came home early from work one day to find a car that looked familiar parked in front of the house. He recognized it as Bruce Condi's car. Condi worked as a mechanic at a local garage. He had suspected for some time that this fellow and his wife had something going on—too many oil changes. He confronted his wife about this. She, of course, denied it, but Rex was not convinced of Melissa's fidelity. Rex pulled up across the street where he could watch the house. After about ten min, Condi walked out of the house, turned on the step, held the screen door open, and placed a quick smooch on Melissa's mouth. She pulled him back into the house. He could see she had what looked like her swimsuit on. Condi came back out of the house in a few minutes, buckling his belt. He jumped in his car and took off. Rex had seen enough and took off right after him; he was boiling. At the first stoplight, Rex threw his car into park, reached into his glove compartment, and grabbed his nine-millimeter. He ran up to Condi's car, opened the door, and let him have it three times."

"Oh my gosh, Goeble, did he kill him?" Mom asked.

"Well, hell, he shot him three times; of course he killed him! He was messing with the family; what did he expect?"

Months later, we learned that Goeble had helped Rex pay for a good lawyer. He mounted a defense that claimed Rex caught this intruder raping his wife. He was so enraged he lost control of himself. Of course, Melissa, to save her marriage, went along with the story. She didn't want to lose her husband and her lover. That's the kind of guy Goeble was—if you were his friend, you could do no wrong. I admired that at the time.

"Our snow bird is not coming north this summer," Dad announced. Looking at Mom and me, he went on to ask, "So how would you two like to go down to see her?"

As always, I was ready to go anywhere. "Who's the snowbird and when are we going?" I asked.

Mom explained, "Aunt Wano—she's our snowbird. You know she lives in Florida during the winter, where it is warm. In the spring she likes to get away from heat so she comes north and spends the summer with us. Then just before the snow begins to fly, she goes back to Florida. Just like the birds do."

Aunt Wano's winter home was in St. Petersburg, Florida. She had a room at the Gotham, a small, very nondescript hotel just off the downtown area. It had a tiny lobby and smelled of old folks. Residents would gather there in the morning for coffee and to swap news from up north. Aunt Wano took us to a little buffet restaurant next door. On the wall hung a video screen with the current stock prices.

"I made enough on the stock market to buy my last Buick," Aunt Wano proudly said. I wasn't sure how that happened exactly, but it sounded good to me. "Buy low and sell high," she would say. "That's all you have to do. Knowing when to do both is the trick." We spent a few days with her visiting Cypress Gardens and some of her favorite restaurants. One night, we went to see Jai Alai, a game I'd never seen before. The game involved players who caught a ball that the other player had bounced off a wall with what looked like a crescent-shaped basket stick and threw it back the other way. It was nothing like baseball or basketball, but it was a very fast game and fun to watch.

The highlight of our visit came crashing down when we finally went to the beach. It was littered with seaweed, dead fish, and smelled rotten.

"Oh, that's too bad! I forgot about the red tide. It comes every so often, and the beach is a mess." I was disappointed; I thought beaches were always beautiful.

After spending a few days with Aunt Wano, we headed north along the gulf coast over to the panhandle to see Uncle Goeble in Valparaiso. It was over a six-hour drive. Mom was driving with Dad beside her in the front seat. I sat in the back right behind Mom. We were going down a busy, narrow two-lane road with houses on the right side and the Gulf of Mexico on the left. I remember hanging out the window, squinting in the sun, pretending I was in a stage coach and shooting Indians along the road. I saw these kids along the side of the road, waiting on the cars to pass before crossing. Just as we got right in front of them, a little girl darted out in front of us.

Mom turned the car quickly across traffic and slammed on the brakes. The right front bumper of the car managed to clip the girl and sent her spinning onto the road. Mom screamed, and she and Dad jumped out of the car. "Stay in the car, Timmy," Dad yelled. The little girl lay on the ground, crying and saying she couldn't move. I was afraid and started crying too, for the little girl but also for us.

"Oh, I am so sorry! She just darted out in front of us. I couldn't stop!" Mom cried.

Several people attended to the girl and some woman said, "Oh, Miss, it wasn't your fault. I saw the whole thing. Sandy just ran right out in front of you." We heard a siren; it didn't take long, and the police were there. They talked to Mom, Dad, and some of the people who were standing around. I could see they were writing stuff down.

I don't remember how we or the little girl got to the hospital, but when we were there, we learned the little girl had a broken leg. The girl's parents kept telling us that Mom was not to blame and that it was just an accident. What started as another beautiful day in the land of sunshine turned into sadness. I learned that day that bad things can and do happen sometimes very unexpectedly.

"Please don't let this ruin your vacation," the girl's mother told us, and soon after, the police told us we were free to go.

We arrived at Uncle Goeble's late that night and told him the whole story. Oh, honey. That girl will be fine, and you'll never hear from them again." Uncle Goeble was only half right. The little girl was all right. But her parents contacted us after we got home and asked for fifty thousand dollars or they would sue us. Dad contacted our insurance company. We never heard any more about it.

THE CRUISE

I am sure it was Dad's idea to take a cruise to the Bahamas. I remember him talking about a beautiful beach they had at a place called Paradise Island. Grandma Susie went with us. I'm not sure why Grandma Stonecash never went on vacation with us. Maybe she was too old.

I was excited. We were going on a big boat to an island that had a great beach. We drove to Ft. Lauderdale to board the Bahama Star for a five-day cruise to Nassau. "This is a dress-up vacation, so don't pack any jeans or cutoffs, Timmy," Mom instructed.

There were lots of kids on the boat, and I had a good time messing around with them. We were all pretending we were rich and were putting on the dog. Most of these kids didn't have to pretend. I was dressed smartly like them and soon began to act like them. It was easy for me to copy their behavior and fit right in. They weren't really that much different than me. But I could tell they were used to this kind of special service and this was all pretty ordinary for them while it was a special, new experience for me.

After about a day and a half on the ocean, our ship pulled slowly into Nassau Harbor. We all stood along the rails of the boat, the water a beautiful blue green that was so clear you could see almost to the bottom.

Young boys and girls swam out to us. Their skin was so black I wondered if it was that way because of the hot sun that shone year-round with no winter. We threw coins into the water, and these kids dived down into the clear blue water for them. It was great fun watching them tread water and dive for a coin we tossed their way. They seemed happy, but I wondered if they were doing this just for fun or if their families needed this money to live on. I thought about black kids I knew of in the US; they were all poor, so these black kids must be really poor. I thought about how different life was for us kids throwing the coins as opposed to those diving for them; neither of us deserved our position. It didn't matter though; it was fun for me, and it looked like it was fun for them.

It was so enjoyable on the boat! I was allowed to run around and play with the other kids on board. Several girls caught my eye, and we had a little flirting contest, which made me feel special. The beach on Paradise Island was everything Dad said it was. Beautiful white sand and crystal-clear water. These were happy times. I was a lucky kid.

TRAVELING WITH PETE

Mom surprised me after my freshman year of high school. "How would you like to go spend some time in New York with your cousin Pete?"

It had been a rough school year, and I was ready for a break from carousing around Miamisburg. I knew Pete was always up for going first-class and to nice places and having a good time, so I jumped at the chance to get out of Miamisburg.

Pete used to say that "Living well is life's best revenge," a quote by popular seventeenth century poet George Herbert. At the time, I wasn't quite sure what that meant. For Pete, it meant that life is certainly a joy and has lots to offer, but it's often full of disappointment and hardship. If you can find a way to enjoy the best things in life even for a moment, that is the best revenge and provides you with some satisfaction. To say that Pete often lived beyond his means to live up to this code was an understatement.

I arrived in New York City soon after the school year was out; I was fifteen. Pete had a one-bedroom on Forty-sixth Street near Grand Central. His fourth-floor apartment was crammed full of books and newspapers he was "saving to read when he had more time." It was never too comfortable in Pete's apartment. If you visited him in the summer, there was a fan in his apartment that couldn't keep up; in the winter, the radiator, which you couldn't control, made the apartment insufferably hot.

150

As soon as you got off the elevator on Pete's floor, you were greeted by a rich, pungent smell of spicy food simmering behind steel double-bolted apartment doors. It felt warm and inviting. I wondered who those people were behind those doors. What kind of food were they cooking? What did they do for money? What was their life like, living in a big building like this? I wondered if they were Americans; I saw a lot of people on the streets who didn't look like anyone I'd seen back home.

There was a place called Chinatown. Pete said that's where lots of Chinese people lived, and there were small shops and lots of Chinese restaurants. One night we went there and picked up Chinese food and brought it back to the apartment to eat. When I saw shrimp on the menu, that was for me. But it wasn't anything like the shrimp cocktail I was used to. The shrimp was cooked in a brown sauce with vegetables and noodles.

"Tim, you need to try some ethnic foods," Pete said when he saw the way I was looking at my food. "New York is a great place to do that. You can taste the world within walking distance of this apartment."

Days in the city were full of lots of walking. We visited art galleries in Chelsea, perused the latest fashions in SoHo, and watched the hippies in Greenwich Village. Then lunch at an outdoor café, perhaps a visit to a museum, or shopping—Bloomingdales, Lord & Taylor, and almost always a bookstore; my favorite was The Strand. They kept a large inventory of used books that were cheap. Then, finally, dinner at a nice restaurant and sometimes a Broadway play. By the time we returned to Pete's apartment, it was late and I was ready to relax, read the headlines and the sports sections in one of the many papers we had collected, and get some sleep.

One night, plans were made with Richard and Emma to go to the Sign of the Dove, a restaurant on the Upper Eastside. Pete had numerous lady friends, but one seemed special: Margarete Buchelle, who lived in Queens. Our family always waited for word that they were getting married, but that never happened.

Pete announced that Margarete would also be joining us for dinner. He frowned as I snapped on my tie. "You're not wearing that thing. Here, let me show you how to wear a tie," Pete said as he stood behind me and draped a long striped blue tie around my neck. "Make sure this end's a little shorter than this end, bring this over here like this, now under here and bring it over, now stuff this down inside and pull it tight—the tip should be at about your belt."

Wow, I had a real tie on now.

Margarete was a good-looking woman with dark hair and olive colored skin. She spoke with a slight accent—Italian I thought.

"Let me look at you, young man." She grabbed me by both shoulders and got up close. My God, I thought she was going to kiss me. She looked at Pete then at Richard, "So do they have lots of these handsome young men out in Ohio? And dressed so sharply for tonight."

I was embarrassed.

There was something exciting and fun about being in a fine restaurant; everyone seemed to be happy and enjoying themselves. The waiters were so courteous, catering to our every need, and people were laughing, smiling, and looking forward to something good. A Coke here was the same as a Coke anyplace, but somehow it tasted different. And I was past getting a Shirley Temple. There was an ambience that said: quality, expensive, first class, only the best here. If you were eating here, you must have done something well.

The Sign of the Dove was a such a restaurant—new for me, but for Pete and Richard, it seemed routine. I hated getting dressed up at home but not here. It felt good wearing a sport coat and tie. I felt important, like I too was somebody special. Appetizers for Pete, Margarete, Richard, and I were shrimp cocktails. Emma had vichyssoise.

She let me taste it and whispered to me, "Cold potato soup." As was usual, I was encouraged to order anything I wanted. I peeked over and saw the bill: it was seventy-six dollars. And Pete left a ten-dollar tip.

I couldn't imagine paying that much for dinner. But everybody seemed to have a good time. Pete and Richard always went first class. I took that to heart and later always questioned if I couldn't go first class, was it worth going?

Pete's apartment had no air conditioning, so the two windows were cracked open, inviting in the sounds of the city. Finally, after some tossing and turning, sleep came. Soon after, the trash collectors began banging and throwing the cans around. How could it be so loud? Did they collect trash every day?

Once the trash cans all found their places, sleep returned. Sirens rang in the distance through the night, preventing any deep sleep. The blast of a car horn sounded, then another, then several at the same time; rush hour had begun. Once the horns stopped, it all got quiet again and good sleep came, but then the low sounds of the radio and Pete scurrying around the apartment filled my ears. The city was ready for us! I was excited—and I was tired.

My time in New York City was like going to another world; it was so different from Miamisburg. The people were more worldly, more in tune with what was going on in the world. There was no mowing grass, eating at fast food places, driving cars. Bookstores, museums, and walks in the park replaced going to drive-in theatres, walking through the mall, and watching TV.

I was a different person there. I was interested in books and museums. I read the newspapers, I watched people and wondered who they were and how they made their way in life.

Pete worked at Avis Rent a Car as a district manager in Mid-town Manhattan. He was able to get most any kind of car he wanted, mostly Chrysler products because that's what Avis featured. He got a really neat red convertible for a trip he planned for us to visit his friends in New England.

"We'll be staying with my friend Dick Ambrose. He's an old Army buddy," Pete told me. "We were stationed at fort Sam Houston in Texas together. Dick has a big soiree planned, and his parents have invited you to go fishing with them out in the bay."

I wasn't sure what a soiree was, but fishing sounded great to me. We got up very early the next day and headed north.

Dick was staying at his parent's summer home on Martha's Vineyard. It was a sprawling windswept shingle cottage right on the water. The kitchen was huge with pots and pans hanging over a butcher-block island. There were glass doors that opened up to large patio.

Pete and I shared an upstairs bedroom that had a little balcony that overlooked the bay.

Dick had a girlfriend Loraine. Pete said she worked part time for the Democratic Party in Massachusetts and also was an adjunct at a big college in Boston. Adjunct—another word I wasn't sure of, but it sounded important.

Dick had taken over his dad's commercial real estate business and was also active in state politics. Pete loved political gossip and was enthralled with any news about the Kennedys. Loraine had met many of the Kennedys, and so as soon as we arrived, Pete began pumping her for the latest about Ted's possible run for the presidency.

The theme for the soiree was Hawaiian, so there was lots of work to do to transform a Cape Cod cottage into a South Pacific island. The main course, roasted pig, was already on a spit in the backyard, tended to by a man with a large white hat. There were men setting up tables, stringing lights, and bringing in fake palm trees.

Dick was a large man with a booming voice and gregarious personality. He had jet black hair and was dark complected, a true New Englander speaking with no r's. He took charge. "Pete, get to work! There's pineapple, watermelon, cantaloupe, and honeydew that needs cut up for a big fruit display. Loraine brought some fresh crab meat to stuff those mushrooms with. Oh no, wait—I know you'll want to get in on this; how about setting up the bar?"

"Yes, sir, Lieutenant." Pete smiled and said, "He's still giving me orders. But this was right up Pete's alley, and he dug right in. First though, Pete mixed a batch of his specialty drink: cranberry and grapefruit juices and a generous amount of Absolut. He called them Pink Peters.

He passed one around to everybody except me and lit up one of his Benson & Hedges—never inhaling, all for show—completely in his element.

Almost as an afterthought, I was introduced all around to Dick, Loraine, Dick's parents, and Loraine's daughter Jeanie. One look at Loraine and you could tell she was a smart cookie. Blonde hair pulled tightly into a tail at the back, still a young woman with a beautiful face and dressed most fashionably.

Jeanie was a knockout, a younger image of her Mom—long blond hair and sparkling blue eyes. And she was perfectly laid out. She was a little older than me, but I was confident that I looked older than my age.

I was anxious to get to know her, but I didn't know what to say. I didn't want her to think I was weird. Shocking me, she came right up and introduced herself.

"Hi." She held out her hand. "Nice to meet you—Tim? Is that what I heard? You're Pete's cousin from Ohio."

This day just kept getting better. "Ah, yeah, that's right, and you're Jeanie, right?"

"Okay, we got that taken care of; wanna walk out by the water? It's so beautiful here."

I nodded.

"So, Tim, what do you do back in Ohio?"

"Your shorts are really short."

"What?"

Oh, shit! What did I just say?

"I mean your shorts are nice—they're very pretty, and I … back in Ohio I … ah go to school somewhere; I think I'm a senior."

"You go to school somewhere, and you think you're a senior?"

Wow, she must think I'm a doof. "Well, you know, not sure how many credits I have. I've been trying to graduate early." I should have said I'll be lucky to graduate at all.

"Oh, wow! You must be a real brain."

"Yeah, well, things seem to come easy," I said, looking down at her legs again, trying to keep from laughing and thinking of a way to change the subject.

She was so familiar. I just met her, and she acted like we were best buds. How could a girl be this nice, be this choice, and be talking to me?

"Tim, don't forget, Dick's Mom and Dad are taking you out fishing and they'll be ready to leave in a few minutes, so don't be long," Pete yelled as we walked out the screened porch toward the water.

Going fishing? What the hell was I going fishing for? All I wanted to catch was right here in front of me. "So, do you live around here, Jeanie?"

"I wish—I live in Brookline."

"So, do you come here a lot?"

"I come out on weekends sometimes when Mom and Dick are having a party fundraiser; they pay me a little to help out." She stopped and spread her arms out to the sky. Her long blonde hair blowing in the ocean breeze. "Oh, just breathe the air; it's so clean and crisp. I love the smell of the ocean. Say, you sure you're from Ohio? You sound like you're from Tennessee."

We weren't that close to each other, but still, what I smelled was her— like my face was smothered in lilacs, so fresh and clean. I thought, *Did I really have a southern twang*?

"Yes, I'm a Buckeye. You sound like you're from England."

"Well, I live in New England."

We both laughed

"Tim, time to go," Pete yelled from the house.

"Oh shit, I have to go fishing. Are you going to be here later?"

She just smiled.

I grinned back and she patted my arm.

Damn fishing.

Dick's mom and dad were excited to share their day with me. She was so sweet—she packed us drinks and sandwiches. He was a hardcore fisherman; I could tell by his tackle and determined demeanor. I loved the idea of fishing in the ocean and had looked forward to it until this Jeanie appeared.

I could be making time with her. Hell, I can fish anytime. Well, maybe not in the ocean. She was so good looking and smart but mostly just nice. How cool would it be to have a girlfriend like Jeanie or any girlfriend for that matter? I don't remember much of what was said until Mrs. Ambrose said we'd better be heading in. My mind was on Jeanie. I did catch a fifteen-pound bluefish.

"You should be proud of that, son. We'll take her in and throw on her on the grill. Wait until Dick sees that baby."

I thought, *The hell with Dick.* What would Jeanie think of my fish? It doesn't happen often, but sometimes you meet someone and feel right off there's something special there. That's the way it was with Jeanie.

By the time we got back to the house, it had filled up with friends and neighbors. *Where was Jeanie? Had she left?*

Pete, who was serving as bartender, got me busy right away helping him. I began taking orders and running drinks. I would ask Pete what each drink was, and then I would have a little taste just to see what it was like. I loved the gin drinks—reminded me of the smell of Christmas trees.

All the talk that night centered on the recent accident Teddy Kennedy was involved in on Chappaquiddick Island. They were all sympathetic to Ted but knew he was a partier, and so they were concerned. Why had he left the scene of the crime? Had it been a crime or an accident? Would this derail Teddy's march to the White House? That night, no one had answers, and I kept busy helping Pete with the drinks and thinking of Jeanie. Where the hell had she gotten to?

I finally managed to ask Pete if he knew where Jeanie was. "I haven't seen her in a while. Check out by the boat house; I saw her headed out that way with Dale."

Dale? Who the hell was Dale?

I made my way down towards the water and rounded the side of the boathouse. There she was leaning on the dock railing and looking out at the water—strands of blonde hair moving in the breeze. She turned to look at me. "Tim, you made it back! How was the fishing?" Jeanie asked.

"Great! I caught a—"

She interrupted with, "Hey this is Dale. Dale, this is Tim, from Ohio."

I had only been vaguely aware of the tall, dark young man beside her until then. She slipped her arm around him after the introduction. This sucked.

Dale smiled at me and shook my hand. I supposed he was a nice guy, and Jeanie was still sweet to me but not as sweet as she was before I went fishing.

I knew they were a thing and I was bummed.

"Dale just joined the Navy—isn't that the most?" Jeanie went on and on about how great that was—Dale volunteering to serve his country in a time of war. So that's how you stood out and impressed someone like Jeanie.

"I'm going to see the world," Dale said.

I wanted to see the world too, but I wasn't sure if I wanted to see it with a uniform on.

I didn't mention the bluefish.

The next day, despite the frivolity from the day before, I was up early. I had my suitcase packed and was sitting on it when Pete finally came downstairs at about eleven. We had a quick lunch with Dick's parents. I never saw Dick, Loraine, or Jeanie. Pete said everyone was up late and sleeping in. He had said our goodbyes the night before.

We headed north to see Pete's friend Peter Fisher, another old Army buddy who was now a high school science teacher in Watertown, Maine. It was a quiet ride; I don't think Pete felt too well. I thought of the bluefish. What had happened to it? But mostly I thought of Jeanie. What had happened to her?

We were warmly greeted by Peter and his wife Ann and invited to quickly join them around the television. We watched in awe as two men landed their odd-looking spacecraft on the moon, got out, and walked around. It was on TV, and it was real!

At first, it was hard for me to believe this was happening, but after sitting in front of a boob tube for three hours nobody making a move, Pete finally broke the silence. "It won't be long and people will be living on the moon."

"I don't know why we're spending all that money going to the moon. What do they think they're going to find up there?" Ann questioned.

I spoke up, "What are they looking for?"

"Both good questions," Peter responded.

"Tim, they're searching for knowledge; Ann, they're looking for what they don't know."

Peter's answer resonated with me, and I thought about it for a moment. It was all cool—men on the moon—but I was getting bored and was ready to move on. What were we going to do here that was fun? Was there another Jeanie out there someplace? We were up late that night, talking, drinking, and smoking—at least that's what they were all doing. I was listening and eating ice cream.

Everyone was up early the next day, TV on, watching more men on the moon stuff.

Pete and I headed back to New York around noon. Another couple days in the city, and I was back in Miamisburg.

Visiting new places and meeting new people were exciting. I was always ready to go. I learned to see things from new perspectives. The people I met had different ideas about things; they saw things in different ways because of where and how they lived. But like me and the men on the moon, they all seemed to be searching for something.

I stared out from car, plane, and train windows and wished I could see into all those houses, apartments, and farms. Who are those people who lived there and what must their lives be like? What did they look like? What was important to them?

Were they like me? Could I live like them? What were they doing right now?

BLACK PEOPLE

John Kennedy said, "One hundred years of delay have passed since President Lincoln freed the slaves, yet their heirs, their grandsons, are not fully free. They are not yet freed from the bonds of injustice. They are not yet freed from social and economic oppression. And this nation, for all its hopes and all its boasts, will not be fully free until all its citizens are free."

In 1960, eighteen million Black people lived in the United States. No Black people lived in Miamisburg, Ohio, that I knew of, and a sign in downtown Miamisburg said, "Don't let the sun set on your black ass." I always heard about that sign, but I never saw it. Most often I heard them called colored or the N-word, and Dad called them Negroes. I didn't call them anything.

The only time I saw a Black person in Miamisburg was when we played a home football game against Franklin, a small town about five miles south of Miamisburg. They always had a couple of Black kids on their team, and their family and friends would sit in the stands. I lived in a white world. Did I hate Black people? No—I just didn't think about them. They were for the most part out of sight out of mind.

Did I know what a racist was? Looking back now, I'm sure I didn't. Was I a racist? I'm sure I was. Did I care? I'm sure I didn't. What I remember

160

most about those times was not understanding what was going on in the world when it came to Black people. What was their problem?

I asked Mom, "Why are the police spraying those Black people with fire hoses, and why are those German Shepherds after them? What's going on? Why's this happening? Why are they all so mad?"

"Those negro people don't like the way things are, Timmy." Mom explained that they wanted to be treated like white people are treated. "They think they don't have the same rights as we do."

"Do they?"

"Well, yes, I think so."

"So why won't the police let them?"

"Let them what?"

"Let them be treated like white people are treated," I clarified.

Mom fidgeted and stood on one foot like she was confused. "I don't know, because they're Black, I guess."

"Mom, what's 'looting' mean?"

"Stealing. Now get away from the TV. Don't you have some math problems to go over?"

The TV showed Black people—mad—in Birmingham, Detroit, and Los Angeles. Unhappy Black people and riots going on in these faraway places caught my attention but didn't hold it for long. I had important things on my mind. I was starting to hit the ball really well, and our team was in first place. My bike had a flat. I had seen the same girl at the pool sitting on the cement bleachers all by herself, twice. My plan was to be cool and just go up and sit near her and see if she noticed me.

But I couldn't get this race thing out of my head. I went back to Mom numerous times over the years. "Why are all these Black people mad?"

When I was in my teens, one day Mom gave me a copy of a letter that Martin Luther King had written when from the Birmingham Jail. He had been arrested and held for eight days for violating a court order against demonstrations and marches that were protesting how Blacks were being treated.

"I want you to read this; I know its long but I think it will help you better understand what this ruckus with Black people is all about. And let me share a quote from the Chief Justice of the Supreme Court Earl Warren that had some meaning to me. He said that 'justice delayed too long is justice denied.' I want you to think about what that means."

This was feeling like homework; Mom was right—it was long. I persevered and read it. The letter helped me better understand why Blacks felt there was no justice in this country for them, that it needed to change, and they were tired of waiting for it to change.

"What is an unjust law?" I asked my mom.

"Well, as you know, I'm not catholic, but Saint Thomas Aquinas said, 'An unjust law is a human law that is not rooted in eternal law and natural law. Any law that uplifts human personality is just. Any law that degrades human personality is unjust.'"

I had always thought of a law as a rule that was to be obeyed and not questioned. I knew this to be true, but I broke many laws of my parents and school that I thought were unjust. Was that any different?

Those are powerful words that resonate with me now. If I had read them when they were written, I would not have grasped their meaning. I wouldn't have tried too hard to understand something that didn't affect me. Likely I would have thought it meant you should be able to do what you wanted to do, something I certainly would have agreed with.

But I was confused, and maybe Dad was too. For he said, "If Martin Luther King is a man of peace, why is it every time he makes a speech someplace, when he leaves, a riot breaks out?" And wasn't that a good point?

I didn't think all this civil rights stuff had anything to do with me; it was all happening in faraway places. I thought Black people were just as free as white people, so why were they so upset? That attitude, while normal, was a part of the problem, but I would not grasp that until many years later. We tend to ignore the things that we think don't affect us. But that doesn't mean those things aren't important.

Just before Labor Day weekend in 1966, the violence, unrest, and injustice all came close to home when a Black man named Lester Mitchell was shot in the face with a twelve-gauge shotgun on West Third Street in Dayton.

Dad brought the day's paper in and began reading. "'Mr. Mitchell was sweeping the sidewalk in front of a small illegal liquor store he operated next to the Christ Holy Temple Apostolic Faith Church. Witnesses said that a white man shooting from a moving car was responsible.'" Dad commented, "I know where that church is; it's not far from Billy's filling station. There's always some derelicts hanging out there with no particular purpose, sipping some wine or whiskey, shooting up a little dope." Dad continued reading, "'Almost immediately after the shooting, a small crowd gathered around the crime scene. It soon turned into a large mob that began destroying their neighbors' property. For only the second time in the history of Dayton, the National Guard was called out to help restore order, and over five hundred people were arrested.'"

The unrest in Dayton didn't end with the Lester Mitchell killing. Visits from nationally known black militants Stokely Carmichael and H. Rap Brown added to the racial tension and civil unrest that continued in Dayton throughout the sixties. As I watched this on the TV news and read it on the front page of the Dayton Daily News, I wondered why Black people were so angry and filled with hate, why they looted and destroyed property right where they lived. I supposed it was just convenient, kind of like when I was little and got mad at Mom or Dad and threw my own toys across the room.

Dad kept Mom and me and anyone else who happened to be in the room informed of things he thought we should know. He would pick out news articles and read aloud. "'At a rally held yesterday at the Wesley Center on the west side, H. Rap Brown addressed the crowd: *Nonviolent against each other, but nonviolence is not the way to deal with whites.* He ended his speech with, *There are those who say Negroes should go back to Africa, if they are not satisfied here; before we go back to Africa, we gonna burn this place down to the ground! Burn it to the ground.* The crowd began chanting: *Burn it to the ground! Burn it down!* And the streets of West Dayton again became inflamed with anger and hate.'"

Dad threw the paper down, "Can you believe what's going on up there?

Why can't those people settle down? We need some law and order."

Mom looked worried and I was confused.

"There's no Negroes here, so there'll be no riots; there's nothing for us to worry about," Dad assured us.

Dad spoke highly of the prize fighter Cassius Clay. "He's Black but a pretty Black," he'd say. Dad seemed confused when he changed his name to Muhammad Ali. I always wanted to change my name to Rick—it sounded better than Timmy. And though Muhammad Ali sounded like a dumb name to a thirteen-year-old kid, it didn't much matter to me.

After Ali refused to go into the Army, Dad wasn't confused anymore—he didn't like him. Dad was a Navy man, and in his generation, most men served their country.

"I got no use for a cocky big mouth draft dodger."

Why didn't Ali want to go into the Army? He couldn't have been afraid to fight; he

already was a fighter and was the most famous person in the world. Everyone wanted to know why Ali would not go into the Army; Dad and I watched his response on TV. He spoke with conviction, and when he was done, my father asked, "Do you understand what he is saying son?"

"Well, I don't know; maybe he thinks that war doesn't affect him, so why should he go fight?"

Dad responded, "Sorta like how we don't think the troubles Negroes have affects us, so we don't need to do anything about it." He sounded like he thought we should be more concerned about how Black people are treated in our country instead of fighting a war so far away.

I watched as other sports figures rallied in support of his decision. Among them the great Jim Brown, Bill Russell, and Lew Alcindor. Was it just Black sports stars who agreed with him? What about white players? I never heard them say anything. Maybe they were like me and Dad.

I thought about what Muhammad Ali had said and what Dad had said about his words. Why would a Black man want to go fight a war on the other side of the world when his real battle was in his own neighborhood? Why, in fact, would any man want to go and fight in that war if they knew the truth?

Dad and I continued to keep an eye on the sports world, particularly my two favorite teams. In 1968 the Reds and Yankees finished fourth and fifth in their leagues with the same record: eighty-three to seventy-nine. The Detroit Tigers beat the St. Louis Cardinals in the World Series just two days before the Summer Olympic Games began in Mexico City.

Dad and I and even Mom watched as Peter Norman from Australia won the silver medal in the two hundred meters, and John Carlos, a Black man representing the United States, won the bronze. Tommie Smith, also Black and from the United States, set a world record and took the gold. But just before the Americans ascended the podium, they removed their shoes, donned black scarves, beads, and raised their black-gloved fists in the air to protest, bowing their heads as the Star-Spangled Banner began playing.

"Look at that what are they doing, disrespecting our flag and country," Dad said.

They were immediately asked to leave Olympic Stadium and made to forfeit their medals. They were booed and razed as unpatriotic and received death threats. Noted sportscaster Brent Musburger called them "black-skinned storm troopers."

Dad and I watched the replay of their protest on the Olympic podium. In my view, they were just like the other Black people I saw on TV—mad about something I truly didn't understand. I learned much later why they were mad.

They were not protesting against the flag or the song or their country. They had removed their shoes and wore black socks to protest poverty, donned black scarves and beads to protest lynchings, and put on black gloves and raised their fists in solidarity with the oppressed black people around the world. They wanted to use this world stage to draw attention to how Black people in America were not being treated with the dignity and respect that whites were. They loved our country, but our country was sick, and the world needed to know it. It takes courage and sacrifice to call out those injustices in a public way.

When I saw pictures of them holding their fists in the air and wearing a black glove, I was angry at them. I thought they were disrespecting our flag and our country, and I felt like they were traitors. Fifty-some years later, Colin Kaepernick kneeled at an NFL game during the playing of our national anthem. Was he a traitor too?

Mom and Dad were not overtly prejudiced toward Black people; they were just indifferent to their plight. I think they saw what was going on as something that wasn't right, but the issue really didn't concern them. They didn't know or have the interest in understanding why Blacks were speaking out and demanding change. Injustice was hard to see then as it is now for those whose justice is not being denied. If you're not directly affected by something, then you tend not to notice it. As someone who has never felt oppressed, it's even harder to accept how difficult it is to recognize how someone else is being oppressed. It's hard to understand something that doesn't happen to you, or at least that you aren't close to, and we were never close to anybody who wasn't white.

I felt bad for them. But that's just the way it was; it wasn't my fault they were Black. When I did see Black people, they stood out—an oddity. There were one or two alone among many whites. And when I saw Blacks on the TV or in the newspaper, they were depicted in ways that made you feel sorry for them or angry toward them. I thought all Black people were poor and mad about something.

My segregation and disinterest in what "all this ruckus was about" with the Blacks kept hidden a prejudice that lived deep within me for many years. I had heard the phrase "all men are created equal" many times. It was a long time before I understood that many Blacks, women, and other minorities felt that they weren't really included in that statement.

To me, freedom meant doing what I wanted on Friday night. It meant going where I wanted when I wanted and being with who I wanted to be. So, I empathized with the angry Blacks. It seemed we were both searching for the same things, but really, we weren't talking about the same kind of freedom. Mom, Dad, and school kept me from my freedom, and everyone kept them from theirs.

Grandma Susie looked out over the river from her back porch, pointed to the other side, and said in a foreboding voice, "That's where the colored live, over there on the west side of the river." The houses were small, in disrepair, and all bunched together. I could see a small playground with a couple boys shooting hoops on just a rim, no backboard.

"Those kids are over there all the time playing with that ball; they must not have anything else to do," she said. I wondered how good they were. Why did they seem to be so much better at football and basketball and just running than white kids? Was it because they practiced so much or were they just born that way?

"Why do they all live over there?" I asked her. "Can't they live over here too?"

"They're colored and they're poor so that's where they live. That's their place. Sure, they're free to live anywhere they like. But they like it over there. They got a little grocery, and they even have a colored church."

That seemed odd to me, but it was a wide river, and I was over here and they were over there. It has been a long process for me to come to a better understanding of the issues that face Black people and other minorities. I had to reach out; it didn't come to me. I had to listen with an open heart and mind and read and try to grasp what the ruckus was all about.

But no book I ever read or lecture I ever heard impacted me as much as simply ending the segregation that I grew up in. Through personal interaction with Blacks and other minorities, I came began to realize how little I knew about their grievances and the injustice that still exists today.

BASKETBALL

The invention of basketball was not an accident. It was developed to meet a need. Those boys simply would not play" Drop the Handkerchief."

-- James Naismith

I loved basketball. So did Mom and Dad. Mom had been a cheerleader in high school, and Dad played on the school team, the Franklin Wildcats. So whether I was playing it or watching it, basketball became a special part of my life that I could share with my parents.

Dad put a basketball hoop up in our driveway, attaching it to our barn. He used a nylon net that's still on the rim. I spent a lot of time out in the driveway shooting hoops and pretending to be all-American Don May of the University of Dayton Flyers. I would score baskets from all over the court, then do a couple layups, a hook shot, and then several jumpers. I also imitated all-American Rick Mount. I would dribble around the top of the key and turn quickly before shooting a fade away jump shot. It was a great shot that was impossible to defend, and if I did it at full speed and didn't think about it, it usually went in, but once I started thinking about the shot, I would miss it.

With basketball, just like with baseball, I had my favorite team: The University of Dayton Flyers. In the fall of 1966, Dad and I really got into following the Flyers. During the season we kept up on all the latest news about our team. We talked about it almost every day. It became something that we both could relate to. Dad was a good basketball player in high school, but now, because of his diabetes, he moved slow and was unbalanced for a man in his late thirties—even when just shooting around. So while Dad and I couldn't play much one on one, we enjoyed keeping each other up to date on how the Flyers were doing.

It was Don Donoher's third season as head coach of the Dayton Flyers.

"Dad, do you think the Flyers can win the tournament?"

"Well, son, that's a bit much to hope for. Its only Don Donoher's third year; he's still a young coach. And they drew a tough first game against Western Kentucky—they're ranked sixth in the country. On top of that, the game is in their home state down in Lexington at Memorial Coliseum."

Dad and I were glued to the TV as the Flyers won the first two games in the tournament. We kept track of the Flyers' run on a big Shoenling Beer poster Dad had gotten from one of his bar-owner friends. We tallied each win and added little boxes with the score and the opponent for the tournament.

"If we win tomorrow night, we go to the final four."

That would be incredible. Dayton had had some good teams over the years. They had even won the NIT back in the fifties. But the NCAA final four? Well, that would be really special.

Wouldn't you know it, the next night our TV was on the blitz so couldn't watch the game. "No sweat," Dad said as he brought the radio from the kitchen to the living room.

Mom made some popcorn, and the three of us huddled around the radio.

The flyers pulled away in the last few minutes and won seventy-one to sixty-six to advance to the final four in Louisville, Kentucky.

"Damm, I can't believe it; Dayton is going to the final four," Dad yelled as he jumped out of his chair. We were beside ourselves with excitement. Our Flyers were going to Louisville! I was surprised how into it Mom had gotten. I don't think Mom and Dad and I were ever any closer than during this time. It seemed we had found something we all loved and could enjoy together.

In their first game, they squared off against fourth-ranked North Carolina Tar Heels coached by Dean Smith. North Carolina was the heavy favorite to beat the Flyers.

"Dad, why are they calling Dayton the 'Cinderella Team?'"

"Well, because nobody expected the Flyers to be in the final four just like no one expected Cinderella to be at the ball."

"Is that a good thing?" I asked.

"It can be if it makes the other team overconfident, and they don't take Dayton as a serious opponent." I didn't care what they called Dayton as long as they kept winning.

Our TV was fixed so Mom, Dad, and I, with bowls of popcorn in hand, were ready for the big game. Don May started hitting shots from all over the court and didn't stop until he had made thirteen shots in a row. Dayton won seventy-six to sixty-two. I went out on our hoop in the driveway the next day and did my best imitation of his performance. Mom and Dad watched from the kitchen window.

There wasn't much time to savor that victory. The next night, the Flyers had to play Coach John Wooden's UCLA Bruins, who were undefeated and winners of the NCAA tournament for the three years prior. Donoher knew his team's only chance was to control the tempo of the game. May was the go-to man, averaging twenty-two points a game to go along with sixteen rebounds. May was a great all-around shooter but was most effective around the basket. The problem with this game was May only stood six foot four, a respectable heigh except when the guy on the other team who liked to play around the basket was seven foot two inches and was the best player in college basketball: Lew Alcindor.

Mom, Dad, and I had our usual setup in the living room. We were on pins and needles until, to our surprise, Dayton's Dan Obrovac out-jumped Alcindor and Dayton controlled the opening tip. It was downhill from there. Obrovac took the first shot, an uncharacteristic jump shot that bounced off the rim. Dayton lost seventy-nine to sixty-four to the best team of the decade. We were all disappointed in coming that close to winning it all, but we were also so proud of our Flyers to have come that far in the tournament. Dad and I could hardly wait for the next season to begin. We were excited and had high hopes for a great season for the Flyers.

Dad surprised me when I got home from school one cold January day. "I got two tickets to tonight's game!" he shouted.

"Oh, wow! Who do they play?" I asked.

"They play Detroit, but who cares, and they're good seats."

Dad bought me a program for twenty-five cents and I kept score. He was right, they were good seats, about mid-court and just ten rows up. It was a special night for us, seeing our Flyers in person, and the popcorn was great.

I read to Dad from my program on the way home. "Bobby Joe Hooper was the leading scorer; he had twenty-eight points, and George Janky had twenty-six points. May only had sixteen points."

"That's okay; it shows they are a balanced team. May doesn't have to be the leading scorer every game. The important thing was that Dayton won."

Dad was such a Flyer fan and loved basketball so much. I hope he saw more than one UD Flyer game, but I'm glad he saw at least one game with me.

After that game, the Flyers went on a three-game losing streak. Dad and I were getting down on our Flyers, as was Donoher, who knew something had to change. While he couldn't control what the players did on the court, he could control who was on the court. So, he shook up the lineup.

That did the trick. They were done with losing that season. The Flyers' record at that point was seven and nine. With a record of sixteen and nine, they were not offered a bid to the NCAA tournament but happily accepted an invitation to play in the NIT. Dad and I were disappointed; we were looking forward to Dayton returning to the NCAA tournament.

"Well, son, I know this isn't what we'd hoped for or really expected from our Flyers, but sometimes you have to accept things and try to make the best of what you got."

Dayton rattled off wins against West Virginia, Fordham, and Notre Dame, and then they met the Kansas Jayhawks in Madison Square Garden. Kansas was led by Jo Jo White, but Don May and company were too much for the Jayhawks. Dayton took the NIT crown sixty-one to forty-eight, and Donoher became the only coach to take his team to the finals of the NCAA and NIT in successive years. Dad and I and even Mom were beside ourselves with joy.

"Son, there are only two college basketball teams that ended this season with a W: the winner of the NCAA tournament and our Dayton Flyers."

I tried out for the ninth-grade basketball team. I was excited and nervous. I wanted the same sense of belonging to something bigger than me that playing on a baseball team had given me. Sure, I had practiced what I thought was a lot in the driveway, but I really didn't feel confident going into tryouts. The tryouts went on for several days, and it seemed like a group of certain players were getting all the attention. They were always the first ones picked to play in the scrimmages, and I asked myself, has this team already been picked?

I didn't say much to my parents about it. Each day, the same conversation went down.

"How did it go today?" Dad asked.

"Oh, okay. Good," I said.

On the last day of tryouts, I got my chance to play with four kids I knew would make the team. I made a couple of baskets and did really well. At least I thought so.

The next day, the names of those who made the team were posted on the locker-room door. I waited to be sure no one was around and ran up to look at the list. The names were listed in alphabetical order, and I scanned it quickly. All the names I suspected to be there were there. But when I skipped to the bottom where my name would be, my heart sank, and my stomach felt sick. Wilson was the last name. I ran my finger up the names to be sure. At least I knew; no more waiting.

I turned quickly, as I didn't want anybody seeing me looking for my name on a list it wasn't on, but Mr. Becker, the freshman coach, was standing in front of me, blocking my way. I looked down and stepped to get around him.

"You know; you have a lot of potential. You were my last cut," he said.

Sure, I thought, *I bet he tells that to all the kids he cut.*

"I'd like for you to be our manager."

I just wanted to get away from there and go home. It didn't feel good to be missing from his list and being manager wasn't what I wanted. "Nah, I have to go."

"You could shoot around and practice at the other baskets when I didn't need you for something."

"Nah, I don't think so—thanks." I got by him and walked away as fast as I could. I was mad, hurt, and disgusted.

When I told Mom and Dad I hadn't made the team, Dad said, "Well, that's okay. You can get on a church team and get out there in the driveway, and next year you'll make varsity." I looked for disappointment to show on Dad's face. I know it was in him as it was in me, but I didn't see it.

My friend Jeff Myers was also asked to be a manager, and he encouraged me to do it with him. I finally relented. Dad didn't like me doing it and said I should focus on playing on the church team.

It worked out that I could do both. I did well in the church league playing for St. Jacobs Lutheran Church. I usually scored ten to twelve points. My friendship with Jeff grew, and we had fun being managers. I learned that while you don't always get what you want, if you swallow a little pride, you might be surprised at how good things can be.

I also had some good games on my home court. Jimmy Zimmerman would come over and play; he was old enough by then that he was allowed to leave his yard. He had grown to a towering six foot seven inches. The only way I could get a shot off was to fake left and then a quick right-handed hook shot under the basket. I never beat Jimmy. Jimmy went on to star at Alter High School and at Wright State University.

Basketball was different from baseball. In baseball, you had lots of time to think about what was coming next—standing in the batter's box, waiting on a ball in the field. In basketball, it all came too quick to think about what you needed to do next.

Constantly searching for fun, I discovered basketball was an easy find. It was on my driveway, on my neighbor Jimmy Zimmerman's dirt court, on the school playground, and in the gym. And Mom and Dad championed it, and that felt good.

Basketball held my interest and helped keep me grounded in something that was all good and pure. After a game, I had a feeling of satisfaction and of accomplishment.

Basketball connected Dad and me. It gave us something we could share. I didn't realize until much later in life how that time with him talking and playing basketball influenced my interest in the sport. The experiences you have, the things you learn during those formative years that we all hear about, do indeed have a lifelong effect on you. Basketball taught me that sometimes you need to take what you're given and make the best of it.

CLOSED

When they asked Yogi Berra how he liked school as a kid, he said, "Closed." I couldn't have said it better. I had a love/hate relationship with school. I was excited to go to school, but when I got there, I wanted to leave.

My early education was not as good as it should have been. Looking back on it now, I believe that was due to a combination of mediocre instruction and lack of interest and motivation on my part. I wish that I would have taken school more seriously early on in my life and put more effort into doing well. I just didn't get it then: how important that would be later on.

I heard conflicting voices that said, "Skip school and don't take it so seriously. It will be fun and exciting, but studying and attending class will be hard and boring. Those voices told me what I needed to do and how much effort it was going to take to get what I wanted. And what I wanted was freedom to do what I wanted when I wanted.

Teachers provide motivation for many young people. Parents and coaches also provide it. Other motivators can be public figures, friends, books, or movies. I was motivated by a combination of all those things, and I was compelled to emulate people I came in contact with, read about, or saw on TV. Those people often were doing things that would not serve me well: smoking, drinking, and skipping school among them. Others were educated, progressive, cultured people doing worthy things. I had choices to make.

And later I learned that the choices you make, make you.

It was rare that a teacher inspired or positively motivated me. Was that me not being receptive? Was it that they weren't very good at what they were supposed to be doing?

School felt confining to me. The obligation to go every day to the same place and do what other people wanted me to do. The lack of freedom. To school at eight in the morning and out at three in the afternoon? The day was about gone by then.

Mrs. Maddox, my kindergarten teacher, began each day with the "Our Father" prayer. And then with my hand over my heart, we recited the "Pledge of Allegiance."

I thought these must be the most important words, as we never missed a day reciting them.

"Gather around boys and girls; we're going to sing some songs," Mrs. Maddox instructed as she sat down at a big green piano. She made sure everyone was singing by looking up in the mirror that was above the piano, then calling out their name.

My attention was drawn to the public swimming pool as our classroom was above the locker room for it. Windows that looked out on this mass of white and blue concrete called to me more than the piano. I would look out each day in anticipation of warm weather and a pool full of water. "Tim, it's a long time to summer. Join in, will you please?"

I started first grade at Kinder Elementary School, the oldest school building in town, on the corner of Central Avenue and Sixth Street. Our house was five blocks east on Central Avenue. It was a pretty easy walk except in the winter. I would walk down Central to Tenth Street, then take a left and walk down the alley, which dumped out right at the side end entrance to the playground at Kinder.

My first-grade teacher Miss Engle was a tall thin lady with black hair and a thick southern drawl. I think she was from Kentucky. She lived across

176

the street from me, was very strict, and used her wood paddle frequently on boys and girls alike.

I thought it odd that there was a toilet that was in the back of the classroom behind the coatroom; only Miss Engle was allowed to use it. And when she was using it, no one was allowed in the coatroom.

Mrs. Engle divided the class up into three reading groups. The Red Birds were the top reading group, the Blue Birds were in the middle, and last, the Yellow Birds. I was in the Red Birds.

When Miss Engle taught reading, she would bring one of the groups up to the front of the classroom and have them sit in a semi-circle around her. She would call you to read aloud from our reading book, taking turns around the circle. She would peek up from time to time to see that the rest of the class was working quietly on a writing assignment.

In general, I was a poor student and a cut up in class, but I liked to read and it was my best subject. I got nervous though, reading aloud in front of everybody.

As kids were taking turns around the circle, I would look ahead and try to guess what paragraph would fall to me to read and read it over, sounding out any words I was unsure about. One day, I was doing just that. "Okay, thank you Joyce. Tim, will you pick up there?" Miss Engle asked.

What? It wasn't my turn. There were two more kids between me and Joyce. I thought, *Why did she call my name*? It was if she knew I wasn't reading along with Joyce.

"Yes, okay. 'Johnny was walking with his mother."

"Tim!" Miss Engel shouted. "We are past that. Begin at the next paragraph."

I heard snickers.

"Oh, sure, that's right," I said. I stammered, nervous, but recovered and the words came easily and smoothly. Until the word "little" appeared on the page. I stopped and stared at that word. I didn't know how to say it. I began to fidget in my seat. I started to scratch the back of my head; I had seen that done by a cartoon character when they were confused. I knew what the word meant, I just for the life of me could not say it.

I tried to sound it out, struggling to know what to do with the "i." Was it a long sound? A short one? Was it pronounced at all? I glanced up at my classmates, who stared at me and snickered again.

"Okay, Tim. We're waiting," Miss Engle said.

I sat silently, scratching my head.

"Well, if you don't know that word, just go back to your seat. You're not ready to be in the Red Birds, and you can read with the Blue Birds."

"It's little. The word is little." I finally got it out.

"Just go."

I got up from the circle and went back to my seat. I hated Miss Engle.

I don't know how this happened, but I must have redeemed myself because one day, Miss Engle announced to the class, "Tim is being moved back up to the Red Birds, but if he doesn't do better, he is going all the way back to the Yellow Birds."

I was happy to be back in the Red Birds but scared about being sent back to the Yellow Birds. If I did badly, why not just go back to the Blue Birds? I didn't think about it then, but I wonder how those kids in the Yellow Birds felt hearing Miss Engle's words.

I liked my second-grade teacher Mrs. Opal. She was older and had a kind and gentle way about her. She was nice to me and reminded me of my grandma. Although I wasn't the teacher's pet. She had two students who filled that role: Carl Apple and Alexis Mays. Mrs. Opal always seemed to call on these two, and they sat up front near her desk. Of course they could do no wrong. I don't know why she liked Carl Apple so much. Maybe because he was smart and didn't give her any trouble; that seemed like a good enough reason. Alexis was one of the cutest girls in the class; she lived next door to Mrs. Opal, and her dad was Miamisburg's mayor. We were all made quite aware of how special Alexis was. I didn't envy Carl and Alexis. I thought it funny though, the special treatment they got. But I understood why. They stood out.

After school was out that year, Mom brought me to the Miamisburg public swimming pool. There was a chill in the early morning air as I got out of the car in my short swimming trunks carrying a towel. A strong smell of chlorine greeted me as I entered the pool area from the bathhouse. Mom brought me here to learn to swim, but my goal was to jump off those diving boards.

For the first week or so I was in the shallow end of the pool. At some point, I was instructed to go down to the swimming lanes, which were in water eight feet deep. I had to be able to swim across the pool, probably about a hundred feet, before I was allowed to advance to the diving boards.

I slid into the cold water, my teeth chattering, and clung to the side of the pool. There were five or six boys and girls, all about my age, and one lifeguard. He motioned one of the boys on the end to start the trek. The boy left the safety of the edge of the pool and began swimming toward the lifeguard as the guard slowly backed up across the pool, staying just out of reach of the boy but close enough to grab him if he stopped swimming. Halfway across, the boy stopped moving forward and began splashing and flailing his arms wildly, his head bobbing under and above the water. The guard stepped forward, calmly grabbed the boy in his sun-tanned, muscular arms, and began walking him slowly back to the edge of the pool. I heard him offer some encouragement to the boy.

"You'll get it next time," he said.

A girl started her trip across the pool as the guard walked back faster this time. It seemed in no time the girl was across the pool. She climbed out using the ladder, looked back at the rest of us shivering and clinging to the side of the pool, and smiled. She headed over to the deep end and the diving boards.

"Okay, who's next?" the lifeguard said. I pushed off into the pool and began stroking my arms and raising my head every three strokes for air and to sneak a peek to be sure the guard was not too far ahead of me. I wasn't cold anymore, but it didn't seem that I was making much progress. I looked to the side, and I was still not yet halfway. I was running out of breath.

My arms became heavy and I was gasping for air with each stroke I made.

I finally realized that I would not make it. I made one last flurry, twitched my arms, and got my feet paddling as hard as I could.

I started to go under and water went up my nose. I gasped for air as water raced over my face when I rose out of the pool into those strong tan arms. "You did good—over halfway!" My heart was pounding as he continued, "You'll make it next time."

He was right; I did make it the next time. I was proud and happy as I looked back at the guard and glanced at those shivering kids across the pool, clinging to the edge, smiling. I had accomplished something. I was headed for the deep end and the diving boards.

I spent a lot of time in the principal's office during my six years at Kinder Elementary School. Mrs. Laveta Bauer served as principal at the time, and oh, was she scary. She looked like Mrs. Gulch from The Wizard of Oz. When she stared down at me with that ragged face and crooked nose, I became stiff with fear.

Recess was my favorite part of the school day, which is why after several run-ins with Mrs. Bauer, that's what she took away. I had to report to her office as soon as lunch was over. Spending recess with her went on for a couple of months. I knew I misbehaved, but I didn't any more so than other kids.

Then one day, as I was sitting outside Mrs. Bauer's office, she came over to me. She looked down at me and in a scratchy voice asked, "Well, Mr. Stonecash, do you think you can behave yourself? Have you learned how to be a good boy?"

"Oh yes, I will be good." I lied of course.

She nodded. "Okay, you go now and don't let me hear any bad reports about you."

I was so excited to get back out on the playground, to play kickball, and hang on the monkey bars. I had learned an important lesson: If I wanted to be free and do some of the things I wanted, I had to obey the rules—or at least not get caught disobeying them—or I would lose that freedom.

At the far end of the playground stood two large buildings where kids from all grades were mixed into the same classroom. Some of these kids were in first grade, and some were in eighth grade. We called these kids "The Tin Builders" because the building their class was in was made of tin. Most of them were really quiet and kept to themselves on the playground. They acted a little odd, kinda different. Somebody said they were below the Yellow Birds, but nobody made fun of them because there were a couple of hoods in those classes, and you didn't want to cross one of them. I stood on the playground staring at the tin buildings one day and Mrs. Engle came up to me.

"You better get with the program, or you'll find yourself in those buildings. "That scared me. Why would she say that? I wasn't dumb. I thought Tommy Abraham was a Tin Builder, and that really scared me.

At the beginning of the year, Mrs. Murphy, my fifth-grade teacher, selected two patrol boys and one alternate. They would be dismissed from class each day fifteen minutes before the bell. Their job was to go to the intersection of Central Avenue and Sixth Street and help kids cross. Each kid got a big red flag that said "Stop" and a really cool silver badge. It looked like a policeman's badge and said, "Patrol Boy."

Mrs. Murphy picked boys who were good students and well behaved, or in other words, the goodie goodies. Since I met neither of those requirements, I never got to be a patrol boy. Maybe she thought I was a girl because none of the girls ever got to be patrol boys either. But I guess that was fair because there were never any boys who were cheerleaders. Not that any boy then would ever want to be a cheerleader—that was for girls; the prettiest ones. Some things were for boys, and some things were for girls; that's just how it was then.

Once in a while there would be a day that one of the regular patrol boys stayed home sick. And once in a great while, one of the regular patrol boys and the alternate patrol boy were sick. During class attendance one day, I realized the "great while" had come to pass. I was excited; maybe Mrs. Murphy would ask me to be a patrol boy that day. Quickly, I did the math. There were twelve boys in our class. Two boys were home sick,

Johnny was still on crutches, Bill and Charlie were goofy kids that she would never pick, Ralph and Felix were always in trouble, Sam never said a word, and Teddy was the other patrol boy. So that meant it was between my friend Jeff, Carl Apple, and me.

I wasn't the best student and I did act up once in a while, but I knew Mrs. Murphy liked me. Maybe

She picked Carl Apple.

Mrs. Murphy kept looking at me all day as if she was going to say something nice. When the patrol boys got up to leave, she looked at me and said, "Tim, would you help me put all the chalk away and take all the erasers out on the fire escape to dust them?"

Why hadn't she picked me to be a patrol boy? It would have been nice to be recognized in this manner. Something endeared me to her, but she didn't think I deserved to be a patrol boy, and deep down, I knew I didn't either.

"Sure," I said as I jumped out of my seat, slamming that math book closed. For that day, school was over for me.

Joining the Cub Scouts seemed like a great way to be around kids and do fun stuff. My friend Jeff Meyer's mother Agnus was our den mother. We met after school once a week at their house.

We learned some basic outdoor skills, did some craft stuff that I hated, and went on a couple of camp outs, which I loved. What I dreaded was report card day. If it fell on a day that our den met, Agnus would insist on seeing our cards immediately and giving her critical assessment of our marks.

"Okay, what do we have here?"

She would start with two smart goody-goodies and work her way down to me, Larry, and her son, Jeff. Larry always had good grades at least compared to Jeff and me.

"Tim, it says here you're not paying attention and are disturbing others in class. You have high marks in reading and spelling but not turning in math homework? 'If Tim has anymore outbursts like he had last Friday, we will need to have a parent/teacher conference.'" Agnus looked at me sternly. "What is that all about, Tim? You better straighten up in class!"

I just shrugged and looked down. I was embarrassed as she read this in front of all the den. Why was she doing this? It really wasn't her business, was it? The report did end on a positive note, I thought. "Tim has lots of potential but needs to buckle down." Now I would have to go home and face Mom and Dad and go through all this again.

I was on the junior high football team, but it wasn't a lot of fun; my uniform never fit. My pants were too big, and I had a hard time keeping them up. It was hard to play football when I was always holding up my pants with one hand. I was never given a chance to play the positions I wanted to play. I always had to play on the line or defensive end—that sucked.

The most memorable part of those junior high football days was a fight. It was no big deal for boys—there were always a couple fighting about something. But one day, two girls got into it. I don't know why these two girls picked the football practice field to fight, but we were all glad they did. A pretty blonde girl and a buxom brunette marched out to the field, and all the players followed, egging them on.

"You bitch, I'll show you!" *Wham*! The blonde landed a clenched fist right across the brunettes' jaw.

"Ah yeah, you slut!" And with that, the brunette made a shoulder tackle on the blonde.

Our team gathered around them as they tore into each other, both squabbling in the mud, pulling hair and swinging wildly. We were all rooting them on and hoping to see as much skin as possible. It was fun watching while it lasted, but soon one of our coaches broke it up. Later I thought how degrading it was for both of them and also for us.

I wasn't a particularly gifted athlete in any sense. But once in a while I did show some ability. In the eighth grade, we had a school-wide wrestling competition. All the boys were divided by weight. I was in the hundred-

and-thirty-five-pound class. My first match was a non-memorable one, which I won easily.

The next kid I had to face was a rough kid named Verlin Manning. He was strong, dark complected, and had what looked like the beginnings of a beard. He was the heavy favorite; everybody said he would kill me. I had spent a lot of fun times wrestling, always with Larry, so I wasn't scared, but didn't think I would beat him.

I surprised myself and everyone else and won the match. The other guy who had won in my division was Mike Van Buren—a husky, tough kid from a bad part of town. He had always been nice to me, but I, as most kids did, stayed out of his way.

I remember that we started the match with one guy on all fours and the other guy on top of him on two knees, holding onto his wrists with one hand with the other arm around his midsection. Then the referee would blow the whistle and we would begin wrestling.

I was a little intimidated and nervous about facing off against Mike. I wanted to beat him, but I was kind of afraid if I did, he would beat me up later. Again, I won and advanced to the finals. Mike was a gentleman; I think I earned his respect. The final would be played out in front of the whole school in the high school gym.

We were encouraged to dress up in some sort of costume or at least colored shirts and shorts. My opponent was Ben Sims, a tall, slim kid who dressed up as Spider-Man. The whole week leading up to the match, he was telling everyone in school how he was going to destroy me. He was a bigger braggart than Cassius Clay.

"Stonecash, I'm going to smoke you, tangle you up in my spider arms, then squeeze you to death with my legs."

"Okay, sure," I responded.

Maybe he really thought he was Spider-Man. He ran his mouth the whole week prior to the match, boasting how fast he was and how many holds he had. I just dressed in some green shorts and a white t-shirt. By now, my confidence was pretty high, and the only person in the school who

I was unsure of besting was Larry, but we were in two different weight classes.

I beat Sims easily. As he jumped and danced around the mat, I finally got hold of him and it was over. Somehow, the big mouth talked the gym teacher into giving him a rematch.

I didn't understand how that happened; I guess he was a better talker than wrestler. It took place at the next gym class. That really pissed me off, and I pinned in the first round.

The wrestling title gave me confidence that there were things I could achieve, that there were things I might even be good at; maybe I just needed to keep searching for those things.

Mr. Newkirk was assigned the unenviable task of teaching me eighth-grade algebra. I think he was the oldest teacher I ever had. I know he was considerably older at the end of that school year. He was a nice man who seemed to really like me. I'm sure I was a disappointment to him as he never got through to me what $y - 2a + 3a$ meant. That didn't take then, and it doesn't make much sense now. I focused on making paper airplanes under my desk, and when Mr. Newkirk turned his back to write on the blackboard, I would let them fly all over class.

The only thing I liked about school was seeing my friends and cutting up with them as much as possible. Doing what I was told and learning something were always the furthest things from my mind.

Looking back on those years, I see wasted opportunities. Most of that was the result of my resistance to being told what to do. I didn't think much about it then, but as I look back on it now, my attitude about school may have been different had a teacher offered some encouragement and showed some interest in me.

My eighth-grade science class was taught by Mr. Allen in fifth period. I liked the class, mostly because of where I sat. The tables were large solid wood with a hard-plastic black top that sat two students. My friend Larry sat right behind me, and he shared a table with one of the prettiest girls in class. I sat directly in front of Larry and shared a table with the other prettiest girl in the class.

Mr. Allen would devote lots of class time to having us read on our own or working on an in-class project while he had his nose in a book or the newspaper. He would periodically peer up from his reading to see if anyone was out of order. As his eyes scanned the classroom, he would pinch his lips together with an up and down movement resembling a fish sucking down a morsel of food. We began referring to him as "Mr. Fish." I don't think he ever knew why we called him that, but he certainly didn't like it. Someone had even stuck a fish sticker on the outside of his door.

At least once a day, he would catch somebody doing something inappropriate during reading time. He would threaten them by saying, "Do we need to take a walk?"

A walk with Mr. Allen meant a walk down to the principal's office for three whacks with his paddle.

One day, as we were putting the last touches on our science projects, I turned around in my seat and looked at Larry's large cardboard display of all these round balls laid out on the top of a sheet of cardboard that said "Solar System."

Each ball was a different size and color. I slapped at one of the balls and said with a snicker, "It looks like a big fruit bowl." Larry pushed me on the shoulder with a chuckle. "Shut up!"

The girls next to us started to giggle.

"What's the disturbance over there? "Mr. Allen inquired.

"Oh, nothing," I said.

But he had seen the whole thing. Larry, do we need to go for a walk?"

"No!" Larry protested

"I think we do; let's go. And, Mr. Stonecash, I think you should come along too. You boys have been asking for this for some time. I have warned you boys; now it's time we took a walk." Mr. Allen glanced at the two girls. They froze. Surely Mr. Allen wouldn't include them. Mr. Allen had never taken a girl for a walk, but The Fish was an odd fellow. Anything was possible; they got a pass.

Mr. Allen marched Larry and me to the principal's office where the paddle was kept, and where he could get a witness. There always had to be a witness. I guess to be sure you weren't hurt too badly, or in case we fought back and he needed some help.

He gave me three quick whacks on the behind. Larry was up next. After the second whack he said, "Mr. Russell, I think you deserve another one. You seem to have been most at fault here."

I didn't know why he said that. Maybe he'd lost count.

He gave Larry one more and that was it. Our butts were burning. He was not a large man but would put his whole weight behind the swing, lifting us off the floor.

Larry and I decided we would go into business selling toothpicks. So, we bought a couple of boxes and soaked the tiny sticks in cinnamon. We brought them to school and told everybody they were bourbon toothpicks. At a nice price of five cents each, we sold quite a few. One girl, a heavy-set blonde bought a dollar's worth.

We also sold them to a couple of hoods, and one of them said, "Oh, this is great bourbon," and nodded his approval.

It wasn't long before we were called into the principal's office and told we were in trouble for selling alcohol at school. We immediately let the principal in on our recipe. "There's no bourbon; we soaked the toothpicks in cinnamon," we explained. He took one and looked it over, put it in his mouth, and agreed.

"No bourbon here, but you can't bring them to school—it's a hazard. Kids could fall on them or get choked."

That was the end of our toothpick business. It seemed everything I did, some authority figure got in the way.

I did my part in the first celebration of Earth Day that Gaylord Nelson, a Senator from Wisconsin, founded. Senator Nelson said, "If we could tap into the environmental concerns of the general public and infuse the student anti-war energy into the environmental cause, we could generate a demonstration that would force the issue onto the national political agenda."

Nelson did not organize a national protest but said it would be "a day for people to act locally." He said, "This is the time for old-fashioned political action."

A friend and I decided to join the effort. We went to the Dayton Mall and stood out in the middle of it and started talking, almost yelling about how we were destroying the environment and the importance of Earth Day to nobody in particular. We just preached to startled shoppers walking by.

We got lots of looks that said, "What are those young nuts doing?"

I don't think we knew much about what we were doing or why we were interested in the environment or even what we said that day. I did remember the unbelievable scene of those huge trash barges going out to sea along the East River, in New York City. How much garbage could our oceans hold? It seemed like the establishment didn't care, and this added to my resentment toward authority.

One night, Johnny Mack—a rough neck little red head we called Red Dog—a couple of girls and I were out drinking and hot rodding in his souped up 1957 Chevy. I think someplace near Germantown, a small village just east of Miamisburg.

We had some altercation with a bunch of guys in another car, and they started chasing us. Just for fun Red Dog had let one of the girls drive but now we were having a hard time getting away from the other car.

"Here, switch seats with me; let me drive," Red Dog demanded. Red Dog, who was in the front seat, slid under the girl, traded seats with her, and took over driving, all while we were speeding down curvy country roads. Red Dog poured it on, passing a couple cars on double yellow lines, running stop signs, and fishtailing around sharp curves. It was a wild ride; we were all over both sides of the road, and in retrospect, I don't know how we didn't wreck. But at the time, those were the kind of thrills we lived for.

"I can't lose them!" Red Dog screamed.

One of the girls said, "Let's go to Strickland's house; there's always a gang of boys hanging out there; they'll help us."

We turned into their driveway and pulled up to the long lane to their house, which was on a hill. "It doesn't look like anyone is home. How could nobody be home?" I said in a panic.

"Look they're still after us," Red Dog said. I looked down the driveway: we hadn't lost them. Car lights were slowly moving up the driveway. *These guys mean business*, I thought.

The girls ran to the house. They screamed and pounded on the door, which Violet, our friend's mom, finally opened. There were none of the Strickland boys around, but their parents were home.

"These guys are after us!" the girls screamed.

"Oh, you poor things! Get in here, girls. Ralph!" Violet called for her husband.

Ralph showed up in the doorway and chambered shells into his twelve-gage pump action while the car continued to creep cautiously up the driveway. I couldn't believe they were coming up to the house after us. We must have really pissed them off. Or maybe they wanted the girls. I couldn't be sure.

Ralph sneaked down the side of his yard, concealed by darkness and some bushes. He eventually reached their car. *Boom-Boom-Boom*! Three quick ones into the side panels of their GTO. That was all it took. They may have been pissed, but they weren't stupid. They hit reverse and booked up.

Everyone wanted to be cool, and having a cool car was a big part of that. Fast, good-looking cars were a big thing. Most cars, even if they weren't cool, could be made to look cool. My first car was a 1962 Chevy station wagon. I think we had it as a second car, so when I got my license, that was the car I used. A station wagon was hard to make look cool, so I took it to another friend's house, Tony Warrick, who had a penchant for working on cars.

"Pull into the barn; it's suppose to rain," Tony instructed. Tony showed me two U-shaped pieces of steel about eight inches long.

"We can bolt these on between the leaf springs and the body of the car to jack up the rear end." Why was that cool? Who knew? But it was.

Tony did most of the work. I watched and handed him tools.

"Wow, that makes it a lot higher in the back. Thanks for putting those on, Tony. What do I owe ya?"

"Nothing man; they been sitting around here for years."

"Let's see how she rides."

We took her for a short ride out in the country.

"Can you get rubber in this thing," Tony asked.

"No, you kidding? This thing is a dog."

"Oh, I bet you can. Stop here; there's nobody coming," he directed. "Now put your left foot hard on the brake; now ease down on the accelerator with your right foot. Now put more pressure on the accelerator; now let up easy on the brake."

The tires began to turn slowly, then faster, then they began squealing. The car moved forward ever so slowly and began to swerve a little. I looked out the widow and smoke was coming from my screeching tires, the smell of burning rubber filled the air.

"Now, let up on the brake."

I did and we took off flying down the road.

"What the hell?" I yelled.

That's power braking, man! You just got rubber in this dog."

At the time, drinking while driving cars was commonplace. We never thought too much about the consequences of doing that. On many nights, we would get somebody to buy us beer and get in our cars and race around town. We did watch out for cops, and we knew the consequences for getting caught with beer in the car were bad, but not bad enough not to do it.

On another occasion, a group of my friends and me were out on the town. Tony was riding shotgun; I was in the back with Larry and Mitch. Red Dog was again behind the wheel. He was showing off, driving like a wild man; he couldn't have been drunk yet, but Red Dog didn't have to be drunk to drive wild. Somebody had a fake ID, and we had just bought an eight pack of Stroh's, some Little Kings, and a couple bottles of Ripple. I think one of the guys had gotten a bottle of Screwdriver too. We headed out of town to do a little riding around and drinking before heading to a party we had heard about.

We were sliding side to side in the back seat every time we made a turn. Red Dog had a method: he would slow down just a bit before hitting the curve, then halfway through it, he would gun the accelerator and fishtail out of it.

It was good thing we were out in the country, and there were no other cars on the road. Still, for the first time on many a wild car ride, I was scared. I knew something bad was going to happen. Those trees close to the side of the road loomed large.

"Slow the fuck down!" Larry yelled in his ear.

Terrified that we might slam sideways into a tree, I reached up and grabbed Red Dog by the shoulder with one hand, while holding onto the back of the seat with the other.

"Come on, Red Dog, you're going to kill us. Calm down."

Despite the seriousness in my voice. Red Dog glanced back at me and just howled, taking a swig of Ripple. The car swerved around a corner and Red Dog tromped the accelerator, which brought the car straight, we were flying now. Then for no reason he flips the wheel and we go sideways. The tires screeched I thought we were going to flip over. I look out and saw trees.

We landed with a jolt and thud in the ditch, stopping beside a big sycamore tree. Red Dog tried to restart the car, but it would not turn over. We were all shook up, but unbelievably no one was hurt.

"Man, the cops are going to come," Ryan said.

"Yeah, we need to ditch this booze," I said. We took all the beer and wine out of the car and threw it out into the fields in all directions as far as we could. My hands trembled as we did, both from fear and exhilaration, which formed a heady mix. Experiences like this—those I knew were wrong, but I chased after because they felt so good—would become lessons later. Much later. Looking back now, it's hard to believe we did such dumb things.

Soon, the police arrived and we were all brought to the station. They had us sit in the cars while they called our parents. They finally led us into a room and told us to have a seat. We all sat around a large table that was full of Little Kings, a bottle of Ripple, and an almost empty bottle of Screwdriver. How had they found all of that? We were released to our parents. They grounded us and told us how bad we were and how embarrassed they were.

The next Friday night, we were all back out looking for another thrill.

Across the street from the Stricklands lived the McAllistors. A strange conglomeration of people lived in that house. Ryan, my friend, was a little older than me and a littler rougher around the edges. He always talked tough but was really a nice guy who tried to stay out of trouble. He and his younger sister Nancy were the only two relatively normal people who lived there.

Ryan had a twin brother named Randy. They were nothing alike—didn't act alike, didn't look alike—you would never know they brothers, let alone twins. Randy was just plain mean and nobody to mess with. He would come to you and slap you in the face for no reason at all.

Ryan also had an older brother Rupert, who was a small-time gangster. Rupert did whatever he wanted, whenever he wanted. Could be a nice guy, but he was so wild and unpredictable that nobody wanted much to do with him.

Their mom seemed pretty old, and I thought for a long time that she was their grandma since everybody called her "Granny." A large man much older than us, always wearing these weird looking sunglasses and always bare chested, also lived there.

Ryan referred to him as "Wide Load."

Their father apparently died a few years back in a house fire that Ryan thought Rupert had started. They lived a meager life but had a neat old house with lots of character that sat back off the road. I had a car, so I would pick Ryan up to go out for the night. I would pull up on a stone bridge that went over a small creek in front of their house and wait for Ryan to come out, hoping to avoid anyone else.

One Saturday morning, when I came to pick up Ryan, I pulled onto the bridge and waited and waited impatiently as always. Finally, I hesitantly honked the horn as I was concerned about alerting Randy or Rupert. Rupert would want to come with us, and Randy might come out and punch me in the head (just for the hell of it) and then make me take him somewhere.

Ryan didn't come out, so I slowly pulled the car back into their gravel driveway, still no sign of Ryan. As I got out of the car, there was Randy, leaning on a fence. He had heard my car door shut and glanced over at me. "Come over here. Want to see something?" he said. No, I didn't want to see anything he had to show me, but I couldn't refuse. There, in a smallish corral, was a beautiful black horse staring at us. Randy picked up a small stone and hit the horse on the behind. The horse reared up and took off running in circles. Randy laughed and looked at my response. I just smiled a little. Randy wasn't just mean to people; he was just plain mean.

"Do you ever ride him?" I asked.

"Nah, he was never broke. Too hard to handle."

I immediately thought of Black Jack and how he acted up at the president's funeral. That's what they'd said about him, and nobody ever rode him. "We're just keeping him for a few more days, then he's off to the slaughterhouse. Not good for nothing but dog food," Rodney said.

"Do they still do that?"

"Not legally, but we know a guy." Randy grinned and picked up another stone.

So that's what happens when you're too hard to handle, I thought. Unless you're important like Black Jack. My mind flashed—was I too hard to handle? Randy certainly was.

I never saw Randy again. I heard later that he'd left with a carnival that had passed through town.

I turned, quickly went up to the house, and pecked on the screen door.

"Come on in!" Granny hollered. "Ryan, your buddy's here."

Ryan bounded into the kitchen.

"Let's go, Ryan," I said. "Are you ready?"

"Oh, settle yourself and have a seat. I've got some pancakes here," Granny said.

"Oh, we got to be going," I said.

"Sit down," Rupert ordered as he walked into the kitchen.

I did.

We had some pancakes and who knows what else. I was nervous and wanted to leave. I looked at Ryan.

"Don't say anything," he said.

"Hey, you guys want to come with me and we can make a little money? Do a little job?" Rupert asked.

"No, we got to go," Randy said.

"Go? Shit, you ain't got no place to go. We can go get a few radiators from over at the used car place on Main Street. They're closed today, so it's an easy job." Rupert snarled and kicked Ryan in the shin under the table. "We can get ten bucks a piece for them at the junkyard."

"Nah, we got to meet some guys," Ryan said.

"You ain't gonna meet nobody, fucker. Come on! It will be easy money."

I wasn't sure what he was talking about... radiators?

"How long will it take?" I asked. "Ryan and I do have some friends to meet." I really didn't want to piss Rupert off.

"Okay, we can just go right down here in Siebert Plat. There are four or five cars parked over at John Cooks' house, and I know there is nobody home; they all went hunting early this morning. We can make fifty bucks real quick, take about an hour or so. I was nervous now. He meant we would steal these out of people's cars.

"Oh, Rupert, leave these boys alone," Granny said.

Ryan put up his hands, palms facing outward. "That's right, Rupert. We want no part of this. We'll get caught," Ryan said.

Rupert held his fist up at Ryan, his face set in anger.

Suddenly, Wide Load sauntered into the kitchen. "Rupert, get out! Your kind of trouble needs to move on."

Rupert jumped to his feet. "You shut the fuck up, Wide Load. I'll bust you up good right now."

Wide Load was certainly larger than Rupert, but Rupert was hard as a rock and had an arura about him that said "beware I'm nobody to mess with." Wide Load looked at us and shook his head, then made his way out the back door.

Rupert was fired up now. "You guys get your ass in the car or you know what's up!"

"Okay," Ryan said. "Let me get some shoes on first."

Ryan disappeared into the back bedroom.

"I gotta take a shit, and then we head out," Rupert said and he shut the bathroom door.

"Now's your chance, boys! Skedaddle," Granny whispered, and motioned us toward the door.

I looked at Granny and then Ryan, who had his shoes in his hand. "Put those on in the car," I said. The sound of the toilet flushing rang out, and we ran out the door, jumped into my car, and took off.

Rupert came busting out of the house, chasing us all the way to the bridge as he hollered obscenities at us. I was looking for fun and wild times, but Rupert was pushing it too far for me.

While Rupert didn't get us that time, I did make the mistake of getting into a car with Rupert one other time. A large black crow tied to his rear-view mirror sat on his dashboard and pecked at bread crumbs.

"He's my pet; he pecks the bread and I peck him." With that Rupert would take his finger and peck at the bird, the bird would squawk, and Rupert would cackle back at him.

All the while we were flying down Old River Road, fishtailing back and forth. The crow flopped and slid around on the dash, the radio blared some rock tune, and Rupert sipped on a bottle of liquor, laughing like a hyena. It didn't matter that cars were coming; they had to slow down and pull off to the side of the road as we slid past them.

I was never so glad to get out of a car.

To say Rupert was a dangerous and unpredictable guy was an understatement. I envied his freedom to do whatever he wanted; nobody was his boss. I hated going to school and resented authority, but there was something about Rupert that scared me.

Another time, I was standing in line to buy some cigarettes at the Point Carry Out and felt a hard jab to my back that almost knocked me over.

"Hey, fucker. Where have you been lately?" It was Rupert.

"Oh, nowhere, just getting some smokes; gotta get right home," I lied.

I never saw Rupert again. Later I heard that he was in prison.

There was a real sweet looking girl I had flirted with at Beachler Field while watching softball games. She lived way out in the country. Not sure exactly what our purpose was, but Mitch and I decided to go out to her house late one night.

Her house sat by itself on a country road a few miles out of town. We drove by real slow in front of an old farmhouse.

"This isn't it," Mitch said.

"Yes, it is," I insisted. We drove to the next intersection, turned right, went down a few houses, and turned around. Then we drove by the house again real slow. No lights were on, but there was a man in the driveway getting into a truck.

"He's got a gun!" I yelled. The truck turned on its lights and started coming out of the driveway.

"Let's get out of here!" Mitch shouted.

I hit the gas on my four-speed Ford Fairlane 500. It had a big three hundred and ninety cubic inch engine and lots of horsepower. "Shit, he's following us!" I screamed.

We flew down Jamaica Road as fast as we could safely.

"He's gaining on us! Get going and open this thing up," Mitch pleaded.

"I bet he's got a four fifty-four in that Chevy," I said.

We came to the intersection and I downshifted and spun through it, making a right turn. Thank God no cars were coming. The road ahead was a straight shot for a couple miles. I gave it all she had. But the truck had made the turn and was again gaining on us.

"Who the hell is that?" I shouted.

I had to decide whether to take Twin Mill Road, which had a winding curve down a hill into town, or take a sharp right turn onto Stony Hill, a straight steep hill leading into town.

At the last second, I chose Stony Hill and downshifted into third gear. We slid around the corner, slowing down, and ran head on into a stopped car.

Mitch hit his head on the rearview mirror and my knee bumped the ashtray, but somehow, neither of us were seriously hurt. I was panicked that the people we hit were hurt badly. What if they were dead? Maybe I had pushed this too hard. What would Mom say? Was this the kind of kid I was? Could I have killed someone?

I jumped out and hurried over to the other car. The front end of their station wagon was smashed in pretty good. I looked inside the car and saw a couple of small kids in the back seat, crying. There was a woman who was trying to comfort them. "Are you all okay? Is anybody hurt?" I shouted.

"We're all fine ... kids just a little shook up and scared," a man standing by the driver's side of the car answered.

They were fine, I thought, relieved. God, was with us tonight. Then I looked up at the shadow of a big man walking toward me. I couldn't see his face because of the glare of his truck lights.

"What the hell, man?" I shouted. "Are you crazy? Why were you chasing us with a gun?" Police sirens began to wail, which meant they must have been close by. The man looked in our car, walked up and looked into the station wagon, then looked at me.

"There's been a lot of robberies out here lately," he said. He turned, got back in his truck, and drove off.

It must have been sometime in early 1969 that I began a never-ending argument with my mom about the length of my hair. She wanted it short like when I was little. A burr with some wax put on in the front to make it stick up. I wanted it as long as God could grow it and as long as Mom could tolerate it because I thought long hair was hip.

It seems like a small thing now, but back then the freedom to grow your hair as long as you wanted was important.

High school was a real blur, mostly because I wasn't there that much. I was an all-around poor student and had little interest in conforming to any rules. Skipping classes became the norm for me. My circle of friends hung out at Red Dog's house who lived just a block from our high school buildings. It was easy to slip unnoticed between two buildings and down the alley to his house. It became the go-to place to skip a class or two or the whole day of school

His front door opened to a small living room taken up by a large three-cushion couch and a TV. A nice sized kitchen with a small red metal table in the center was where we all congregated. No one ventured upstairs to the two small bedrooms unless on a rare occasion you stayed all night.

Red Dog's dad died soon after we became friends, so it was just him, and his mom Mabel, and his little brother. Mabel worked until early evening, so we had free run of their house during the day. Mabel was always welcoming and would feed us whatever she had. Lots of baloney sandwiches, and once in a while, fried hamburgers. She didn't care if you smoked as long as you used an ashtray. There was, however, absolutely no cussing or drinking allowed in her home.

On many an early morning school day, I would give a quick knock on the door, and if it was unlocked, and it almost always was, let myself in.

"Hey, who's cutting first period today? I'm beat, man. I need a break from that French class," I whined.

"Yeah, I'm cutting first period too," Larry said. "We were supposed to have had this whole chapter read and I haven't even started it."

"Shit, I'm cutting the whole day; you guys should too," Tony said.

"No, I can't. I have to keep my grades up; football coach is on my ass about it," Larry said. Larry was the only one of our gang who was concerned much about grades.

"I'm going to class," Red Dog said as he headed out the door. "You guys can stay but don't have any girls in here and stay out of the refrigerator."

The other friend's house that was fun to hang out at was Tony's. His parents never seemed to be around. And when they were, they never paid much attention if you were smoking or drinking or who was coming and going or when. Tony had no curfew, so it was always a good idea to tell Mom I was staying all night with Tony. Then, you pretty much were free for the night. It's hard to imagine as a parent now, giving this kind of freedom to a child.

Friday was always the best day of the week. It was full of anticipation for the night ahead when we'd go to the football or basketball game. My curfew was always eleven p.m. on Friday or Saturday nights. But if I begged hard enough, I knew Mom would always give in to eleven-thirty. She must have considered I was up to no good, but she hoped for the best.

Jeff Myers was a fun kid to hang with, but he was quite clumsy, and if you ever wanted to get caught at doing something, then make sure Jeff was with you. One night, Jeff, Larry, and I decided to sneak into the basketball game.

At the entrance door, the security guard had turned his head to talk to somebody, and Jeff and I just slipped right by him. We were shocked he hadn't caught us. Larry, however, didn't get through as the guard had returned his attention to the door.

"Go around to those bathroom windows and we'll hoist you up," I told Larry, making sure the guard didn't hear me.

"Hell, those widows are eight feet high," Larry quietly protested.

"Then find something to stand on."

Jeff and I headed to the boy's bathroom. I opened the window, and there was Larry standing on top of a trash can.

"Hold it, Jeff. Shut the widow. The guard's coming," I yelled.

Jeff slammed the window shut and quickly took a spot next to me at a urinal. The guard came in, looked around, did his business, and followed us out the door.

After the guard was out of sight, we went back to the bathroom and tried again. Larry got back on top of the trash, peeking in the window. I kept watch at the door." The coast is clear; get him in," I called to Jeff.

Jeff hurriedly ran and jumped up on the interior window ledge, putting his knee right through the window and shattering glass all over Larry, who was still teetering on top of the trash can outside. Terrible noises rang out, glass flying all over. Jeff screamed about his knee, and the trash can went tumbling over Larry as he fell to the ground, cussing.

We hightailed it out of the bathroom and disappeared into the crowd. Jeff got away with a bruised knee, and Larry gathered himself from the fall and just came around to the entrance and bought a ticket.

If we could sneak into a game and not get caught, we thought we had accomplished something. It's not that we couldn't afford to pay the ticket price for admission to the game, it was just an easy way to get a thrill.

After the games, a gang of us guys would head to Ron's Pizza House. Some of us would take the shortcut through the graveyard and see who got lucky while walking with a girl. There was hope that you would stop for some smooching behind one of large gravestones or mausoleums. I was never so lucky.

One night after a football game, I was walking with a number of friends out to Ron's Pizza, including John Thompson and Roberta Stone. Roberta was a short brunette who wore her hair pulled into a ponytail. She was full of life and always kidding around and telling jokes.

"Hey, Tim! You coming with us?" Roberta asked as she flashed me an inviting smile. She had given me that smile a couple of times at the game that night.

Was she flirting with me? I smiled back. "Sure; we going by way of the graveyard?"

"Yep," John answered, giving me a wary look.

She was clearly John's girl, and he was going to walk her through the graveyard. I was just a tag along. We stopped along the way, and John took Roberta in his arms, kissing her long and hard like I had never seen before.

How could they breathe? Were they going to pass out? When they finally came up for air, Roberta looked at me over John's shoulder, our eyes met, and she smiled.

Soon John and Roberta broke up, and Roberta and I became something of an item. Were we boyfriend and girlfriend? Probably not—but we were more than friends.

One day at school she passed me a note that said: Tim, you're shy! Did you see the way John kissed me that night in the graveyard? That showed how much he liked me.

I was a little embarrassed, and at the same time, excited. I couldn't wait until Friday night; there was another home game. By Friday night, however, Roberta and I were no longer an item, and I never did get to show her how much I liked her.

In 1969, I was sixteen years old and things were moving very fast but too slow for me. Not sure *where* I was going, it only mattered *that* I was going.

One thing that helped me feel as though I was going was our barn, which I turned into party central. I bought small strips of carpet in all different colors—red, green, black, blue, and yellow—for fifty cents each and nailed them down on the floor. We hauled in a big couch and a couple of old chairs. We even built a bar. I hung Christmas lights all around the rafters and put in a great stereo with big speakers that rocked the place. We lined the walls with dead solders as we consumed them, mostly Stroh's cans. At the top of the main cross beam, I placed a large, framed poster of one of my heroes Robert Kennedy.

Mom was not happy with most of what went on in the barn, but I think she figured it was better to have me there than out on the streets somewhere.

There were some wild nights in the barn. It attracted some strange characters. There never needed to be a reason for a party in the barn. The word would get out, and before you knew it, the place was full of smoke, loud music, and a wide assortment of Miamisburg's off-the-wall characters mixed in with our usual group of friends.

"Who the hell is that?" I asked Mitch, pointing over in the corner to where a potbellied, balding, older guy sat stomping his feet and slapping his hands in time with the music.

"That's Wayne Myers; he's a little spacy, but he is unreal on the harmonica." Mitch yelled over to him, "Hey, Wayne! You got your harp? Play us a tune!"

"Nah, man, don't play anymore. Just groovin' to your sounds here, man. Just groovin' man, just groovin'." That's pretty much all Wayne ever said other than "no" when we offered him a beer. That was about the extent of a conversation with him.

Wayne would show up once in a while and hang out. He was of a simple mind. Some said he was a real brain in school but had blown it out on booze and acid years before. By the time we came to know him, he was alcohol and drug free, but he was a lesson to us about what drugs could do to you.

David Brooks lived with his dad and three younger brothers. His dad was a nice guy but didn't keep track of him–where he was or when he was coming home. DB—that's what he went by—said his mom had booked up a few years back. I envied DB's freedom but felt bad for him not having a mom around.

One night he and I made a date to pick up a couple girls. They were staying together all night and were going to sneak out after everyone was in bed. It was sometime after midnight when we picked them up. We rode around for a while, then went to the barn. We hung out, listened to some tunes, and put away a few beers. The girls were antsy about being gone too long and getting caught out. So, for some dumb reason, we decided we would walk them home. Hell, it must have been five miles all the way through town, across the river, and out in the country.

Less than a mile into our walk in an alley behind Library Park, a police car pulled up beside us. The window rolled down and a large policeman eyed us suspiciously. "Kinda late for a walk, isn't it?" None of us spoke.

"How old are you kids?" The policeman asked as he got out of his car and stretched to his full height.

"I'm sixteen," I said.

"You?"

"Me too," DB answered.

The big policeman looked at Sandy.

"I'm seventeen."

"And how old might you be, young lady?" he asked Marsha.

"Ah..."

"Truth, now. I am going to check," he said.

"Fifteen," Marsha said meekly.

"Hey, you're Sargent Meyers, aren't you?" I asked.

"That's right."

"Are you Wayne's dad? I heard his dad was a cop."

"You know Wayne?"

"Yeah. What a great guy! We're all friends with Wayne."

Everyone nodded.

"That so? Okay, well, I want to make sure all Wayne's friends are safe out here, and at three in the morning, it's not safe. Get in the car; we're going down to the station."

We pleaded with him all the way to the station to let us go. He took us into the police station and called our parents. It was bad news. Those girls were grounded for life. Mom yelled at me. DB's dad didn't say much. He and I were back out on the streets the next night.

Hanging out in the barn gave us all a sense of freedom. We could do whatever we wanted in there—smoke pot, drink beer, play loud music, have girls over, have parties—as long as we could keep most of what was going on hidden from Mom. In the barn, I was free.

One morning, DB and I slept in late in the barn. Mitch came over around midday and thought it was time for us to get up. He turned on the stereo system, and it came on at full volume—as loud as it had been playing the night before.

I thought a train was coming through the barn, it was so loud and frightening. I jumped up and opened the door to the loft, jumped out, and took about three steps before I realized that I was standing in the yard wearing nothing but my underwear shorts. Mitch was standing in the doorway to the loft, laughing his head off. I was so pissed, I cussed him out a good one... and then I started to laugh my head off too. DB didn't even wake up.

The only teacher that had any positive impact on me was Mr. McIntyre. I had him for psychology. Thinking about it now, I'm surprised they had a high school class in psychology in 1969. I liked the class because we studied human behavior. Why did people do the things they did? Why did people act so differently from one another when faced with the same situation?

There was also no math in his class, so that was nice, and what Mr. McIntyre said rang true to me. It gave me a better understanding of who I was and a glimpse of who I might be. Mr. McIntyre was nice and encouraging. He respected me and I him. Without saying it directly to me, I understood that I could do something, I could be good at something. I could be successful.

He was dealing with a rowdy bunch. I don't remember who else was in the class, but DB and I would have been more than most teachers could have handled.

One day in his class, DB asked Mr. McIntyre if he could go to the restroom.

"David, this class is not that long; you can wait." A few minutes later, DB interrupted the class a second time and asked again to go to the bathroom.

"DB, I'm not sure I can trust you to go to the bathroom."

"Yes, you can. I will be right back; it won't take me long. I just have to, you know."

Mr. Macintyre gave in. "I'm timing you, and you got three minutes."

DB hustled out the door. One minute, two minutes, three minutes went by. Once five minutes had passed, a door banged, somebody cussed, then a scuffling sounded in the hall. Mr. McIntyre ran out the door. Some of us followed. DB was in a fight with some kid, both of them rolling on the floor, gouging and pulling at each other. Mr. McIntyre was a big man. He grabbed both by the collar, pulled them to their feet, and hauled them off to the principal's office. Mr. McIntyre arrived shortly back at our room. "Yeah, I'll trust him again," he said sarcastically.

In high school, I spent my fair share of time in the principal's office too. Sometimes it was for talking and being disruptive in class. Most of the time, however, it was trying to explain to our truant officer Mr. Robinson, a tall man with a grey mustache and salt-and-pepper hair, why I was not attending class.

One day, DB and I were riding around in my new car—a lime green Plymouth Barracuda. Of course, we should have been in school. We were coming down Fifth Street right in front of Red Dog's house and turned left into the alley by Library Park.

"Oh, shit! That's Schmidt!" I yelled. He was the Miamisburg cop who was assigned to the high school to help out with kids like us.

"And there's Robinson standing by his car," DB added.

I threw the car into reverse, turned, and took off back down the street. Schmidt spun his cruiser around and was coming after us. I checked the rearview mirror; his lights were not on, and I heard no siren.

I stopped quickly at Linden Avenue as I didn't want to add to my lawlessness by running a stop sign. I made a quick turn up Jefferson Street, then cut through an alley back and out onto Linden.

"You lost him," DB said.

I pulled the car to a stop on Linden just two blocks from school. We jumped out of the car and began to run back to school. I glanced over my shoulder once to see that my car was about three feet from the curb.

"Should I go back and move it closer? I don't want to get a parking ticket!" I yelled at DB.

"Fuck! You just outran a cop, and you're worried about a parking ticket?" DB laughed.

I found a note on my car later that day. It was from Officer Schmidt. "Nice park job, fast foot. Don't ever run from me again." I didn't; I knew he gave me a break that day, and I respected him for that.

The first real party I remember going to was at Paul Bedford's house. At that time, I really didn't know him very well, and I'm not sure why he invited me or even how he knew me.

Paul's parents were gone for a few days. He was seventeen, so they figured he was old enough to manage on his own for a couple days. He invited about ten guys over to his house. It was to be an all-night deal, so I told Mom I was staying at Tony Warrick's house.

When you came in the door, you paid five dollars and had a choice of three beers or a bottle of Wild Irish Rose. I made the mistake of choosing the Wild Irish Rose, which was some kind of cheap wine.

Most of the action took place down in his basement, a dark room lit mostly by a strobe light. We had a good time laughing, smoking, and drinking until the basement started to spin. After that came throwing up, then dry heaves, swearing at the wine, and vowing never to drink again before finally, mercifully, falling asleep. I should have learned about temperance that night, but I didn't.

We seemed to always be doing something wild in cars, and in one case, on top of one. It all started on a Saturday night, arguing about my car.

"That station wagon you got is a real dog," DB said.

"Yeah, it's faster than what you think," I replied.

DB came back at me with, "Hell, I bet your mom had a governor put on it. You'd have a hard time passing me on my bike."

Mitch came to my station wagon's defense. "Okay, let's take it out and see what it'll do."

"That's lame. What fun is that? Let's kick it up a notch and do something wild," Mitch challenged.

I had an idea. "I'll tell you what—DB, you drive, Larry, you come with us and ride shotgun, and Mitch and I will sit on top of the of car and hang onto the luggage carrier, and you open it up."

"Big deal," DB said.

"In our underwear!" Mitch added.

"Now you're talkin'! Let's go," DB said.

Larry spoke up. "I don't know, man, somebody could get really hurt here."

Mitch laughed. "Bullshit! Let's do it!"

We put our feet up against the front cross bar and held onto the side bar with one hand. We locked arms and held onto each other with the other hand. It was a warm night, but the air blowing against our bare skin was cool, and the excitement we had was intense. The country road was dark, lit only by our headlights. Trees were rushing by faster and faster as we kept gaining speed; thank God we had the road to ourselves.

"How fast?" I yelled at DB.

"Fifty!" he yelled back.

"Push her all the way."

"That's sixty."

I looked over at Mitch, his hair blown straight back and his face wrinkled from the wind.

"WOW!" he yelled

I thought, just for a second, *What if I lost my grip? What if the car top carrier broke lose?* Then suddenly the car slowed and DB pulled it over to the side of the road. I was surprised our wild ride was over but I'd had enough.

"How fast did we get?" I asked.

"We got to sixty," Jim said.

"Oh, come on, we had to get to at least eighty," Mitch pleaded.

"Let's go with seventy," I said. "Right, DB?"

"Okay, shit, it was seventy. You can tell everybody it was eighty if you want."

Like most of our weekend exploits, by school on Monday morning they got stretched and embellished considerably. Sometime much later, we realized how stupid we had been and how lucky we were.

The school day was filled with planning and anticipating our exploits after school. I saw school as an impediment to doing what I wanted, when I wanted. It was the discipline and regiment that school required. You had to be there at a certain time, had to do what teachers said, and you could not leave until a certain time. I wanted to be free from all that structure and do whatever seemed fun at the time. I didn't realize then, but for me, school was closed. I didn't use the opportunities that school presented to help me reach my goals until many years later.

I wish I would have been aware of and taken to heart so many more things that school had to offer. As time went on, my love/hate relationship with school became mostly hate. At times, I wasn't sure what I was looking for, and if I would recognize it if suddenly I found it. I was impatient and wanted it now. I developed a passion to push things to the edge and look for meaning in places outside of the confines of school.

Oprah Winfrey once said many years later, "Education is the key to unlocking the world and a passport to freedom." But Oprah was only ten years old herself when I needed her words of wisdom.

JUST ME

"Faster than a speeding bullet! More powerful than a locomotive! Able to leap tall buildings at a single bound!" *Superman* was one of my favorite TV shows. I would tie a towel around my neck and run around and pretend I was flying. In scary dreams, if I was falling out of control from a high place, I would tell myself, "Hey, I'm Superman and I can fly and nothing can hurt me." I had the freedom to go anywhere; nothing could stop me. Nobody could tell me what to do. My fear would go away, and I would swoop down and land safely on the ground.

I also learned to love some of Grandma's favorite western shows: *Gunsmoke, Wagon Train, Bonanza, Rifleman, Maverick,* and *Have Gun – Will Travel.* Mom and Dad's favorite show was *Peyton Place,* a soap opera, and *Ben Casey,* a show about a brain surgeon. Ben Casey always started with an old doctor Zorba, writing on a blackboard very slowly and methodically the symbols for man, woman, birth, death, and infinity. Dr. Ben Casey was a neurosurgeon who always had difficult cases he was working on. He was very serious and very smart, so he had everyone's respect. I wondered if I could be like him.

I was so excited when I got the invisible man model for Christmas. It was a large model skeleton that had all the body parts to put together. I spent hours working on it. After watching a *Ben Casey* episode, I couldn't wait to work on my model. If you wanted to be important, you had to be smart. Where was I going to get smart? Were you just born smart? Or did you get smart from going to school?

Ben Casey came on at ten p.m., my bedtime. Mom and Dad would always be watching the show so intently they didn't notice me edging down the top of the stairs on my belly just far enough to see the TV. Every once in a while, I would make a sound, and Dad or Mom would suspect I was there and call my name. I would never answer as to not give away my presence, only move up so they couldn't see me.

From time to time, the TV would go on the fritz and wouldn't work. Dad would unscrew the back of it.

"I hope it's not the picture tube," Dad said as he peered into the jungle of tubes and wires in the back of the TV. "If it is, she's shot." He pulled a couple tubes that looked burnt out.

"Betty, take these and get them tested."

Mom would take them out to Revco drug store where they had a tube tester. Dad was the tube puller, and Mom was the tube tester. Teamwork, I guess. If that didn't work, they called the TV repairman, who sometimes came that very day, but never in time for us to see our favorite show. The repairman brought a huge tool box that carried lots of tubes and began pulling and replacing and adjusting until the TV finally came to life, and *The Ed Sullivan Show* or another favorite show appeared.

"It's a good thing it weren't your picture tube, or she'd be shot then," he'd say just like Dad. Not sure why the TV was always referred to as a "she."

Our family was not much different than the average family. It didn't seem like that though. Most of my friends had a brother or sister, and most had several siblings. There was nothing more fun for me than to be around other kids, but that wasn't always possible, so Mom was my best friend. She was the one I went to if I was hurt or wanted something. Often I complained to Mom that I wanted a brother. She smiled and said, "Well, I don't know."

"I don't have anybody to play with, Mom."

"Well, play with Chubby," she replied.

Chubby was the first dog I remember. He was a big dog—part Alaskan Husky and part mutt. He could pull me in my wagon or in the winter on my sleigh. He was fun to play with, but he was a dog.

Later, another dog appeared named Boots. She was a cross between a Beagle and Springer Spaniel. She was a sweet little dog and I loved her, but there was always something on the other side of the road that grabbed her interest. And one day she met a car crossing that road. She lived but then always walked with a limp and smelled like pee. Mom said she had lost her control.

One day, I saw her in distress out under the apple tree where we tied her by her doghouse. She was pawing at her mouth and gagging. I ran out there. She had gotten a stick from the yard wedged crossways in her mouth. I couldn't get it out since she wouldn't hold still, so I ran and got a pair of long nose pliers and pulled it out. She squealed a little but was glad to be rid of that stick. I felt like Ben Casey.

Mom and Dad loved going out for dinner, and I grew to look forward to it as well. Mom would put on a nice dress, and Dad always wore a coat and tie.

"We're looking spiffy tonight," Dad would say, beaming at Mom and me. I too felt special with my white shirt and clip-on tie. One of our favorite places was way out on North Main Street in Dayton. It was a Polynesian restaurant called The Tropics. We only went there on special occasions as it was quite expensive.

The first time we went there was on my birthday. Mom said we had to get dressed up real special, that "We're going to The Tropics." I first thought she meant in Florida someplace. The restaurant was decorated with grass huts and palm trees, and the waiters were dressed in flowered shirts and hula skirts. I was handed a large menu with lots of stuff on it I'd never heard of.

"Now, Timmy, you can order anything you want," Mom said.

I looked at Dad and he nodded. Dad always ordered a shrimp cocktail for an appetizer. So I followed, and it started a lifelong love for boiled shrimp and tangy cocktail sauce made with a serious amount of horseradish. I knew going out to dinner must have cost more than eating at home. It was nice though seeing Mom being waited on instead of always being the one who did the serving and the cooking. I enjoyed it too, choosing new foods, seeing all the different looking people. I hoped I could always come to nice restaurants and be waited on.

We all had steaks, and they were delicious. At the end of dinner, they brought me a small birthday cake with ten little candles on it. As we were leaving, I noticed a big bowl of matches at the check-out. Each matchstick was a cute little hula girl in a grass skirt made of wood. They were free, so I grabbed a handful, catching the eye of a questioning waiter as we left the restaurant. His face said, "What are you doing? Those aren't for you. You're a little young to be smoking." As if matches were only used to light cigarettes.

It seemed like Dad spent lots of time going to doctors and was in the hospital numerous times. Dad had diabetes, which Mom and he referred to as having "sugar." Diabetes didn't mix well with Dad's penchant for drinking and smoking. His circulation was bad, and cuts or injuries always took a long time to heal.

At a gas station where he was working, a heavy-duty truck jack fell on his foot, and it took forever to heal. He would soak his feet in Epsom salts at night. Eventually, he had to have a couple toes removed, and he began to have trouble bending down and using his right arm. I often tied his shoes for him. He had had lots of health issues before, but this was different. The doctors said his arteries in his neck were clogged and that he needed an operation to clean them out. Kettering Hospital was new, and his doctor told us it was serious, but the surgery should go well.

I overheard Dad telling Mom, "Maybe I can play some ball with Tim if I can get this fixed." I was at his bedside the night before his operation.

He took my hand and said, "Tim, be a good boy and study hard." It was almost as though he knew he wasn't going to see me for a while.

Aunt Katie came to my school the next morning and asked the principal for my immediate release. Something didn't go well during Dad's operation, and she drove me straight to the hospital. When I entered the room, it was cold and had an antiseptic smell. Dad was lying in bed with a tube in his throat that was moving in an out, making a sucking, pumping sound. I walked over to him. His eyes were open but he didn't see me, just stared at the ceiling.

"What's wrong with him, Mom?"

"He's in a coma; he had a stroke during the operation."

I looked at Dad and expected him to see me and say something but he didn't move. We spent the next couple days in the hospital, taking turns sleeping on the couches in the waiting area near the elevators. The pumping and sucking noise continued. I didn't like to see Dad not moving, just lying there still.

It was seven days before Christmas. I was standing near the large picture window looking out into a cold, snowy night. A big, lighted Christmas tree stood below. Singing rang out in the distance as carolers strolled through the hospital. My mind took me to family times at Christmas. Dad so loved wrapping those packages. I wondered if I would be getting anymore baseballs for Christmas. Why did it have to be like this? I felt so alone. Why couldn't we all just go home? I squeezed back tears. Virgil touched my arm.

"You better come on. Your dad is going."

My life changed abruptly and forever on December 18, 1968. Dad had been my biggest impediment to doing the things I wanted to do. The sometimes harsh discipline he imposed kept me in line. I only remember shedding a couple tears at the time of his death, no details of his funeral. I had just turned fifteen years old, which seems old enough to remember something as important as that, but I don't. I do remember Aunt Katie and Lisa kneeling at Dad's casket, holding some beads and reciting a long prayer. I wasn't sure what they were doing, but it seemed important and I felt good that they were doing it, that maybe somehow it would help Dad.

A mass was said at St. Mary's Catholic Church in Franklin where dad had been an altar boy. I checked the sports page the next day. The Flyers beat Providence ninety to sixty-three.

George Janky had twenty-seven points, Dan Sadlier had a monster game with twenty points and eighteen rebounds, and Don Mays' little brother Ken May chipped in with eight points and eight rebounds. Dad would have been pleased.

Sometime, soon after Dad's funeral, we were riding in Dad's Lincoln. It was raining, and I was in the back seat, staring out the window, my mind adrift with wandering thoughts; I would never have to hoe onions again or study algebra. I could now do what I wanted pretty much. I felt free but alone. I thought of the Kennedys; I knew now what it was like to lose your dad. I would never have a dad again. I cried a little.

A week or so after Dad's funeral, Mom and I went to the backyard where we had built the golf green. We dug out a piece of sod about four feet by eight feet. We took it out to Springboro Cemetery and laid it out on Dad's grave. We carried water from the well pump and gave it a good soaking.

Mom said, "Your dad would have wanted to lay under this familiar ground, that he so loved."

I wish I would have had Dad longer than I did. I wonder if I would have turned out much differently. It just didn't seem that I had enough time with him to learn from him, other than "be good" and "study hard." It would have been helpful to have a model as I grew up. I had uncles and aunts and Virgil, but I don't think it was like having a dad.

Virgil, the quiet fisherman, offered these words to me: "Timmy, your mom is going to miss your dad a lot. Now you're going to have to step up and be the man of the house." I wasn't sure what that meant exactly except that now I was considered a man.

Whatever I learned from Dad about being a man or how to be a father must have come about innately. I don't recall my father telling me, "Well,

Tim, when this happens, you do this" or "this is how to handle that." If I
learned anything from my dad about being a father, it was to be there.

WORK

My first job (aside from passing papers) was after my dad died. I got a job mopping floors at a small men's store in the Plaza Shopping Center Paul Harris. A sharp looking girl with bangs almost to her eyes, always wearing a mini dress, worked there, and they played good music. That was enough to hold my interest for a couple of months over the summer.

I had a distant cousin Butch Willow, who had a good job at Woody's All-Night Market in West Carrollton, a small town just north of Miamisburg along the Miami River. Grandma Susie asked Butch if he could get me a job there.

Butch was the Dairy Manger and in charge of all the milk, cottage cheese, cold juices, and cheeses. I was hired to be his overnight stock boy. The back of the cold case opened up to a big walk-in cooler. Everything was stocked from the back so that the older products moved to the front. To this day when buying milk, I reach and get the container closest to the back.

I was allowed to have all the milk and cheese I could eat as long as I marked it down on a little clipboard. I tried all different kinds of cheese including some stuff that had a thoroughly rotten smell. I developed a real love for sharp, cheddar, and Swiss cheeses.

I made the minimum wage, a dollar sixty an hour. I liked having the money to do as I pleased and bought cigarettes, rock albums, and beer. It

216

didn't take long for me to tire of working the eleven p.m. to six a.m. shift and the obligation of having to go in.

After working there a couple months, I called Mr. Willow about two hours before my scheduled shift, stammered around, and told him I quit and that I would not be coming in that night. I was embarrassed when I was talking with him. I knew I should have given him more notice. After all, he had done Grandma a favor by giving me the job. I felt relieved though after I hung up. I felt free.

That feeling didn't last long, and a feeling of disgust and disappointment in myself set in.

I learned two things from working at Woody's. At home, we had one kind of cheese: American. Working in the dairy, I gained an appreciation for many different types of cheeses. Swiss cheese, blue cheese, mozzarella, feta, cheddar, and brie. I also learned if you want to quit a job, do it in a proper way. Give them plenty of notice, and do it in person so you won't feel like an ass about it.

Dad had always been the brains of the outfit, the big picture guy, but Mom was the income producer and money manager. She was hardworking and always had a job that provided a steady income for our family. Dad was never able to work a full-time job for any length of time because of his health. But he was successful in making a little money here and there, doing the books for a small business. He even had a lawn mower repair shop for a while. We relied on his disability pension from the Navy. Somehow, Dad managed to buy a Lincoln Continental. It was used, but that was still considered a big deal. Mom always said Dad had a "champagne appetite on a beer pocketbook."

Maybe it was because WWII had only ended about twenty years ago. Or maybe I just had an interest in armies and fighting, but I was always asking questions about the war. One day, I was sitting on our bench in the kitchen, watching Mom prepare dinner and leafing through one of my large big picture books of WW ll.

"I know what Dad did during the war, but what did you do, Mom?"

"I was working, like most people," she told me. "I had a job at NCR."

"So, what was that?" I asked.

"Well since you're interested, NCR is a large company in Dayton where they made cash registers. But during the war, they started making war material. We were building carburetors for Liberator planes and bomb sites for B-29 bombers."

"Wow, you worked on bombers?"

"Sure did; I worked a twelve-hour shift. I ran a drill press and would come home covered in grease and oil. It was a tough job—really a man's job—but most of them were off fighting."

"So, where you work now? Is it in case we go to war again?"

"That's a good question."

Mom worked at Mound Laboratories. The Mound, as it was referred to, was located on a big hill on the south end of Miamisburg. It was operated by the United States Atomic Energy Commission. The Mound included many buildings and a couple big smokestacks, but most of the plant was below ground to keep it from being seen and to protect it from an attack.

"You know, it was about six months after I applied to work there," Mom went on. "I had given up hope of getting on when I got a call from the FBI. They told me that they would be doing a background check on me for possible employment at Mound Laboratories. I was so excited; I knew it would be a great job. They went to family members and neighbors in Franklin where I grew up and asked them all kinds of questions about me. They even went to my high school and talked to my teachers. I guess they wanted to be sure I wasn't a communist. It was all very secret, and once I was hired, I could never tell anyone what I did. They told us to tell people we made windshield wipers for submarines. Uncle Goeble began calling me the Atomic Lady."

UNCLE BILLY

Chuck Miller was a Vietnam vet who had moved in with his grandma just a few doors from me, just past the Zimmerman's. He was a wild sort with long red hair flowing down to his shoulders and a thick, bushy—but well-trimmed—mustache. He always wore a muscle man t-shirt highlighting his muscular build.

One day, Chuck and I were standing in our drive when Uncle Billy pulled in. "Hey, son, how you been?" He reached out to me as he nodded at Bud and gave him a long look. It had been a while since I'd seen Uncle Billy. He looked thin and weak and unsure of himself. He had filled his life with "hard living," as Mom would say– too many cigars and too many long nights with Jim Beam.

"I'm fine. Still have that little Beatle, huh?" I asked.

"Oh, yeah, she gets thirty miles to the gallon and starts every day; can't ask for anything more." There was silence, Chuck slouching up against the Beatle, me feeling really uncomfortable, and Uncle Billy sizing up Chuck. No one seem to know what to say.

Chuck broke the silence, pulled out a joint, and lit it up. "Wanna toke old man?" Uncle Billy waved him off. Then Chuck offered it to me, and I just gave him a frown and shook my head.

219

I could tell Uncle Billy didn't think much of Chuck and my associating with the likes of this guy. I was embarrassed for him to see me with Chuck. It wasn't that Chuck was such a bad guy, but he sure looked it. Uncle Billy's eyes sent a message: "Is this what you're becoming? It's not good. You're headed down the wrong path, and your dad would not have allowed this."

When I looked at Uncle Billy, I was reminded of Dad, but I didn't fear him, and I knew he had no power over me. Dad was gone now. I paid scant attention to Mom's wishes, and Uncle Billy did not have the strength to demand my attention or influence me.

"Hey, I'll leave you two; you look like you need to talk," Chuck said as he smiled, flashed the peace sign, turned, and booked up.

There wasn't much for us to say. Uncle Billy didn't stay long. I never saw him again.

OUT ON THE TOWN

It was a humid summer night. Larry had the top down on his convertible. He and Mitch and I were tooling around town looking for some action.

"Let's check out the west side," Mitch suggested.

"We're going to go way up there? That's crazy; for what?" I asked.

"For kicks man; what else?" Larry chimed in.

Was surprised Larry was up for something this wild.

So off we went to the west side of Dayton, about a twelve-mile trip up Route 4. The west side was a notoriously rough side of town; that's where all the riots had been. It was dark since the street lights had long ago been shot out. There were people yelling at each other from porches and sirens in distance. It was a foreboding neighborhood; we all felt uneasy. The top was down, but we still locked the doors.

"There—turn onto Home Avenue and slow down," I told Larry. "I heard this is where they're at."

We hadn't gone two blocks.

"Hey, baby you want to party?" A black girl in short pants said as she came up to our stopped car.

Two other girls with beers in their hands, smiling, waving their arms, came over to the other side of the car.

"Hey, boys, whatcha all doin' over here? You wanna have a good time?"

None of us said a word. Things were moving too fast, and we weren't sure what was happening.

Just as the first girl reached to put her hand on the car door, Larry hit the gas and we spun out laughing, hooting, and hollering. The thrill of that little tease was enough for us. We headed back to the Burg. That was about as close as I ever came to a black person.

Back in Miamisburg, nothing was happening at the bowling alley as we didn't recognize any cars in the parking lot. We drove around the Pizza King; it was dead.

"Hey, let's get some beer and go out to the cabin; maybe there's a party going on," Larry suggested.

"Larry, you got your brother's ID?" I asked.

"Oh yeah always."

Larry's brother was twenty-three and Larry looked just like him, so we could get six percent beer not that weak three-point-two percent shit.

"Yeah, let's go down to the Point Carry Out. That old guy in there don't look at IDs too close," Larry said. The cabin was actually an old barn that stood at the back of our friend Tony Warrick's place. It had a separate entrance off a side road, so you didn't have to go by their house and alert his parents. Tony's older brother and his friends were always out there drinking and partying.

We were all set; we had our night planned. Everything went smoothly at the Point and Larry carried out two eight packs of six percent Stroh's and a bottle of Ripple. There were only a couple cars parked at the cabin, but we were excited. There was a real blaze going in the fire pit. JD Booker was there and some other guys I didn't recognize and a couple of chicks I didn't know. JD was much older than us and was known as a real hell raiser and tough guy.

They were smoking weed and passing around a bottle of whiskey. One of their cars had all the doors open and Iron Butterfly pounding out In-A-Gadda-Da-Vida from their eight-track. We hung out there for a while but we could tell JD didn't much care for us being there. We didn't want to cross him, as he was nobody to fool with.

Mitch suggested we hit the Riviera, a small bar on the edge of town. The Riviera Lounge was known for free peanuts and liberal, or no, ID checks. A long bar stretched the length of the narrow place with little room between the barstools and the side wall. At one end, there was a small space just large enough for a bumper pool table. The bathrooms and a back entrance were at the other end. The front and back door were always propped open on hot nights like this.

Tonight, there were only a few customers, so my two friends and I had plenty of room to belly up to the bar. It was cool hanging out in a bar. We felt like we were big stuff, and they served free peanuts in a shell. You could just crack 'em and throw the shells on the floor.

George, the owner, gave us all a stern look. He was a large man with big features and always looked like he was mad about something, always wearing a plain white t shirt. He was older now, but you could tell in his younger days he was a stud of man. He had a thick neck and broad shoulders connected to what had been muscular arms. He still looked intimidating standing behind the bar as gatekeeper of the spirits that lay behind him. But when he got to know you and flashed his big smile, his gentle ways broke through that rough facade. He had opened the bar last winter and seemed to be struggling for customers.

"Need to see some IDs, boys," George demanded. That surprised us. Mitch and I had been there many times before, but it was Larry's first time.

We dug out our billfolds and flashed George our driver's licenses. He barely glanced at them, but looked closely at Larry's, then looked at him hard, and glanced at all of us, not saying a word. Larry did look like his brother, but there was a four-year age difference. We were in Larry's car, so if he didn't get served, we had to leave.

A big smile finally came over George's face. "Got Falstaff on draft—or you all want bottles of Stroh's?"

"We'll split a couple of pitchers, George; where's those peanuts?"

I don't know if George really thought we were all of age, if he couldn't add too well, or if he just needed the business.

There wasn't any more action in the Riviera than there was at the Cabin. Then suddenly two hot looking girls walked in and sat at a table next to the bar.

"Check those chicks out," Mitch said.

"I think I will do just that," I said.

Both were knock outs; one was taller with dark hair, maybe a little older. The other a brunette with a sweet smile.

"Hey, anybody sitting here?" That was the best line I had.

"I guess there is now," the dark haired one said.

"I'm Tim and you are?"

"Jane."

I turned to the other girl. "And you are?"

"Ann."

It wasn't long before Larry and Mitch had joined us, and surprisingly, we all seemed to hit it off. Ann and I seemed to really click. She was a little older than me and was on break from college.

"So, Ann, what are you studying at UD?"

"Oh, I don't go to UD; I go to a little college in Indiana."

"Really? What are you doing here?"

"I'm just visiting my sister for a couple days." She pointed to Jane.

"Oh, cool, you two are sisters?"

"Yeah, she's my big sis. I'm going to be a teacher," Ann said.

Wow, a teacher, I thought. Not my favorite thing, but wished I had a teacher this good looking.

A couple of really young chicks in short-shorts came in and went straight to the bumper table. George winked at us as he brought them a pitcher. No ID check for them.

George grinned at us and said, "They're good for business."

It was uncomfortably hot, and the small fan that hung over the bar did little to cool us. The cold beer felt refreshing; it went down easy, and we quickly put away two pitchers when, to our surprise, JD Booker stumbled in with a couple of friends—and just when things seemed to be moving along with Ann and Jane.

He came straight to the bar and ordered a pitcher and three shots of Old Grand Dad. George looked at the three roughnecks with a little snarl on his face. "I oughtn't serve you, JD."

"What? How come, George?"

"I know what you did the other night."

"I didn't do shit, man. Just pour us the drinks and get some peanuts over here." JD gave us a glance that said "mind your own business, punks; you shouldn't even be in here." He and his friends wandered over to check out the chicks at the bumper table.

"Hey, George, what's up with you and JD?" I quietly asked.

"Some bitch dropped acid on me the other night. I was so messed up I had to close and couldn't open the next day. It was some bad shit."

"Wow, that's crazy, George. Did you call the police?"

"Nah, what they gonna do? No way to prove anything."

"Hey, George! Set us up with five shots down here," JD yelled.

George just winced and paid no attention to him. "I'll get the motherfucker back; you can bet on that."

JD yelled again, then came around to where George and I were. "Your ears plugged up, old man?" JD confronted George. "You heard me. I said set us up five shots—or are you still buzzing from the other night?"

George was sweating. He'd had enough." Okay, you're done in here, JD. Get the hell out and take your friends with you."

"I said, set me up. Old Grand Dad, right here!"

"Get out of here, you piece of shit."

JD grabbed a big glass ash tray and shook it at George. "I'll kill you, old man right now!"

George turned away toward the cash register, then whipped around quickly. "You will, will you? Well take that, you son of a bitch!"

Crack. George fired a quick shot into JD's stomach. *Crack* then another.

We all jumped up from our seats. The girls at the bumper table screamed. JD clutched his stomach, blood oozing out over his hands. He staggered out the front door.

"You guys all clear out; we're closing." George turned to the cash register and returned his little friend to its hiding place.

JD's friends rushed him to the hospital—it was too late.

"We need to split before the cops get here, and we get caught drinking," Larry said.

"Yeah and I've got a bag of weed in the car; let's move it," Mitch added.

All of us moved quickly out to the parking lot. I looked at Ann.

"Let's go, Tim," Larry yelled. He and Mitch were already in the car.

I wanted more from Ann. This was ending too soon. I didn't want to turn her off. I hesitated. I reached for her gently and gave her a kiss. She was so warm and smelled so good. She hadn't resisted, so I added another quick one.

Still holding her, I said, "I hope I can see you again." I didn't want to let her go. She smiled, turned, and walked away.

In the rush, I didn't get her phone number, but there was something about this moment and this girl—a feeling that someday we would meet again. But it wouldn't be at the Riviera; it never opened again. It was time to move on. We had run out of wild things to do; this town had gotten too small. There were lots of witnesses who saw JD threaten Charlie, so he was never charged.

HELTER SKELTER

It was less than a year after my dad passed when I ran away to California with Larry and Mitch. We didn't need much of a reason. Larry had just gotten a speeding ticket and was going to have to go to court. Mitch had gotten into trouble with his parents when he got caught (again) smoking his mom's Old Golds. And me? Even though I had mixed feelings about my dad, I could acknowledge I was still reeling from his death. Who imagines their parents dying? So, I was up for an adventure, ready for anything that would allow me to do what I wanted, with whom I wanted, and when I wanted to do it. California said all that to me and would allow me not to think of Dad, so I was in.

After a summer of baseball and hanging out at the swimming pool, we snuck away early one morning in late September, got on I-70, and headed west. We only packed a few things. I brought my swimming trunks, a couple of t-shirts, some Reece's Cups from the fridge, and Mom's Visa that I found in her purse. Larry brought his toolbox and drill set. Mitch contributed the most important thing to our escape: his dad's old red station wagon. It had no radio, lots of rust, and of course, no air conditioning, but all the windows rolled down, and it ran great.

We drove for hours, stopping only for gas and snacks that we purchased with Mom's Visa. We wanted to put as much distance between us and Miamisburg as quickly as we could.

I felt bad about using Mom's Visa as she would be in a panic about me being gone, and in all honesty, we were stealing from her. But we only had fifty dollars cash among us.

At a filling station near St. Louis, a hitchhiker with hair down to his shoulders and a thick mustache approached us. He was carrying a duffel bag and a guitar; he asked where we were going.

"California," Mitch answered.

"Me too. Think I could ride along with you guys?"

"Well..." Mitch raised his eyebrows, questioning me and Larry. I appreciated the sentiment, but it was his dad's car, so it was his call.

"Hey, I got a little weed, and I can chip in for some gas."

Mitch smiled. "Hop in."

The hitchhiker seemed like a good guy. He had a guitar; he wasn't a great player, but he kept us entertained. And true to his word, he chipped in for gas and food stuff along the way. During the day, we took our shirts off and rolled the windows down, baking in the car as it crossed through the deserts of New Mexico and Arizona.

One night, someplace in the desert, Mitch pulled over. He was tired and suggested that we all should get some sleep. The air was cool, and we all stretched out the best we could in the station wagon. But Mitch couldn't get comfortable. "Hell, I'm sleeping on the roof," he said.

About an hour later, Mitch climbed back in the car. "It's fucking raining; we're hitting the road. "Mitch jumped behind the wheel and we were off again. It took about forty hours to travel the 2,194 miles from Miamisburg, Ohio, to Los Angeles, California.

Soon after we crossed the California state line, a road sign announced the distance to Los Angeles: Two hundred miles. "Holy shit!" I said. "I thought we were almost there." Had I known how long the journey would take, I might have considered not going. But really, what was time? I had all the time in the world. And a few hours here or there didn't seem like that high a price to pay for freedom.

But soon, palm trees lined the roads and convertibles were everywhere.

Just as we came to an exit sign that read "Santa Monica Pier, three miles," the car started to shutter and groan. "Hell, I think this thing is out of gas," Larry said, as he frantically pumped the accelerator. Luckily, we were at the top of the ramp, so we all jumped out and pushed the car. With some momentum behind it, and Larry sitting halfway in the car, pushing with his left leg, we moved it down the ramp, around a corner, and onto a side street.

"Here, let me try it," Mitch said as he got behind the wheel.

After a few minutes of grinding, the battery finally went dead.

"Nope that's it; ain't gonna start." Mitch took a rope and fed it down the gas tank.

"Hell, it's still got gas," he said as he pulled out the wet end of the rope. "You can't trust that gas gage."

"Well, it won't start, so what should we do with it?" Larry said.

Mitch rubbed the back of his neck. "Dunno."

The hitchhiker guy spoke up. "You don't want the police to trace it back to you or your dad, right, Mitch? They'll know where you are."

We stripped the car of both the license plates and registration plate on the door and dropped them down the sewer drain. Was that our freedom swirling down the drain too? Were we being stupid for not trying to get some gas? That remained to be seen. We were convinced that if we made it to the beach, everything would somehow work out. Now without a car, we had to hoof it or hitch a ride.

The hitchhiker looked at all of us; his main reason for being with us was gone. "No one is going to pick up four guys together. We might as well split up...maybe meet back up at the pier, on the beach?"

"Split up?" Larry asked.

"Yeah. I'll go first. You count slow to a hundred, Tim, and then you can follow. Then after Tim leaves, Larry, you count to two hundred and then start hitching. Mitch, after Larry leaves, you count to three hundred and then go. That should space us out enough."

"So, wait," Mitch said. "If I'm the last guy to go, then I'll be the last guy that's picked up. That's crap! What if I don't get picked up?"

The hitchhiker looked at Mitch. "You don't know, you might be the first guy picked up; besides, you look like you have some new tennis shoes there, and the sign says it's only three miles to the beach." He smiled at the rest of us. "Good luck, guys," he said, and with a wave, the hitchhiker took off. We never saw him again.

The three of us discussed the hitchhiker's plan. "What if we can't find each other down on the beach?" I asked.

"What if somebody picks me up and has a gun and robs me?" Mitch asked.

"How would they rob you? You don't have anything to rob," Larry said.

How exactly did we make it to the beach? I can't be sure. But when we did, we collapsed on the warm sand, lifted our faces to the sun, and drank in the freedom.

Eventually, Larry sat up. "We need money and some food."

"A place to sleep would also be good," I added.

Mitch, always the optimist, had a solution. "Hell, we can camp on the beach or a park somewhere and...yeah! Let's sell those tools."

Larry wasn't about to leave his tools, so we'd taken the toolbox and drill set from the car before we abandoned it. We agreed that Mitch and Larry would look for jobs and buy some food with the little money we had while I would try to sell the toolbox and drill set. *No problem*, I thought.

I had sold stuff before—flower and vegetable seeds from a catalogue, boxes of candies for Cub Scouts. These tools were pretty new, so it wouldn't take too long. And it sure beat trying to find a job.

I took off, a spring in my step and zero thoughts of Miamisburg in my head, stopping at filling stations and car repair places, peddling the tools. Or trying to anyway. One station attendant didn't say a word as I approached, just pointed me off the property.

After several hours of rejections and many strange looks, I was hungry and tired. With only a couple dollars in my pockets, I bought a pop and a bag of chips at a filling station and took a seat on a curb next to an air hose. As I sat crunching chips, an old yellow van pulled up, and a wild-eyed guy with a scruffy beard and long red hair yelled out his window, "Ay, do you mind getting your ass out of the way? I need some air."

I took a swig of my Mt. Dew and swallowed. "Air?"

"The air hose, man. Can ya fuckin' move?"

The guy had muscles, as showcased by a white sleeveless t-shirt that also covered a brace of some kind. He was using a cane and had trouble bending down, holding the air hose on the tire.

"Hey, you need some help there?" I asked.

"Sure, man, if you don't mind. Those back two are really low."

I put a little air in all four tires and hung the hose back on the rack. "Say, you don't have a smoke, do you?" I asked. Freedom meant a pop and chips for lunch and smokes whenever I wanted them. I just had to find them.

"Hell no, that shit's no good for you," he said.

I started to walk away.

"Hold on kid—Sandy, gimme a smoke for this kid." He reached into the van window and pulled out a Kool.

"What's your name, kid?"

I didn't answer. I might have helped him with his tires, but I wasn't sure what else, if anything, I wanted from him. And despite my best intentions, thoughts of Mom and Miamisburg crept into my head. What would Mom think about talking to a stranger who looked like that?

Okay, I'm Bud."

Stranger no more, I answered, "Tim."

"So, what's your story, Tim?"

That was a question I wasn't ready to answer. I really didn't know what my story was other than I was running away from home, looking for an adventure, to be free to do what I wanted. Life until then hadn't been bad, but I still sought something more. More connections, more happiness.

And of course, more freedom. I looked down at the ground then up at the sky, my gaze finally reaching Bud's face. But I didn't say anything.

"We're headed to the beach to catch some rays; you want to go?"

At least I'd have a ride back. "Sure. I just came from there, but..."

"What's up with those tools? You steal them?" Bud asked as he gestured to the van.

"No, they're my friend's. I was trying to sell them. He said it was okay."

"And where's your friend?"

"Down at the beach."

"My Gramps might buy them. Go with us to the beach and then we'll go back to the house and see if he wants them." With no other plans in place, I grabbed the toolbox, my little duffel bag and hopped into the van. I could almost feel my mother cringing two thousand miles away.

When I got in, the woman in the passenger seat introduced herself properly, "Hi, I'm Sandy, Bud's sister." She was skinny and had a pretty face, with fair skin, small red freckles, and long stringy, unkempt, red hair. It was easy to tell she was Bud's sister. "How old are you, sweetie?" she asked.

"Eighteen," I said.

Bud looked at Sandy with a grin and then to me. What were they thinking? I hoped they would let me go with them. "Well, you can hang out with us for a while, but don't do any stupid shit." I frowned a little at him; I knew how to be cool, and eventually, we made it to the beach.

We walked a hundred yards or so to reach the water. The sun was blazing and the sand almost too hot to walk on. I expected the ocean to be warm; it was cold. The surf was rough and wild looking. We walked along the beach for a while. I looked all over but saw no sign of Larry or Mitch. Bud lit up a joint and started smoking it right out on the beach. Heat flamed in my cheeks; behavior like that wouldn't happen in Ohio. He gave me a hit, and I choked while Sandy snickered.

I looked out over the beach, full of tanned, long-haired guys and sweet looking chicks, radios blasting, kids playing volleyball, frisbees flying. *So, this is California. I had made it here—now what?* I shook my head, trying to put away the negative thoughts, but still they came. *I've got nothing but a drill and a tool box. No food, no place to sleep, and I don't know where Larry and Mitch are.* But then, another thought took hold: *I don't wanna give up and go back to the same old shit back home.*

Maybe I would have to get a job. Maybe I could hang out with these people for a while. Maybe something good, not great, would turn up. Maybe I just need to bide my time.

We sat along the beach, allowing the water to tickle our feet. Nobody talked. We just chilled and looked out over the surf, taking in the salty, fishy smell of the sea, warmth of the sun, the laughter of folks having a good time. The pot was good, and in the moment, life was good.

We walked up to the pier, turned around, and started walking back, just checking everything out from a different point of view.

"I got the munchies," Bud said. "The house should be open by now. Let's go." He cocked his head in the direction away from the beach.

"So, where are we going?" I asked.

"Beverly Hills, sweetie," Sandy said.

"Beverly Hills?" When he'd said we'd go to the beach and then to find his grandpas, I assumed he meant on the beach. But Beverly Hills? "So do you think your grandpa will buy these tools?" I asked. I really hoped for a yes.

"Yeah, maybe we'll get there later. We got to go check on something first," he replied.

My spine tingled. I wasn't sure I should be going with these people. I had this uneasy feeling that Bud wasn't being completely straight with me. Even though they seemed cool, I'd just met them. These were Californians. Mom always said there were a lot of weird people in California. I shook my head as I got in the van, one word on my mind: freedom.

We drove up into the hills through some real swanky neighborhoods. From time to time, Bud slowed down by a big house and then sped off as if he didn't know where he was going. We finally turned onto Cielo Drive, pulled through some gates, and rolled up to a sprawling house on the side of a hill.

"Wow, man. This your grandpa's place?" I asked.

"No." Bud looked at me, straight-faced, and laughed. "I said we'll go there later. Relax, now. We got to make a stop first."

A stunning babe with bushy blond hair and big blue-green eyes greeted us at the door. This time, my spine tingled in a good way. *Who do you belong to?* That was soon answered when Bud swallowed her face as we entered the house. Bud finally came up for air. "This is Terry. She's my realtor."

I might have been from Ohio, but I wasn't that naïve. "Realtor my ass."

"What do you mean? Don't realtors find houses for people? Isn't that what you do for me?" he asked Terry.

"Well, most people are looking to *buy* the house, not shit in them and leave," she replied.

Bud waved her comment away. "Okay, enough. Let's check this place out!"

The place was huge, with a sprawling living room that led into a kitchen and glass doors that opened up to a large patio and pool. The whole place was white, from the carpet to the walls, couches, and chairs.

"Who are you, kid? And where are you from?" Terry asked me, tipping her chin in my direction.

"Ah, my name is Tim. Ohio."

"Wow, cool. Tim Ohio, what are you doing out here?"

That was a good question. What was I doing out here? As interesting as I found this place and Terry, I had a nice home and pretty much everything I wanted. A loving mom and grandma cared for me. Next to some, I had an enviable life. But loving easily morphed into smothering, and I didn't want to be told what to do. No one, not Mom or school or anyone else, needed to be the boss of me. I craved freedom, and I was pretty sure once I had it safely in my grasp, I'd be happy. That's not what I told Terry though. "I just needed a change. That's all."

"You have any money?" Terry asked.

"Well, not really, but I have a credit card." Terry laughed.

"Hell, ditch that, they can trace it," Bud said, then leaned over to me and sniffed. "Man, you need to get cleaned up. Check out one of those bathrooms upstairs and get some clean clothes on. We're going to party tonight."

"Clothes? Party? This is about all I have right now."

Bud motioned me toward the stairs. "Look in the closets upstairs; you can find something there."

The hot water warmed my body; getting the crud off felt good. I sat down in the large shower and washed the sand from between my toes. It was the first shower I had had since leaving home.

After toweling off, I put on my swimming trunks and a t-shirt, the only clothes I had brought in my duffel. Wearing somebody else's clothes didn't appeal to me. I found my way downstairs and followed the music out to the pool.

My foot tapped a steady beat as a crowd grew. People dressed a little different out here, bright flower covered shirts, patched blue jeans and sandals. They brought bottles of wine and cases of beer and walked right in like they owned the place and lingered everywhere. *Who were all these people and where were they coming from*? I wondered. Bud found some wood and built a fire on the cement right by the pool. I took a ringside seat and just soaked it all in. A couple of dudes were playing guitars, and another was pounding on some little drums.

A striking tall girl with long, dark hair suddenly appeared and began wailing on a harmonica. She wore a multicolored band across her forehead. Her eyes were dark, almost black, but I couldn't tell if it was her actual eye color or all the eye liner she wore. Her face was porcelain white, and she wore a long linen dress that was slit up the middle. She danced and spun around and made that harmonica sing. I couldn't keep my eyes off her: her face, her body, the way she moved. She was mesmerizing. I wanted to be close to her. And then I thought she looked right at me. I hoped she was flirting.

Everybody seemed a lot older than me; most had scruffy beards and long hair. Everyone gathered around the harmonica girl, some singing, some laughing and cutting up, and everyone drinking and smoking pot. I thought of Wayne Myers playing the harmonica back at our barn; these were his kind of people. They all treated me swell. I was having a great time. I fit in like I was meant to be here. Freedom and this. *This* is what I was looking for.

The girl finally gave the harmonica a rest, and to my shock, came over and sat next to me. "What's up, dude?" she said as she leaned over and planted a kiss on my cheek.

Oh, shit. "Ah, nothing—just enjoying all this. You know, you're great on the harmonica."

"Thanks. I can play really good, can't I?" she asked and then blew out a few notes.

"What's your name?" I asked.

"Pearly."

"That's kind of a strange name, ain't it?" She hummed a few bars. "What's yours, little boy?"

I straightened my back. "Tim," I said.

"Well, ain't that cute. I bet you go by Timmy, don't you?" She winked at me. "What are you drinking, Timmy?"

I didn't like people calling me Timmy, but she could call me anything. "Just beer." I showed her the can.

"Here, try some of this." She handed me her glass, which I took, then hesitated. "What's the matter, boy? Think I have cooties or something? Don't you trust me?"

My thoughts flashed back to everything my parents had taught me, everything teachers had drilled in my head. "Sure," I took a big swallow and choked.

"A little rye for Timmy boy."

After a few rounds of throat-clearing, whereby I tried my best not to cough, I managed to settle myself. "So how did you learn to play like that?"

"Oh, my dad used to play, and I messed around with it when I was a kid. I saw Canned Heat at a concert in Monterrey a couple of summers ago. We snuck behind the stage afterwards, and I got to meet the Blind Owl." She sighed and closed her eyes. "He was phenomenal, sort of inspired me to get serious about playing."

"Who's the Blind Owl?" I asked. We didn't have music like that back in Miamisburg.

"Come on, man. You never heard of the Blind Owl?" She took a long swig from her glass and handed it to me as she began softly singing. *I am going up the country, baby, don't you want to go, I am going up the country, don't you want to go,*

I am going up the country to a place I never been before, I am going where the water tastes like wine. We can jump in the water and stay drunk all the time."

Pearly stood up and swayed back and forth amid the smoke from the fire. Her long hair splashed across her face; she began to blow on the harmonica. The guitar guys joined in, and everybody formed a circle around Pearly, belting out the lyrics. Her voice was strong, clear, distinctive, and somehow familiar. The lyrics about leaving and freedom called to me in her voice.

"I am going to leave this city got to get away,

All this fusing and fighting you know I sure can't stay, so, baby, pack your trunk

We've got to leave today, just exactly where were going I cannot say, but we might be even leaving the USA.

It's a brand game that I want to play."

Bud came by and kicked my foot. "I think this song's for you. Having any fun, kid?" He had no idea; this was about as good as it got. Sitting by a pool, drinking a beer, a beautiful chick singing to me, the smell of smoke from the fire laced with burning weed... I was smack dab in the scene I was looking for.

"No, I'd rather be in Ohio!" I yelled back.

Pearly sat down and gave me a squeeze and another peck on the cheek. "You smell like campfire."

"So do you," I said, and we laughed and that was it. I grabbed her around the shoulder, pulled her close. Her warm lips tasted like raspberries, and now this close, the smell of smoke was replaced by the distinctive smell of hash. I squeezed her tight.

She pulled away. "Hold on, Timmy Boy. Don't rush it. Let's just enjoy the party." She stood and grabbed my hand. "Come on. Let's walk over here—and grab that bottle of wine, will you?"

We leaned up against a rock wall that bordered the pool area. She fired up a joint. "Come here and just breathe in." She put the lit end of the joint in her mouth, held my face close to her mouth, and blew a strong stream of smoke in my face as I breathed in. I took in as much as I could and then stumbled back and started coughing, my head spinning.

"Oh, what the fuck was that?"

"Ha! That's a shotgun, man. Now do me."

I would have rather just given her a long kiss, but this might be as close as I would get to that face again.

"You ever been out in the canyon before?" she asked.

"I thought we were in Beverly Hills?"

"Well, we are, sort of... just north." She looked up at the sky.

"No, this is the first time. I've really never been to this part of LA before."

"Oh, what part have you been to?"

"Mostly on the coast, southern California and Hollywood; that area." Based on her lack of response, she knew I was full of shit, and she knew I knew she knew.

She grinned and passed me the joint. "You see the house up there?"

I was staring at her and feeling a little high, so I missed what she was talking about.

She turned my head. "On the hill...up there—see through the trees?"

"I see. It looks nice, so"

"That's where Sharon Tate, you know...she was..." Pearly looked at me and raised her eyebrows. "You know, the movie star?"

"Oh, really? Maybe we should invite her over. Does she know we're having a party here?"

Pearly scowled at me, then grinned, and then burst out laughing. "Sure, good idea kid. Maybe she can bring Charlie with her!"

"Charlie?"

"You know who Charlie Manson is, don't ya? He's from Ohio, ya know."

"Sure...well, I've heard of him."

Pearly shook her head. "Stop lying. Just be honest and don't be a dumbass. It's okay to say you never heard of these people. But let me enlighten you, Timmy Boy. You wanna hear?"

I really couldn't have cared less who the hell Manson or Sharon Tate was, but I would listen to anything she had to say to stay in front of that beautiful face and those dark eyes.

"Okay, let's sit up here and poor me some of that wine." she said.

We crawled up on the stone wall around the patio, which gave us a good view of all the partying around the pool. And then she told me the story about Charlie and his girls.

"Come on, how do you know about all this shit?" I asked.

"She was there, Timmy Boy," Bud said over my shoulder. "She was one of Charlie's girls, until Charlie ran her off."

"That's not true." Pearly huffed. "This stuff has been all over the papers the last few days. Don't you read? They arrested some of the girls, and they already had Charlie. Anyway, let me finish."

Minutes before, I didn't care about this guy. Now, I still didn't care about anything but Pearly. She continued, "I had met Charlie at a party in Venice, and he told me that he and Dennis Wilson were buds."

I frowned, my brow wrinkling. *Dennis Wilson?*

"Dennis Wilson." Pearly looked at me. "Like the Beach Boys' Dennis Wilson? Come on, man. You live under a rock out there in Ohio?" Pearly looked straight at me with those eyes and said. "Are you for real?"

I nodded. "I know who he is. Go on."

And so, she did, but I could not keep from staring into her eyes, trying to conceal my desire for her body and make her believe I was interested in what she was telling me. The music was getting loud, so I leaned closer to her, pretending I couldn't hear her. My eyes closed, my cheek touched her nose, then I turned my face and began kissing her. She took my head in both her hands, and she was so warm and soft. I hugged her tight and started to slide my hand into the slit in her dress.

She jumped back. "Oh great! That's red wine, and this is new!" She pointed at the red spot I'd dripped onto her dress from my cup. "It won't come out! What the fuck are you thinking?"

"Oh shit, I'm sorry."

She stood up and wiped the wine off her dress. "Big stain. You're a goof, you know that?" Like any hot-blooded young man, my thoughts were still on her, not the stain, but I apologized again and grabbed her a towel.

"Now, where were we?" I whispered as I put my arm around her waist.

"Well, not there," she said, unwrapping my arm from her.

She went back to talking about this insane scene she'd just described. "So, as I was saying, it just got too weird, too intense. I knew there was some serious evil there, and it was too much for me."

Evil. My mind flashed back to Miamisburg and my family and friends. We did some bad things, and there were lots of fights, but we sure didn't encounter evil much there. Confusion, frustration? Yes. Evil? No. I thought of the Kennedys, Martin Luther King, Malcom X, all the killings—that was evil, pure and simple. Now I was out in the world with it.

She stopped talking. "Are you listening?" she asked.

I shook my head, focused on her beautiful face. "Sure, what happened then?"

"Well, some of them are in jail. You know that, right? Never mind, they all got arrested and one of the girls ratted them out. That's all been in the papers here."

"Wow what a bunch of crazy people." My response seemed so Ohio, so inadequate, but I didn't know what else to say. I switched gears. "So what do you do now?"

"I split, came into town, and got a waitressing job at a joint on the strip. The tips are great, and I'm sitting in with some club bands on the weekends. That's where I met Terry."

I thought of Mom—what would she think if she knew what I was doing right now and how close I was to where all that shit happened. A tiny bit of remorse climbed up my neck, but then Pearly grabbed my arm and asked me to dance. "Oh no, I don't dance. You go ahead." She smiled and drifted away. As she left, a tingling sensation began creeping over my body. I had only a couple of beers and a few joints of grass, but the music became garbled as Pearly danced with Bud and Terry. Were they dancing on top of the water right in the pool? They motioned for me to join them, so I got up, but I couldn't feel my legs moving or feet touching the ground as I moved over to them. Pearly had her hand out for me, smiling. My head spun; then wetness surrounded me. Strong arms wrapped around me, and my mind flashed to the lifeguard in my swimming lessons, lifting me up as I coughed and spit up water. Voices sounded around me.

"Is he okay?"

Then Bud's voice, "What'd you do, Pearly?"

"Nothing I didn't do for me," she said.

I recalled her saying. "Don't you trust me?" and felt like gagging.

The voices faded away. My stomach heaved, my mouth felt like a desert, and an awful pounding throbbed in my head.

I strained to open my eyes, realizing that the pounding wasn't just in my head. A big fat guy wielded a baseball bat, slamming it down on the bed right next to my head.

"Get out of my bed!" he screamed.

I jumped up and realized I was naked. "What the hell happened?" I said, scratching my head.

"You tell me, you little punk!"

I focused on the man as best as I could. "Bud said I could crash here."

"Bud who? I've called the police. You get your ass out of our bed, or I am going to bust your head." He waved the bat at me, taking aim at my head.

"Okay, okay." I held my hands up, palms out. "Who are you, man?"

"Who am I? Who the hell are you? You've trashed our house! What are you doing here? You punks think you can just come in and take over somebody's house?" He took a swat at me with the bat. "Get out of here!"

He began chasing me around the bedroom as I was trying to get my still-wet swimming suit on, one foot in and hopping around on the other while dodging the bat. He swatted again, just missing my arm, and I managed to get my suit on, grabbed my duffel bag, and beat that crazy man to the bedroom door and down the stairs. But everyone was gone. *Where was everybody? And how the hell am I getting out of here?*

Bud yelled from outside, "Come on, kid. We're cutting out!"

I found my way to the front door and stumbled out as Bud was revving up the van. I jumped in the side door. Sandy grabbed me and pulled me in. The questions tumbled out, one after the other. "What the fuck? Who was that guy? Whose house was that?"

Bud shrugged. "Who knows? We just knew it was empty and thought we would make ourselves at home for the weekend. The owners came home early." I shook my head and laughed.

Bud drove like a madman through the neighborhood, and we soon hit the highway with the windows down, music blaring. Bud relaxed, and Terry lit two joints, giving one to Bud and passing one back to Sandy and me. Sandy gave me a mixture of beer and tomato juice. "Hair of the dog," she said.

My stomach settled, and my head started to come back around. So I sat staring out the window, sipping the beer, and smoking a joint. In a short amount of time, I'd made friends, found some people. I felt good, better than I had in Ohio, but at the back of my mind, images of Larry and Mitch nagged at me. I had no money, and I should have been looking for them. My thoughts turned to Pearly—what had happened to her?

"Hey, don't bogart that." Sandy reached over and took the joint from me, ripping me from my thoughts. The neighborhood slowly changed from mansions to small houses and strip shopping centers, then back to nice homes into a neighborhood much like mine. We pulled up to a tidy-looking home with a long driveway. Red roses, neatly trimmed and in full bloom, lined the walkway. A skinny little guy with more hair on his face than on his head greeted us at the door.

"Gramps, this is Tim. He's going to hang with us for a while," Bud said.

I smiled. That's just what I was hoping he would say. If I could hang out with these people for a while and figure some shit out, like a way to make some money, I could make it out here. I could say goodbye to Ohio forever.

Gramps walked slowly over to me, looking me in the eye, and with both his hands shook my hand warmly. "Glad to make your acquaintance, young fellow. Come here, have a seat, and tell me about yourself."

We sat on the stoop, and he launched into a series of questions, "Where are you from?"

"Ohio."

Gramps put his hands in the air and looked down. "You by yourself?"

"Well, sorta."

One-word answers never garnered favor at home, but Gramps didn't seem to mind. He shook his head and smiled. "Kind of young to be so far from home. What are you doing out here?" He shook his head again, his smile growing bigger. "Wait, don't tell me...you're Terry's cousin." He looked toward Terry and raised his eyebrows. "Let me see...heard about the summer of love, and you've come out here to be free. You've had it with school and parents telling you what to do; you're looking for easy sex, free drugs, and wild times. "You want to turn on, tune in, and drop out. You're a runaway... that's it, isn't it?"

An itch started at the back of my neck and wound its way around my entire head. He'd pegged me, so what could I say?

"Well, I'm not Terry's cousin. And I have some tools and a nice drill set. Bud said you might be interested in them."

Gramps sat back and crossed his arms over his chest. "Bud said that? Where'd you get that stuff? You steal it from your dad?" He picked at the thread on the bottom of his t-shirt and then looked me in the eyes. "Kid, I got a shed full of tools. And you might as well know that Bud might say anything, anything at all. You know he's a dumbass, don't you?" I looked over at Bud and he just shook his head.

Bud comes over and says, "Hey, we're going to a rock festival up north, man. You wanna come?" There was no question in my mind; I wanted to go with them. But my need to make some money struck me. I needed it. Maybe if I could get in with them, it would lead to something good, like a place to live, a way of making some money. A feeling of belonging pulled me once more.

"Sure, why not? But I have a great idea—why don't we make some t-shirts with the name of the concert on them and sell them?"

Bud looked at me, then winked at Gramps. "Hey, not a bad idea. Kinda late for that, though. We're going to be selling shit, but it ain't going to be t-shirts. We don't have time for that."

Gramps stood and dusted off his thighs. "Well, I'm ready; just let me get my shoes on. I already put some supplies in those duffel bags."

Bud threw up his hands. "What are you talking about, Gramps? We already talked about this, and you're not going." He turned to Terry, who was messing with something near the van. "Terry, what the hell are you doing?"

She stuck her tongue out at Bud. "I'm giving this van some character." She pointed to the peace symbol on the side of the van. "This makes a statement about the kind of people we are, what we stand for!"

Gramps tipped his head toward Terry. "You know the hippies stole that from some guys in England. It was the anti-bomb movement symbol in the fifties. Bet you smart asses didn't know that. Anyway, you're going to have to paint over that when we get back. I use that van to go to work…can't have no peace sign on there."

244

"That's nice, Gramps," Bud said. "Thanks for the history lesson, but you ain't goin'!"

Gramps put his hand on his chin and scratched it like he was thinking. "You think I'm going to let you go see Gracie Slick without me?" He cocked his head and glared at Bud.

Bud crossed his arms over his chest. "No way you're going."

Gramps pleaded. "She's going to sing White Rabbit, and I'm not going to miss it."

"The Airplane is not even going to be there."

"Bullshit! You know that's bullshit! They're going to be there. And I've packed all kinds of shit—blankets, a tarp, a hatchet, cans of food, some beef jerky, flashlight, chips, and two cases of Lucky Lager. I'm ready to go. We should've left last night; there's going to be a huge crowd."

I wasn't sure what to make of this argument and was thankful when Sandy took my hand.

"Let them sort that out. Come back here—I want you to see something."

I walked to the back of the van, and she pulled a blanket back to reveal small plastic bags, lots of them.

"What is it?" I asked.

"Weed, dumbo."

"Wow." I didn't know what else to say and probably sounded like the hick from Ohio that I was. But honestly? Was that shit real? Was this a dream?

"Hey, I just want you to know what we got here. My guess is that this shit is what Bud's trying to hide from Gramps, but don't worry about it and don't say anything to Gramps."

I was surprised to see so much grass, but it made me nervous when I saw the butt of a rifle sticking out from under a blanket. Why would they be taking a gun along?

I nodded as Bud yelled, "Gramps, it's too far! There'll be a lot of wild shit up there. This is for kids. Believe me, you won't like it."

"You know; just because I let you drive that van, it's still mine. So, tell you what now—if I don't go, it don't go."

Gramps won. The five of us piled onto the old VW van with Bud at the wheel, Terry riding shotgun, and Sandy in the middle of Gramps and me on the bench seat.

The old van wasn't much, but it had a great stereo, and Bud had it turned all the way up as we drove. Between the beers, the smoking, the wind blowing in through the windows, and Sandy snuggled up to me—I was in heaven. *This* is how I thought California would be.

But then, the uneasiness deep inside me sparked. This was not good at all. I shouldn't be doing this. I was getting too far out, too far from Larry and Mitch, and what would happen if we got caught with all this grass? And what about that gun? It felt like when I skipped school—when the doom of getting caught tainted the freedom. Maybe Sandy knew what I was feeling, maybe not. She squeezed my fingers and I pushed those chicken shit thoughts away.

"We're going to see the Stones, man. Can you dig it?" Bud screamed.

Just to sound cool I said, "Hey, groovy man," as one last thought that maybe I shouldn't be there bubbled to the surface and then popped.

After an argument over where the concert was—Bud said Sears Point Speedway and Gramps insisted it was at Altamont Race Track—we made our way, drunk and stoned.

"It's a good thing I brought plenty of Lucky's; y'all are drinking like fish," Gramps said.

"Tell me you're not going to do that," Terry said, looking at Bud, disgusted.

"Hell yes, we're not stopping." Bud had emptied his beer can, took a last swig and put the empty can between his legs. With one hand on the wheel, he unzipped his pants. "Oh, shit get me another can!" he yelled.

"You're a dumbass," Gramps hollered back. Terry took a long swig of her beer.

"Hurry, damn it." They exchanged cans. "Don't drink that now."

"Fuck you, Bud." Terry gave it a wide toss out the window.

Gramps was right; the concert was at Altamont, and somehow, we made it there. I couldn't believe all the people. First there was nobody, and then the closer we got to the track, there was everybody. The traffic had slowed us down to a crawl, and people who were walking passed us by.

We finally caught sight of a mass of people and what looked like a stage in the distance. We pulled the van over on the side of the road, parked it, and loaded up with as many cans of beer that we could carry. Terry and Bud stuffed two backpacks full of bags of pot. Bud barked out, "Ten dollars a bag, good stuff."

Gramps just shook his head. "Just stick with me and stay away from that shit."

But Bud pointed to Sandy and me, "Hey, you two get your asses over here and help us push this weed."

"Bud, he doesn't have to do that shit!" Gramps said.

"The kid has no money. This way, he can earn some. I'll give ya two dollars for every bag you sell."

I didn't see myself as a drug dealer, but it was only grass. It didn't look like cops were around, and it might be fun. Plus, I needed some cash.

By the time we had sold all the bags of weed, I had twenty bucks in my pocket. We'd made it close enough to see the stage and we took the beer we'd been hauling in plastic bags and loaded it up in the two packs, one of which I was assigned to carry.

"See that American flag up there? Let's head for that," Gramps directed.

"What flag?" Bud asked. "I don't see any flag."

"Bud, you're either blind or you can't see—its straight ahead!" Gramps barked.

The closer we got, the more people there were. A wild scene drew my attention: a naked couple on a mattress getting it on in front of everybody. They were all wet and covered with mud. The crowd cheered them on, paying no attention to what was happening on the stage. I never saw anything like that in Ohio. And probably never would. This whole scene was out of sight.

Gramps gave me a push. "Keep going! Fuck those nuts."

We snaked our way around people until there was literally no ground to stand on. The music was loud, but I had no idea who was playing.

"How's this? We can't get much closer," Bud said.

"Bullshit!" Gramps yelled. "Keep going! We can get up there. I wanna see—let's get to that flag. Boy, I hope she sings White Rabbit."

We wiggled our way up to about a hundred feet from the stage just in time to see Santana playing Evil Ways.

And talk about evil ways. People stood and lay on top of each other. They danced, yelled, passed bottles of booze and joints around. We were all smashed together, swaying to the music. I had never been this close to people I didn't know. The strong smell of sweet perfume from one person and a whiff of bad body odor from another wafted by me. I loved the feeling of togetherness, but it was odd not having any personal space.

Carlos Santana's guitar was on fire. It was so loud we had to scream at each other to be heard. The smell of grass filled the air. Bud offered a green pill to me. Gramps nudged me and looked at me hard, and I passed. The Hells Angels stood around the stage with what looked like pool sticks acting as a shield between the bands and the crowd. They were rough and mean-looking dudes and didn't look like they were having much fun. And finally, Jefferson Airplane came on. And Gramps got to hear "White Rabbit."

"Man, that made it for me. We can go home now as far as I'm concerned," Gramps said.

It was dark by the time the Stones came on and everyone was completely blitzed. The Angels kept telling people to move back and settle down. Several fights between the crowd and the Angels broke out. At one point the music stopped. The Angels were swinging their sticks, and people were screaming and throwing cans of beer at the stage. I was someplace I shouldn't be; I grabbed another Lucky from the pack. Somehow, we finally managed to sit down.

Bud took out what looked like a chunk of green dirt. He stuck it on the end of a knife and heated it with his lighter. He then crumbled it up and mixed it with tobacco from a cigarette.

"You have to do this to keep it burning," he said. He poured it into a pipe and lit it. A cloud of smoke encircled his head, and he passed the pipe to me. It had a distinctive odor, stronger and earthier than grass. My mind went to spring in Miamisburg, the smell of freshly cut grass, the look my mom gave me when she said she loved me. Then to Pearly—that smell was her.

After the Stones sang, we hung out and tried to get some sleep, but finally Gramps yelled, "I'm freezing! Let's get the hell out of here."

We made our way through what had become a cold, smoky mush of a boozed-out, drugged-out mass of people back to the van.

Gramps, Sandy, and I slept most of the way back to L.A. Bud, high on White Crosses, drove the whole way. He was staring straight ahead, hands tightly gripping the steering wheel, his eyes fixed on the road, not saying a word. Was he in any condition to drive? He certainly seemed alert.

When we got back to the house, Bud, Terry, and Sandy crashed, and Gramps offered to cook me some food. We moved to the kitchen where I sat on a stool.

"Look out the window here. See those damn squirrels? They're eating all the bird seed I just put out! Can you go out to the van and get my gun out of the back?"

"What?" That was Gramp's gun I saw?

"Go, but be quiet. I don't want to scare them off."

I slipped out and then back in the house quietly and as fast as I could. "Wow, I thought this was a real gun," I said as I handed the BB gun to Gramps.

He hit one with the first shot, and they all scattered. Then, he got down to cooking.

The bacon and eggs hit the spot, but Gramps wasn't done. "Hey, you making what I think you're making?" I asked, the aroma in the air very distinctive.

"You up for some biscuits and gravy?"

I rubbed my belly. "I was raised on my grandma's biscuits and gravy. She makes them every Sunday morning." Today was Sunday.

Gramps stirred the mixture in the bowl. "I put a little something special in my gravy. Family secret."

Despite the hunger and the thoughts of Grandma, my mind turned to Pearly. She was sweet. What happened to her?

"So, kid, tell me ... what are you doing?"

"Ah, nothing. Why? Just eatin'," I said.

Gramps leaned down to me, his weathered face about an inch from mine, and looked me in the eye, saying softly with conviction, "What are you doing in California?"

Easy question. Easy answer. "I'm doing my thing. I needed some place to be free," I said. "I couldn't hack that school stuff—too many rules. I can read, write, do some math; that's all I need."

"So, you think quitting school is going to set you free?"

"Hey, it has! I can do whatever I want."

Gramps laughed and slid two large biscuits on my plate. I poured some gravy on them and lapped them up. They were soft on the inside, a little crunchier on the outside than I was used to. But oh, that gravy—he had made it with milk just like Grandma.

"Kid, are you sure you don't have this all backwards?" He got close again and looked at me hard, like he was looking right inside my head. "You've got some clear eyes, kid. There just might be something worthwhile behind them." He took a bite of biscuit. "You up for a little advice? Now, I won't give you any unless you want it and you ask for it."

The old man had made me breakfast, and I really didn't know what the heck I was doing, so I would give him an ear for a bit. "Okay, sure. Whatcha got?"

He sat on the stool next to me and spoke in a low voice. "An educated man is a free man. He's not bound by all the constraints that're put on a dumbass. He will have an opportunity to do the good and fun things in life. Education makes you aware of all that life has to offer. Being a dumbass—

like you are now—you will be limited as to the work you can do, where you can live, the type of people you will meet, and the friends you're going to have." He paused, but I said nothing.

My eyes wandered into his living room; he had a nice pad with a big leather couch and a mamasan chair in the corner. One whole wall was shelves filled with books and albums. An easy chair with stacks of books on each side of it sat by the picture widow. Then a plaque on the wall caught my eye:

"Don't let the past remind us of what we are not now."

Stephen Stills

"What's that supposed to mean?" I asked.

"Think about it," Gramps said.

I thought for a long moment and repeated the words in my mind. "It means I don't have to be what I was."

"Hey, you got something up there," he said as he poked me in the head.

"Do you read much?" Gramps asked.

No, not really."

"You seem like a bright kid, but you're uneducated. You know school is not the only place you can become educated. There's travel, life experiences, and lots of reading. I know you're too busy. You want to hang out with the kind of trash we saw at that concert?"

I swallowed another bite of biscuit before answering. "Everybody was just having a good time."

"Having a good time is one thing—drinking yourself sick and blowing your mind out on drugs? That's another. You can do that a few times, but the more you do it, the harder it will be to get your shit straight. That's not how life is, kid. It's not just going from one party to another."

He talked a good game, but I'd seen him. "What's with you? You went to the concert. You were drinking and partying. I thought you were a free spirit! Bud said you were cool about everything."

"That's all true, but I'm going to work in the morning. What are your plans? Sell some more pot?" Well, I sure as shit wasn't going to work, but even that would be better than school.

Gramps tapped the countertop. "Kid, Bud's a dumbass right now, just like you. I pray he won't always be a dumbass, but he's been a dumbass for a while now, and the longer he stays a dumbass, the harder it will be for him to change. Same with Sandy. She's got a good head for math but thought smoking pot and hanging out was better than staying in school."

Gramps had me cornered; it was just the two of us. All his questions and preaching were beginning to make me uncomfortable.

"So, what are you searching for, kid?"

"A place where I can be free to do what I want when I want with whoever I want."

"I understand that, but real freedom doesn't come easy. It can't be given to you. You can't steal it like a credit card—you must earn it." Gramps tugged at the end of his beard and looked at me hard. "Are you ready for this freedom you're talking about?"

I looked away. I didn't have an answer.

"You know, kid, you can do anything you want if you're smart about it."

"And how's that?"

"Well, you have to learn how to be smart about things. If you're where you're supposed to be, doing what you're supposed to be doing, and you do that consistently and long enough, you'll eventually earn that freedom you're looking for. Most of the time anyway."

I thought that made sense. "But how do you know what those things are and how long to do them?"

"That's the hard part. You have to look and listen and then recognize the truth and follow it. Some people get it right off; others it takes time."

"Yeah, well, some things that maybe I'm supposed to do aren't cool, and I'm not interested in them anyway."

"Kid, you said you want to have fun and be cool, right? Do you feel like you're a cool dude right now?"

"Sure, I'm in California, going to rock concerts, hanging with chicks, smoking, drinking, nobody telling me what to do."

"Okay, you're cool all right. But you have no money, no means to get any, no place to live; who's making your breakfast tomorrow? Not me, and it sure isn't Grandma. You know what you smell like, don't cha?"

"Yeah," I mumbled.

"What?"

"A dumbass, but maybe I like being a dumbass."

"Only a dumbass would say that! How do you think your mom and dad are taking all this?" I was sure Mom had called Grandma right away, probably went down and got her so she wouldn't have to be alone with all this.

"I hope they don't think I don't like them." I sat my fork on the plate and looked at it. "I don't know; she won't like it."

"Were you all together? I mean your mom and dad—not divorced or anything?"

"No, they were all together. Why do you ask that?"

"Well, with a kid like you, there's bound to be trouble in the nest," Gramps said.

"Well, my dad's dead. It's been about a year."

"Were you a dumbass before your dad died?"

"Some before."

"Let me ask you something, kid. Would you be here if your dad was alive?"

"Oh, shit no. He would have killed me."

"You know your mom knows that too. She doubts herself. She knows your dad would not have allowed you to be such a dumbass. She hopes that her love for you will be enough to make you a good person. If she gives you what you want, you will do the right thing. She doesn't get it right now, but that love is what is enabling you to do the very things she doesn't want you to do."

Why was this old man hassling me? I didn't need this shit. I felt bad enough about Mom—she had no brothers or sisters, Dad was gone, and all she had was me and Grandma. She deserved a better kid than me.

"Kid, what are you afraid of?"

"Me? Well not much of anything."

"Really? That sounds like bullshit to me. You were running from something. People don't run away unless they're afraid of something. Fear is very powerful. Fear, you know, that's what caused this war we're in and that's what keeps it going."

"What, we're afraid of Vietnam?" I asked.

"We wanted Vietnam to have a government like we have. Our fear was that if they didn't, it would be bad for the world and that they would be our enemy. So we go to war with them to make them be like us. Now we have this fear of losing the war, but we're also afraid to really go in and throw everything we got at them and win the war. Does that make sense to you kid?"

"Sorta."

"Think of it like this. There is this little kid who is different than you. He doesn't look, think, or act like you. And that bothers you and you become of afraid of that difference. So you get into a fight with this kid who is much smaller than you, so you fight him with one hand tied behind your back. You're afraid if you beat him up too bad, his big friend who is standing next to him will jump in on his side and then you might lose that fight. Fear gets the world into big problems, and fear causes big problems in our personal lives—so what do you fear?"

"Well, I'm afraid of going home. I'm going to be in big trouble."

"Come on, get honest, dig deeper."

My mind raced. What was he looking for? "I'm afraid… I'm afraid that I don't know who I am. I'm not sure who I want to be."

"Good; that's good, kid—really good. Now what do you think about most of the time?" He sat back and looked at me with a hard face.

"I don't know, a girl, I guess. Any girl, a nice car, lots of money, fun times, and the freedom to do what I want."

"So, you're always thinking about the same thing, really."

I looked at him and frowned, thinking, *Just leave me alone.* What was he trying to tell me?

I stood up, ready to leave.

"You think you're going to find all that here in California? Kid, do you think you're smart enough to do what you want to do?"

"Look man, stop hassling me. I need to do my thing and do what I want to do. I'm old enough and I'm smart enough; I know what I'm doing. And look, I'm open to learning new stuff."

Gramps leaned in. "An old philosopher once said, before you can learn anything, you must first admit you know nothing; are you ready to do that?"

I sat down, his words hitting home. Dad had once said those same words to me. I felt unsure. I knew I was screwed up. But I wanted this. I didn't want to go back home to the same old shit. But Dad had said those very words to me more than once, and there was truth in them. Now this old man seemed to have my number, and he wouldn't let go.

"Sometimes, kid, it's as simple as taking the first step in the right direction."

I shook my head and held up my hands. "Okay, I surrender. Just tell me what I should do—which way, what direction I should head."

"Okay. Go in that little hallway there." Gramps pointed down the hall.

"What? What do you mean?"

"You asked for direction, didn't you? I'm giving it to you."

I went into the hall, listening for more direction from Gramps.

"Okay, now turn to your right. See that black thing on the wall with the dials on it? Pick it up and stop being a dumbass."

I was soon back home. And the following Sunday, Grandma's biscuits and gravy were especially good. I thought of Bud, Terry, Sandy, and Pearly but mostly of Gramps. My freedom, my wanderlust if that's what it really was, was short-lived.

I was lucky.

THE REINS ARE BROKEN

Blackjack continued his spirited and wild ways up through his teenage years. He was averse to training and resented being confined. He continued to demand that his handler keep a tight rein on him. But his personality endeared him to people. People liked having him around. He became a favorite and go-to horse for national public funerals.

I was sixteen years old when Black Jack celebrated his twenty-first birthday with a butter pecan cake. He was sixty-two years old in horse years.

A few more funeral processions, and Black Jack would be retired and perhaps then he would earn his freedom. His last major public funeral was for President Lyndon Johnson. He tugged on the lead line most of the way and pranced along as spry as ever.

My handler was losing her grip on what were by now loose reins.

There was more searching for new highs, new experiences, more wild car rides. School was a drag almost more than I could bear.

Country Joe and the Fish (whom I'd never heard of before or since), Creedence Clearwater Revival, Crosby, Stills, Nash &Young, and Jefferson Airplane were all singing about the Vietnam War at the greatest rock concert in the world, and I missed it. When Richie Havens looked out over four hundred thousand people and played every song he knew, the word freedom sprung from him. That's what was ringing through my mind too.

Even though the Beatles, Led Zeppelin, Rolling Stones, the Beach Boys, or the Doors were not at Woodstock, their music was always with us. It made everything seem cool. It was a big part of what we did. We played it on our eight tracks in our cars, at our parties in the barn, and we played it loud.

The idea that the freedom these people sang about and the freedom I was looking for had to be *earned* had not set in with me yet. I continued to feel that I had the right to do the things I wanted, and that nothing should hold me back from that. Gandhi said, "People tend to forget their duties but remember their rights." Did I have a duty—to who?

There was a reckoning that I must have with myself. And every once in a while, I could see clearly and do things that opened the way for what I was looking for. But I was not ready for all of that. I struggled with accepting discipline and recognizing its value in attaining what I wanted. I wanted to be who I was going to be now. I was confident that I would do well and achieve great things, but I don't know why I would have thought that. I didn't realize the thing I wanted most, I was not ready for.

In the fall of 1970, I was out of school almost as much as I was in school. Yet deep within me, I knew that education was the key to finding out who I was, and if I knew that, maybe I would have the freedom I was searching for.

I lived for Friday and Saturday nights, and now every night seemed to be a Friday or Saturday night. I had done about as much in Miamisburg as I could do. I had left home a couple times with really not much intention of staying gone or really any purpose in going; I went for the thrill of going. What was next?

I had a steady girl, so maybe I would get married or just run away again or join the Marines or get a real job; was I going to go to college? My world was spinning fast and at times dangerously out of control. I began the sixties as an ornery seven-year-old and now it was ending, and I was a confused seventeen-year-old wannabe hippie.

I was always glad when school began in the fall, and 1970 was no exception. It was all fresh new classes, new teachers, old friends who somehow I didn't see over the summer, and new kids that looked odd and seemed quirky. Some new teachers and some old cranks.

After a week or so I was doing the same thing: going to a couple classes, then down the alley to Red Dogs to see who was skipping class and joining them for a little break in the day.

Football or basketball games, cars, girls, Stroh's beer, parties, and of course, doing anything really worthwhile was to be avoided at all costs. Days were becoming all the same. Searching as I did, nothing much different occurred, and any newness wore off quickly.

A couple of my friends began talking about joining the Army. You could join on the buddy system and stay together. You could join even if you weren't eighteen. You didn't even have to graduate from high school; you just had to get your parents to sign. We had just about exhausted what Miamisburg had to offer; maybe we could go to Vietnam.

What had I not tried? Maybe there was something more out there. Something I could not explain, a place I needed to go. A couple of my buddies and I decided it was time to do something. So, we went to downtown Dayton. The Navy/Marine office had a sign that read, "Gone to Lunch." Right next door was the Air Force office—same sign. No sign on the next door, and it opened easily. An Army staff sergeant greeted us enthusiastically.

"Have a seat, boys."

I thought just for an instant that if my dad would have been alive, I would not be taking that seat. The idea of joining the Army would never have come up. But maybe I would have had the courage to remind him that he and his buddy had taken that same seat only a few years before.

Mom's initial response was, "I think you need your head examined. Who would join the Army when there's war on?"

"Dad did," I answered.

She quickly acquiesced; she knew something had to change. Grandma didn't say much because Mom probably told her to be quiet.

My friend Red Dog pleaded with me. "Man, you don't want to do this. You don't know how long your grandma will be around. She might die while you're away. Don't be stupid, man. Stay here and go to school."

Red Dog wasn't right about most stuff, but I was afraid he might be right about that. But I was not to be deterred. I was worn out searching for who I was and the freedom I thought I didn't have, for that belonging I needed. It wasn't here for me. I was ready to search elsewhere, and this could be the ultimate adventure, something only a few (at least from my world), had done. I also got the message that while the love I felt at home was warm and real, the discipline I needed wasn't there for me.

The sun was shining brightly on the bitter cold February morning that Mom took me to the bus station. I hoped it wouldn't be this cold in Fort Leonard Wood. She grabbed my arm as we walked out to the car and looked up in the sky.

"Do you remember that night?"

She startled me at first, then I looked up in the sky and then at her.

I wondered what the future held for me. Could my search for freedom and who I was be realized in this new adventure? Would things stand still here until I got back? My thoughts turned to Mom and Grandma, then to all my friends. What would they be doing while I was gone?

"Yes, I remember, Mom."

Acknowledgement

I want to thank my early readers Autumn Coleman Purdy, Christa Stewart and my close friend Donn Burrows who also gave me good doses of needed encouragement and motivation. A special thank you to Christina Consolino, without her critical review of the manuscript it would never have gone to print. I want to thank my son Matt Stonecash for his last-minute review and advice and also Joy Niu.

My gratitude to Abby Macenka my publisher who took a chance on an unknown author and made my day when she offered to publish my book.

Tim Stonecash grew up in Miamisburg Ohio during the 1960's. He lives in the nearby community of Springboro with his wife, Kathy. Tim earned his master's degree from The University of Dayton. He retired from there in 2015. He enjoys traveling, studying history, and spending time with his four children, their partners, and his two grandchildren.